Reform The American Police Eliminate Slave Catching Tactics

Darrick D. Muhammad

Dedication

I dedicate this book to all the "good" police and security officers who fulfill their duty every day to "serve the community; to safeguard lives and property; to protect the innocent against deception, the weak against oppression or intimidation and the peaceful against violence or disorder; and to respect the constitutional rights of all to liberty, equality, and justice" (IACP, 1957). There are far more good police officers than bad ones.

I also dedicate this book to the many victims and to the loss of innocent lives at the hands of those who are or were supposed to protect and serve them.

Lastly, I dedicate this book to my children, Britney, Darrick, Makal, and Malik, who continue to inspire me to stand up for truth and justice in an attempt to make the world a better place for all in the pursuit of freedom, justice, and equality.

Preface

I understand there will be much debate and controversy surrounding this book. It has never been an easy discussion about race relations and the police, especially in dealing with America's biggest nightmare - slavery. Having spent 40 years in the field of law enforcement and security, including 8 years as chief of police of a Michigan Commission of Law Enforcement Standards (MCOLES) sworn agency, having obtained a Master's degree in Criminal Justice from Wayne State University, and writing several unpublished academic papers on several facets of racial justice and equality and policing, I feel obligated to disseminate my understanding, assessments, and conclusions. With any luck and God's blessings, this scholarly work will increase public awareness and spark a conversation that could lead to significant police reform and a reworking of the criminal justice system. We will all gain from this, as we will all live longer and healthier lives—ourselves, our children, our loved ones, and society at large. I would like the police in America to be not heedless and non-reactive to crime in the Black community, but rather a system of equal justice based on a process of understanding the subconscious effects that race and slavery have had on the inferior and superior complexes while interacting between Whites and Blacks in society.

Two distinct reading levels are possible with this book. First of all, it could be read by regular people with little to no experience in law enforcement or criminal justice. The work was written with this readership in mind from the beginning to the end. At times, the incidences of police brutality, misconduct, excessive use of force, and killings presented might seem overwhelming. Some may argue that it is race-baiting and that "Black Lives Matter is becoming more powerful by the hour, and they know it," as Tucker Carlson warns (Sollenberger, 2020). I'm hoping you won't give up easily. The scientific evidence provided, the citations from primary sources, the findings reached, and the suggestions offered can all be easily understood, even if the police racist content of a particular chapter is difficult to understand. One of the book's key characteristics is that, while the chapters must be read in the correct order to be understood, they do not all follow the formal textbook empirical study framework. Honestly, you can begin the adventure at any chapter, depending on your preferences, tastes, and areas of interest.

Professionals from the law enforcement sector, academics, government organizations, police unions, and even some security groups will represent the second set of readers. I don't expect every member of the security and law enforcement community to concur with the concepts and information presented in this book. However, I do hope that the knowledge and information shared will serve as a wake-up call for the general public, lawmakers, regulatory bodies, business executives, and police administration, bringing to light how direly the current state of affairs needs to be corrected.

There are six chapters in the book. Chapter 1 is a general introduction to the inequality in policing based on race and a thorough introduction to me and my career in security and policing. Chapter 2 presents the problem with overwhelming evidence to support the premise that police brutality, misconduct, excessive use of force, and killings may appear to be the most daunting monstrosity confronting police - community relations, particularly in terms of law enforcement engagement with African Americans. Chapter 3 introduces a literature review of research data that suggest that African Americans are disproportionately stopped by police and victims of aggressive force far more than other racial groups and provides an explanation as to whether it's a problem of "the bad apple" or "the bad apple tree" which argues that the entire police agency is corrupted. Chapter 4 introduces the concept that the Civil War was about slavery, and it took this bloodiest battle on American soil to put an end to chattel slavery in the United States. Chapter 5 could come as a shock to an unwary reader. However, it is critical for the overall understanding that the origins of modern-day policing can be traced back to the "Slave Patrol" since it explains how and provides examples. Chapter 6 concludes and sets forth conceptual solutions to the policing problem in the United States with innovative reform according to leading police administration and the urgency of the changes proposed.

I hope a lot of people read this book. We must reorient police and begin to utilize the body of information established by professional administrators if we are to escape the dangers of the past. This was not our opportunity several years ago. George Floyd's police death sparked a national movement against the ongoing use of force by the police against African Americans and heightened calls for structural reform in American law enforcement. This is the ideal moment. I hope and pray that you enjoy reading this book.

Acknowledgment

In the name of God, most gracious, the most merciful.

First and foremost, all praise and thanks are due to the cherisher and sustainer of the world - almighty ***God***, for giving me life and inspiring me to take on this topic.

Secondly, my gratitude goes to my late father, *Lenton J. Muhammad Sr.,* and my late mother, *Franceno B. Muhammad*, who taught me, without theoretical insights, to always do what is right, to stand up for justice, and to appreciate being an independent, brave thinker.

It is not possible to express my thanks to all those who have, directly and indirectly, helped me to develop these ideas, been a mentor to me, and or helped to develop me in my career. However, I must recognize *Dr. Curtis L. Ivery*, Chancellor of the Wayne County Community College District, for encouraging me to write the book. I must remember *Dr. Bradley Smith*, Professor & Chair, Criminology and Criminal Justice, at Wayne State University; it was his class (Advanced Law Enforcement Administration) in April 2002, where I initially wrote my paper, Reform the American Police - Eliminate Slave Catching Tactics which is now this book. I'd like to thank *Amazon Self Publishing* for their constructive feedback, valuable suggestions, insightful comments, and careful editing of this manuscript.

This was a very enlightening and rewarding experience for me, and I thank anyone who has honored me by reading this book.

About the Author

Darrick D. Muhammad, a metropolitan Detroit *renowned public safety and security leader*, was featured in the February/March 2013 issue of Campus Safety Magazine as a *2012 Director of the year finalist.* He transitioned a private security department at Wayne County Community College District (WCCCD) to a fully sworn MCOLES police agency. He served as the *campus safety director* and *police chief* for the college from 2004 to 2022.

Darrick began his career as a volunteer Detroit police reserve officer from 1984 to 1989. He was hired as a security officer at

Fairlane Town Center mall in Dearborn, Michigan 1985. He shortly became the *"first" African American sergeant* in the department, which became a security police agency under Public Act 330. Later, in 1994, he served as lieutenant of a private security department assigned to Tel Twelve mall in Southfield, Michigan. He joined WCCCD campus safety as a sergeant in 1999.

Darrick holds *MS* and *BS* summa cum laude degrees from Wayne State University, an AAS degree summa cum laude from WCCCD, and a certificate from Northwestern University School of Police Staff and Command. He is a member of the faculty at WCCCD and has taught *Law Enforcement and Respect for Religious Diversity*, *Introduction to Criminal Justice*, *Introduction to Security*, *Physical Security*, *Asset Protection and Incident Response*, *Security Administration*, *Security Capstone,* and *African Americans and Islam*.

Darrick developed a keen interest in criminal justice and its intersectionality with race and religion. His key areas of work and research focus on race, religion, policing, and equal justice. Darrick has four children: *Britney, Darrick, Makal,* and *Malik*.

Contents

Chapter 1: Introduction

It was approximately five o'clock in the morning when I suddenly looked at the clock out of fear and shock. I was inside my residence, which I didn't recognize, but it felt like home. My son Darrick Akbar apparently grew fond of animals and pets. He had collected a dog, a rabbit, a guinea pig, and lots of fish. There was a fish tank with several breeds of aggressive fish. The most aggressive were piranhas, who were jumping out of the fish tank, scaring the other animals and pets. We had to capture the piranhas and get a new fish tank. I and all four of my children (Britney, Darrick, Makal, and Malik) got into my unmarked Chevy Tahoe police car, where my four brothers (Lenton Jr., Roderick, Gerard, and Marvin) met us and got inside, too.

We ran into a large crowd of "Black Lives Matter" protesters as we drove. As some were protesting, a few began to loot and commit acts of arson. I got out of the car and told my family, "I'll handle this," and told them to call 911. A hostile crowd began to surround me, and all of a sudden, the cavalry arrived. Arriving just in time were many marked police cars, mounted units, K-9 units, and police on motorcycles. A Black policeman in charge asked me, who are you? I told him, "I'm a chief of Police at a college," and showed him my badge and ID. He said, "I don't recognize you, but okay." About three White policemen approached me and demanded to see my badge again. I showed it to them, and they handcuffed me and told me I was under arrest for impersonating a police officer and carrying a handgun. They tied me to a pole inside a horse stable, and one of the White policemen demanded again, "Tell me who you are!" I replied again, "I'm a police chief." He grabbed a cattle prod from a burning flame and said, "You say police one more time, and I'm going to burn this prod into your back. Niggers are not police!" Suddenly, I woke in horror, looked at the clock, and finally realized it was a dream.

Maybe it was the side effects of my medication, or maybe it was something subconsciously in my mind that was telling me that I'm not like some of the police officers that I've seen or read about over the years. While I continue to believe that the majority of police officers are decent human beings who chose a noble profession, there are a few "bad apples" that made it bad for all officers Nationwide. For example, while serving as the chief of police for Wayne County Community College District (WCCCD), I was pulled over at least 9 times while driving an unmarked Chevy Tahoe police SUV. Was I speeding sometimes? Sure. But the vast majority of the time, I was pulled over for nothing more than driving an unmarked police car and being a Black man. However, I would never indulge in such outright devilish behavior.

I'm not like the so-called police officer who kneeled on the neck of the dying George Floyd as he pleaded, “I can’t breathe.” I’m not like the so-called police officer who entered the wrong apartment and shot and killed Botham Jean. I’m not like the so-called police officer who beat Malice Green to death with a metal flashlight because he wouldn’t open his hand, hiding crack cocaine. I’m not like the so-called police officer who used fire hoses and unleashed vicious police dogs on First Amendment protesters fighting for Civil Rights like Bull Conner. As a matter of fact, I wrote extensively against police brutality and racism throughout my academic studies.

In 1998, I wrote an unpublished paper in Dr. Brad Smith’s class at Wayne State University titled “Reform the American Police - Eliminate Slave Catching Tactics,” which is the inspiration for this book. The class was required to give a five-to-ten-minute presentation to the class about our paper. I was a bit nervous because I was aware of how controversial my topic was, and at the end of my presentation, I took questions or, in this case, comments. A White off-duty suburban police officer raised his hand. When I acknowledged him, he said, “I have some friends on the Wayne State police force, and I’m going to tell them to pay you a visit on your way home tonight.” I smiled and replied, “I have some hungry attorney friends who are waiting for a good lawsuit.” I realized at that moment that police reform is a real problem because the mindset of some of the White police officers is in arrogant, serious denial. It is that warped White supremacy mindset that has led to many African Americans becoming victims of police brutality.

Some young African Americans grow up either witnessing or becoming victims of police harassment or brutality (Hudson, 2014), and it encourages them to join the police to foster change from within the ranks (McKinnon, 2020). Former Detroit Police Chief Ike McKinnon recalled this horrible trend from his teenage days in Detroit:

> ***In 1957, I was a freshman at Cass Technical High School. As I walked home after speaking with my favorite teacher, four White police officers jumped out of their cruiser, threw me against it, and beat me severely. I hadn't done anything wrong. Officers in the feared "Big Four" were well-known in the Black community for brutally maintaining their kind of "Law and Order." The more I screamed, the more they beat me. Time seemed to stand still as I saw the anger on their faces and the horror on the faces of Black people who gathered around us, yelling for the police to stop. After what felt like hours, they told me to get my ass out of there. I ran home crying but did not tell my parents, fearful that it would put them in danger. I was 14, the same age as Emmett Till when he was killed in Mississippi two years earlier. I was scared, angry and***

> ***confused. Why did they hurt me? That day, I promised myself that I would become a Detroit police officer and change the Detroit police force from the inside. (McKinnon, 2020)***

Conversely, former Chief McKinnon's savage beating by Detroit Police was a law enforcement nightmare and could only be resolved by African Americans becoming leaders within the police department.

For some others, it's the dream of becoming a police officer. Some became police by being fascinated with the shiny, fast, and pretty police cars with the shiny emblems on the side, the meticulous uniforms, and the guns (Dulaney, 1984). I became interested in security and the police profession because of the status of authority and paramilitary structure.

I grew up in the Nation of Islam and watched my father, Lenton J. Muhammad, who served several roles within the Muslim community. My father was raised in Columbus, Georgia. At the age of nineteen, he migrated to Detroit, Michigan. in 1954. He joined the Nation of Islam under the leadership of the Honorable Elijah Muhammad. There, his accomplishments included being caretaker of Muhammad's Temple number one, squad leader, first lieutenant, and eventually Minister. In 1957, he served a one-year prison sentence at Milan Federal Correctional Facility for being a "conscientious objector" due to his religious beliefs. The United

States Supreme Court would later rule that members of the Nation of Islam's "beliefs are founded on tenets of the Muslim religion as he understands them" (Court clears Ali, 1971). After his release, he began setting up Temples in Saginaw, Michigan, and Toledo, Ohio.

He served as the head Minister of Toledo, Ohio, until the Nation of Islam transitioned to Orthodox Islam under the leadership of Imam Warith Deen Mohammed, where he took on the role of Imam until his health slowed him down. He made his transition to Allah (God) on November 20, 1998. I was accustomed to observing the rank of authority within the Temple and the Nation of Islam.

Since its inception in the 1930s, the Nation of Islam maintained the "Fruit of Islam" (FOI), a paramilitary unit that all men members must join. The FOI were known to possess self-discipline and trained for self-defense and karate. The leaders in the FOI were assigned military ranks (Evans, 1999). The hierarchy of the Mosque included a Minister in charge of the entire structure and a Captain who drilled the men and taught defensive tactics (Lincoln, 1961). According to C. Eric Lincoln, "inside the temples, there is a constant movement of young men with military bearing; they move quietly but with an unexaggerated dignity and the inescapable suggestion of latent force" (Lincoln, 1961). Empiric research sustains that parental behaviors and personality traits will influence a child's future social conduct (Kagan, 1999). Ideally, a child watching this form of religious military structure would possibly engage in a similar environment as an adult.

I reminisce as a boy watching the FOI wearing distinctive blue or White uniforms and caps and recognizing different ranks of Captain, Lieutenant, Squad leader, and soldier. The rank designation was by the number of stripes on their sleeves at the Temple. I recall Captain Roscoe Muhammad Jr., of the Detroit Temple number one, referring to me as "Chief" as I was a little boy. I reflected on my childhood memories of how my older brothers and I, after the Mosque meetings, would pretend that Lenton Jr. was the Minister, Roderick was the Secretary, and I was the Captain. It is possible that in my subconscious mind, it turned into a huge inspiration for me to become the Chief of Police at Wayne County Community College District.

My journey in the security police profession began in 1984 when I joined the Detroit Police Reserves, a volunteer unit within the police department. Shortly after joining, I recall riding down Jefferson Avenue in a passenger car, in uniform with a fellow reserve officer, when a white traffic police officer spat on our car as we sat at a traffic light. I did not equate this to the blatant racism within law enforcement at the time and simply naively viewed him as a dumb cop. My eyes would become wide open after obtaining employment at Fairlane Town Center Security-Police.

I was hired as a security officer at Fairlane Town Center shopping center in 1985. The mall hired and added several Black officers to a nearly all-white department due to the NAACP calling a boycott against the city of Dearborn for banning Blacks from using their parks (Sternisha, 2010). Fairlane Town Center is a regional shopping mall in the Detroit suburb of Dearborn, Michigan. While Dearborn is in close proximity to Detroit, it has a terrible history as it relates to race relations. The former Mayor Orville Hubbard had a phrase, "Keep Dearborn Clean," a code for keeping Dearborn White while keeping Blacks out (Kapilango, 2019). Malcolm X said, "I know Dearborn, I'm from Detroit, I used to live out here in Inkster. And you had to go through Dearborn to get to Inkster. Just like driving through Mississippi when you go to Dearborn." (Breitman, 1965). Racism in Dearborn did not die with Mayor Hubbard; city and mall officials fostered a climate of racial intolerance and abusive and unjust practices.

Racism and discrimination at Fairlane Town Center security police were widespread and rampant throughout my employment there. For example, on one occasion, I overheard a White male lieutenant refer to Black officers as "dumb niggers." After another officer and I complained, he was promoted to Assistant Security Director at another mall. On another occasion, I, as a shift sergeant along with a White male lieutenant, witnessed three White officers using excessive force, constantly kicking a Black male while he was on the ground. The next day, I recommended disciplinary action, which was denied because the lieutenant claimed it never happened. The racism was so pervasive that in 1991, nearly the entire force of African American officers agreed to walk off the job. There was a practice of skipping over African American officers on the rotating overtime roster, and at that time, African American officers were constantly passed over for promotion.

In November 1988, I was the first African American promoted to the rank of sergeant. However, Fairlane had no intention of ever promoting me. I made second place on the promotion list that was valid for a year, and the position was given to a White officer. This newly promoted sergeant came to me after a few months and told me, "They (Fairlane Town Center) never plan to promote you. They only put your name on the list to keep you quiet. I'm going to promote you by resigning, and they'll have no choice but to give it to you." Soon after, he resigned as a sergeant, and I was promoted to the position. As an African American security police sergeant, I was never able to escape my racial identity while serving in this official role, and the Dearborn police department reassured it by their racist, hostile actions.

On September 28, 1990, I, several off-duty Fairlane Mall security police officers, and an off-duty Detroit police officer were racially harassed at a nightclub by Dearborn police. A White Dearborn police officer (later identified as Dennis Kenny) approached me and struck me on the shoulder with a large metallic flashlight, and stated, "Start the bike up and go home nigger." Several other uniformed Dearborn officers walked towards us in a threatening manner, shouting racially derogatory remarks and making threats to assault us (Williams, 1994). My Detroit police officer acquaintance identified himself as an off-duty officer, and the same White officer replied, "You one of Coleman Young's monkeys. Your Black ass got no jurisdiction in the city of Dearborn." While one of the men in our group wanted to challenge the Dearborn police officers physically, we decided it was in our best interest to leave.

We met up at a safe location once we were in the Detroit city limits and noticed that the off-duty Detroit police officer was missing. I and another acquaintance returned to Dearborn. We observed the same White Dearborn police officer talking to the off-duty Detroit police officer. The White Dearborn police officer had the off-duty Detroit police officer's handgun stuffed in his pants, holding his badge, and he pointed his handgun at me when we arrived. I asked him to call his supervisor, but he refused. Fairlane security police officers at that time were certified under Public Act 330, which granted officers misdemeanor arrest authority while on active duty, on their employer's premises, and in full uniform. I had worked earlier that night, made an arrest, and booked the suspect at the Dearborn police station. I knew who the officer in charge was of the Dearborn police that night, and I pleaded that he call him by name. He refused again, stating, "he doesn't have time for this." The White Dearborn police officer put his arms around the off-duty Detroit police officer in a friendly manner and told him, "We're all cops here, and this got out of hand. Tell your buddies to just forget the whole thing" (Williams, 1994). The off-duty Detroit police officer retrieved his handgun and badge, and then the three of us left the area.

I was so upset and shocked that I couldn't forget it. I intended to bring this to the attention of the Dearborn police department. I just wanted the White officer to apologize, and then it's over. However, the second in command at the Dearborn police department refused to take my complaint. He told me to write a letter, which angered me more. I told him that I was assaulted and wanted to do a police report, but he refused. I went to the city attorney's office and told her about the incident. The city attorney, after telling me the White officer's name just from my description of the incident, sent me back to the Dearborn police department, where they finally took the report. The Dearborn police initiated a so-called investigation, which appeared to be an interrogation when a Dearborn lieutenant interviewed me and other Fairlane officers while we were at work. It was at this point I decided to consult with an attorney.

The entire group of nine individuals filed a federal lawsuit due to the unlawful stop by Dearborn police. Federal judge Bernard Friedman held a pre-trial conference with both attorneys present in an attempt to settle the case without going to trial (Williams, 1994). The city of Dearborn did not take this racially motivated assault and harassment seriously. The administrative assistant to the mayor said, "It's a frivolous case. They're manipulating the media…If they're looking to make a quick buck, they should buy a lottery ticket" (Runkle, 1994). The treatment by Dearborn police against me and my friends made news, and the story was extensively carried throughout the metropolitan Detroit area. The City of Dearborn and Fairlane Town Center management was fearful of a lawsuit from this incident. While the Dearborn police chief told the media that he could not comment because he was "not familiar with the lawsuit" (Williams, 1994), he and some members of Fairlane Mall management were orchestrating my termination.

The penalty for police whistle-blowing is drastic, with "the full force of the agency, formal and informal, is brought to bear on the [informant]…, including scorned, shunned, excluded, condemned, harassed, and almost invariably, [termination]" (Johnson, 2005, 80). In late November of 1990, Dearborn Police Chief Ronald Deziel attended a ceremony at the Fairlane Mall to introduce the Wayne County Sheriff's Mounted Division to patrols at Fairlane Mall for the holiday shopping season. This ceremony was attended by the Fairlane Security Police Director and Assistant Security Police Director. The Assistant Director told me that at this meeting, Chief Deziel told the Director to "keep Muhammad quiet and to do something about him." On several occasions after this meeting, the Assistant Director told me to be careful because the mall intended to get rid of me (Muhammad v. Taub-Co Management, 1996, 1). At the same time, I was fully aware that police agencies "have a vested interest in protecting the integrity of their profession and, thus, not perpetuating the perception that the police are engaged in this discriminatory practice" (Barlow, 2002).

I continued working at the mall during these stressful days. On February 18, 1992, my other friends and I filed a suit against the City of Dearborn and its police department. The suit alleged violations of our constitutional rights. Immediately after filing the lawsuit, I was called into the director's office, and I was told that my lawsuit was creating great hardship for the mall and its relationship with the Dearborn Police. He also asked if there was an alternative to filing the lawsuit. After this conversation, I began to experience great difficulties at work (Muhammad v. Taub-Co Management, 1996, 2).

Although there were no problems with my performance prior, in April 1993, I received a negative employment performance evaluation. Of course, I protested the evaluation as unjust and unsubstantiated. The evaluation was subsequently changed.

I was informed by the White male Lieutenant who conducted the erroneous evaluation that I would not be having these problems if I had not caused the department so many problems with my lawsuit against the city of Dearborn. He also told me that the Security Police Director was controlling things at the mall. Of course, in my pomposity, I told him that "he may run things here at the mall, but God is in charge of the Earth and universe." In late April of 1993, the same Lieutenant recommended that I be disciplined for talking to another Black Security Police Officer who was on duty at the time. After an investigation, no charges were filed against me. In May of 1993, I was disciplined for allegedly smoking while on duty. However, it was a common practice, and none of the other White officers who were seen smoking were ever disciplined. In addition, I was disciplined for writing a message on the daily schedule in September of 1993. The message read: "Justice was served" in reference to the 1993 convictions of two Detroit police officers (Larry Nevers and Walter Budzyn) for killing Black Detroit resident Malice Green (Muhammad v. Taub-Co Management, 1996, 2-3).

In late 1993, I was approached by a fellow White female Security Police officer, who informed me that Mall management was asking her to support a false sexual harassment claim against me. She publicly denied that I sexually harassed her and had to retain an attorney to warn Fairlane to discontinue a complaint on her behalf. Although she never filed charges against me, a second White female did make allegations of sexual harassment against me. At the time of the allegation, she was dating a Dearborn Police Officer. An investigation by the Vice President of Human Relations found the charges to be unsubstantiated. However, during the investigation, a Black female mall executive told me that this charge was a "calculated plot to fire me" (Muhammad v. Taub-Co Management, 1996, 3).

Finally, on December 1, 1993, I was scheduled for an interview for promotion to Lieutenant. Before the interview started, I was terminated for writing a check with insufficient funds to the company to cover a hardship withdrawal from my 401K by a White general manager named Michael Finley. Despite the fact that the check was honored before the interview, I was still terminated (Muhammad v. Taub-Co Management, 1996, 3). I was terminated for allegedly "misappropriating company funds" by failing to repay a loan that I received from my very own retirement account in a timely manner. I immediately filed complaints with the Equal Employment Opportunity Commission (EEOC) and the NAACP and came to the conclusion that they both, to no avail, neither appeared interested in helping a Black man complaining of racism.

I filed a lawsuit in Wayne County Circuit Court on Judge Brian Zahra's docket, case number 3 96-635097-CL, against Fairlane Town Center and the Taubman Company. My attorney at the time was Charles M. Lowther, who later became an Administrative Law Judge and is now deceased. In my opinion, I was the victim of legal malpractice because my attorney failed to disclose that my case was dismissed within the 21 days for my right to appeal. He claimed that he had sent me a letter, which I hadn't received in the mail. I was advised that Judge Zahra dismissed my case by a friend and former Fairlane co-worker, Thomas Balentine, who was told at a meeting at the mall. Judge Zahra wrote in his opinion, "The court was reluctant to grant defendants' motion [for summary judgment] because providing an employer with an NSF check does not seem to be sufficient reason to terminate employment" (Muhammad v. Taub-Co Management, 1997). Referee Carol D. Little of the Michigan Department of Labor opinionated that my actions did not willfully disregard an employer's interest, constituting misconduct and awarding my contested unemployment benefits.

On October 24, 1998, I wrote a letter to the U. S. Justice Department requesting that they investigate the Dearborn police department and Fairlane Mall. An FBI agent visited me at my residence, but they indicated that my claims were found to have insufficient proof to pursue. A community NAACP associate named Mr. Stewart told me that since the police didn't kill me, it would be difficult to find community support or initiate a governmental investigation. It was around this time that I became a community activist and started attending meetings held by Belinda. She started an organization called the Coalition Against Police Brutality. At one of those meetings, I met Minister Malik Shabazz and became a member of the New Marcus Garvey Movement.

My first impression of Minister Malik left me suspended in judgment. I was somewhat suspicious of a Christian minister with a Muslim name. However, my doubts were wrong. He became a community activist after his mother, who was addicted to crack cocaine, shot and killed his stepfather. She was convicted of murder and sent to prison. Minister Malik was devastated and began his crusade (Kaffer, 2005). The New Marcus Garvey Movement was founded in the early 1990s by Minister Malik. The group registers voters, stages protests and public actions, including against crack and drug houses and grocery stores that sell rotten meat, promotes education, visits homeless shelters, and seeks a society promoting Black entrepreneurship and empowerment and the elimination of White supremacy. I recall a march I attended with him and about 10-15 others at a crack house when I saw how much peril we were in and how much faith he had in God. While protesting at a crack house and chanting "Shut it down" and "up with hope and down with dope," two Detroit fire engines with lights and sirens blocked each end of the street at each intersection. A group of about 3-5 men drove up in a minivan beside us and stopped. The rear door pops open, and one of the men is reaching into his jacket and looking around as if he is about to pull out a gun and start shooting. Minister Malik shields himself by raising his Bible in the air, and they drive off with no incident.

I would later become a close associate as we became good friends and brothers. One day at one of his public meetings, his introducer did not come and he asked me to take his place. I was nervous, but I reflected on my father, who I watched in my youth as a fiery Minister for the Honorable Elijah Muhammad. With a few borrowed words from Minister Farrakhan, I lit the place up. After that night, I became the person to introduce Minister Malik to many of his public meetings. We both would unleash rhetoric and insults at elected leaders, pastors, imams, or anyone we thought was selling the Black community out. One day, my mother came to a meeting, and after hearing me speak, she told me that I reminded her of my dad but advised me not to put people down and to focus on being positive. Her words changed my perspective on public speaking forever.

I recall a massive snowstorm in Detroit with at least 12 inches of snow in about January of the late 90s; we marched on the

African American Museum. We were protesting that the museum was giving an honorary inauguration to former Governor John Engler. Governor Engler was not liked by most Blacks in Detroit. Attorney Geoffrey Fieger, infamously known for being Jack Kevorkian's lawyer, said, "I don't know how African Americans can vote for Engler. That's like Jews voting for Adolf Hitler" (Stodghill, 1998). The Michigan State Police executive protection advance team asked Minister Malik to meet with the governor when he arrived. Minister Malik asked me to accompany him to the meeting. There we were in a secluded room, Minister Malik, Governor Engler, I, and 2-3 plainclothes officers. Governor Engler offered Minister Malik his telephone number and told him that instead of marching on bad, filthy stores that only "sell alcohol and lottery tickets" to the Black community, he could have the Department of Agriculture close them down the next day. Like most politicians, he asked Minister Malik for something in return to support his takeover of the Detroit Public Schools. Minister Malik told the governor that he could not do that, and the meeting was over. I was convinced that Minister Malik was not a "sell-out."

In 1997, former Detroit mayor Dennis W. Archer decided to award three city's gambling licenses to Motor City Casino, MGM Grand Detroit, and Greektown Casino instead of a black-owned developer, namely Don Barden, in a city with a 76 percent Black population, a black Mayor and a predominantly black City Council. Dennis Archer said, "Making one African-American richer does not constitute Black empowerment" (Dennis told City Council, 1998,

1). Archer's decision caused dissension and division in the city, and community activist Helen Moore said, "The ones who voted against us in the community are definitely traitors" (Pulley, 1998). Minister Malik Shabazz and other community groups called for Mayor Archer's recall, and they marched at his mayoral residence. I was one of the marchers at a protest at the Manoogian Mansion led by Minister Malik, as many shouted, "Recall Archer." Some of the protesters referred to Mayor Archer as "the devil" and a "national disgrace" for his attempt to take over the Detroit Public Schools, refusal to award a casino license to a Black entity, and neglecting his duties for snow removal (McGraw, 1999). I once saw Minister Malik as a sole protester at a local theater featuring a movie called "Booty Call." He was by himself and told me that they were disrespecting the Black woman, and somebody got to stand up. Examples like these and the bold positions I saw Minister Malik take led me to protest the city of Dearborn and Fairlane Town Center's racism.

My first protest against Fairlane Town Center and the city of Dearborn was passing out "Boycott Fairlane Mall and Dearborn" leaflets throughout metropolitan Detroit. The flyer started with quotes from Marcus Garvey, Susan B. Anthony, Dr. Martin Luther King, and Malcolm X. I then stated, "Don't be fooled by Black mall managers." At this time, Fairlane had a Black mall manager and a Black security director. I would later regret making this statement and have since apologized to Aj Jemison for making her job harder. I believe that she really tried to make things right at Fairlane;

however, she was fighting the legacy of Orville Hubbard and decades of racism. I mentioned other racist customs and practices at the mall, and Dearborn described my 1990 incident with Dearborn police and my unfair termination from the mall. I later staged a one-person protest outside the mall perimeter at Southfield Service Drive and Hubbard Drive, strategically because that's where the majority of African Americans enter the mall from. Another terminated African American officer named Eric Dupin joined me as we attracted the attention of the Dearborn police.

One day, Mr. Dupin and I were carrying signs and passing out flyers when approximately 3 to 4 Dearborn police cars arrived and questioned us. I urged African-Americans approaching the mall not to shop there, and some agreed and drove away. The Dearborn police chief, Deziel, came and watched us from across the street. I did not have much respect for Chief Deziel, who I considered incompetent due to suspending Officer Brian Yinger for 3 days for writing the number seven in European style. Brian Yinger's story "was widely reported on ABC's World News Tonight, Newsweek, Harper's magazine, the New York Times…Nickelodeon network" and maybe even Russian newspapers (Deep, n.d.). Interestingly, a Dearborn police officer, Wilson, gave me his card and asked me to visit him. I went reluctantly, and he told me if I edited my flyer and added information about Fairlane allowing gangs to hang out at the mall, I would not be harassed anymore by the police when I wanted to protest near the mall. Needless to say, I agreed, and they never came again. However, it was inevitable that I would have a confrontation with the mall security.

In September of 1998, I went inside Fairlane Town Center and handed the flyers for the protest "Boycott Fairlane Mall and Dearborn." That's when a Black officer named Terrill Myles told me to leave. As I was leaving, he commented, "You must be one of those mother-fucking Farrakhan bow-tie men." After exiting, I requested to speak with his supervisor and was falsely arrested by another Fairlane officer named Damon Moseley. An accomplice of mine was taking pictures, and they attempted to arrest him. The accomplice knocked the officer to the ground and fled the scene. I went to a local hospital and was issued an appearance citation for trespassing and soliciting without a license. The matter was taken under advisement by the 19th District Court and later dismissed. The Dearborn police went to my residence and stole my car from my driveway. I later recovered it (Siegel, 1998); however, the Dearborn police filled my air vents with White fingerprint powder. After having a meeting with the mall general manager Aj Jemison, security director Harold Scott, and Minister Malik Shabazz, I decided to back down on protesting and eventually deleted my website calling for a boycott of Fairlane Town Center.

After deleting my website alleging racism in Dearborn by police and at Fairlane Mall in June 2000, Frederick Finley, who we will discuss later, was murdered by Fairlane Lord & Taylor. This happened a few weeks later after they accused his daughter of shoplifting a $4.00 bracelet. The mall management had told me that "things had changed over the years." After Finley's unjustified killing, I began to be questioned as to why I deleted the webpage. "One of them accused me of being a sellout." I decided to reinstate the webpage, and it began to receive enormous hits and traffic (Bagwell, 2000). The killing of Finley brought 7,000 people to a rally protest outside the Lord & Taylor store in the Fairlane Mall parking lot. Leaders and speakers at the mall protest included Reverend Al Sharpton, Martin Luther King III, Horace Sheffield of the National Action Network, Detroit NAACP leader Wendell Anthony, Congressman John Conyers, Geoffrey Fieger, Washington DC radio personality Joe Madison and Dick Gregory. A follow-up march was held with approximately 1,000 people outside the Federal Building in downtown Detroit (Randall, 2000). I felt sorry for Aj, who had to be under intense pressure to improve the mall's image amidst this tragedy. Minister Malik and I attended the rally, but the NAACP security wouldn't allow us to be on the stage. We both criticized the organizers of the rally strategies.

As reported in the Michigan Citizen newspaper by journalist Ron Seigel, Minister Malik Shabazz called the rally regarding the Finley murder a "ho-test, rather than a protest." Minister Malik was referring to the decision of the NAACP, the SCLC, and the National Action Network to move the protest from Dearborn to Detroit. Minister Malik said, "We decided this was ridiculous — a complete and total sellout. Twenty-first century Uncle Tom foolery". Minister Malik and I both criticized the organizers for asking Black people to buy stock in Lord & Taylor's. "The only people who can exercise power in a company are the majority stockholders." The organizers also refused to allow Minister Malik Shabazz, Councilwoman Brenda Scott, and State Representative Kwame Kilpatrick to speak (Seigel, 2000, A5). They wouldn't let Minister Malik speak because he's likely to say anything without any compromise. I should've been allowed to speak because I spent 9 years as a security police officer and sergeant at Fairlane Town Center and had firsthand experiences about the racism that existed there. Unfortunately, the inescapable truth is that Black Lives did not matter in the city of Dearborn and Fairlane Mall. Some officials at Fairlane warned me that due to my protest and public criticisms of the mall, I would be blackballed and never work in security or police again.

I had no doubt that it would be difficult to find suitable employment in the security police profession when I went to an interview, and the first question the interviewer asked me was, "Are you the Darrick Muhammad from Fairlane Town Center?" However, during my brief times as contract security manager at Tel-Twelve mall, driver for Metro Cars, and driver for President Clifford Dimmitt of Dimmitt and Owens Financial, I always had a vision of being back into my profession. I received my Bachelor's degree in Criminal Justice from Wayne State University in 1998, and Mr. Dimmitt passed away the same year. I responded to an ad I saw in the newspaper for the Lead Officer position at Wayne County Community College District (WCCCD). I had an interview with Chief James Baylor and Lieutenant Edward Blackburn and was offered the position of sergeant. I nearly did not take the position.

Upon Dimmitt and Owens Financial receiving my two weeks' notice of resignation, they offered me a few thousand more dollars a year to stay. I agreed and withdrew my acceptance to the position at WCCCD. However, the demands of inconsistent shifts and upon the advice of a good friend and co-worker at Dimmitt and Owens, Mr. James Gillespie, who told me, "There's probably more and better opportunities at that college," I reconsidered. Mr. Baylor always reminds me that I sent him a letter asking him for a second chance for the position. I will always remain grateful to Mr. Baylor for giving me an opportunity, even after I explained to him that I had previously filed a lawsuit against the city of Dearborn police department and Fairlane Town Center. He told me that he understood, and by being in law enforcement as long as he had been, he knew why someone might file a lawsuit against a municipality.

I started my employment at WCCCD in September 1999. On my very first day, Mr. Baylor took me to meet the Chancellor, Dr. Curtis L. Ivery, and told him, "This young man is going to help you." The campus safety department, as it was called, was a hybrid of in-house proprietary security officers at the northwest and downtown campuses and contract security at the eastern, downriver, and western (Ted Scott) campuses. I was assigned to the northwest campus, and there were tremendous challenges to the safety and security of the campus. Upon my arrival, the northwest campus would experience 3-6 breaking and entering into automobiles a day. We tried many tactics, such as roof look-out or surveillance, foot and vehicle patrols, and gatehouse, but they still continued. A female officer by the last name of Williams told me that if I wanted to stop the break-ins, all I had to do was stop the audio shop across the street from buying the radios after the thieves stole them from our lot. I went to the Detroit police 6th precinct, met with a community police sergeant, James White, who would later become chief, and asked for their help, and surveillance break-ins stopped cold turkey. I was shocked and surprised to hear that Mr. Baylor would be retiring in the year 2000.

As Mr. Baylor was leaving, he gave the new chief Blackburn and me, now lieutenant, marching orders. He told us to turn the campus safety department into a professional public safety department. We both agreed. However, due to an internal conflict between Chief Blackburn and myself, I was reassigned to the northwest campus administration office as Evening Dean and later Director of Campus Business and Operations. Shortly after joining the campus safety department, some officers and supervisors from Fairlane Town Center went to Chief Blackburn and told him that I was a troublemaker and that there were other malicious lies. I am so thankful that I was able to call Fairlane General Manager Aj, and she put a stop to it immediately. Not only is she a talented and respected leader, but I also consider her a friend. Mr. Blackburn was able to transition the campus safety department to 100 percent proprietary at all the campuses. They were doing so well that the Administration and Finance department decided to return back to contract security as a cost-saving initiative. As a result, the crime statistics accelerated upwards, and we watched what Chief

Blackburn built begin to collapse.

Chief Blackburn was reassigned to WCCCD's Michigan Institute of Public Safety Education, and I was appointed Chief of campus safety in September of 2004. Upon my arrival, the department had about 24 contract security officers and 10 proprietary security supervisors. Mr. Baylor returned from Dallas, Texas, and Detroit to introduce me to the supervisory staff as the new Chief. I was aware that the supervisors were extremely loyal to Chief Blackburn and considered me the enemy. My speech was very brief; I said, "Change is inevitable, but growth is optional." I asked, "Who among you want to grow with me?" Lieutenant Dwayne Page stood up and said, "I'm with you." The others remained silent and seated, some with their arms folded. My first assignment was to transition the department back to proprietary (in-house) security. The first group of five officers was hired in early 2005, including Officer Koreathia (Dandridge) Williams. I'm very proud of her for eventually leaving the department and becoming a Human Resources associate at WCCCD. The transition process took longer than I expected, nearly 2-3 years. Having a department of in-house officers was good, but colleges began to become soft targets for active shooters.

There were approximately four college shootings between 1966 and 1991, but for us, the first was Virginia Tech on April 16, 2007. The shooting at the university campus in Blacksburg, Virginia, was the deadliest one ever. At least 23 other people were hurt, and 32 people died. During the shooting, the shooter committed suicide. Less than a year later, on February 14, 2008, at Northern Illinois University in a lecture hall on the Dekalb, Illinois, campus, an active shooter shot five people dead and injured 16 others before committing suicide (Welding, 2023). Next, it occurred very close to WCCCD; it happened right in our backyard, an active shooter at Henry Ford College in Dearborn, Michigan. On April 10, 2009, a male student fatally shot a female classmate before turning the gun on himself in an apparent murder-suicide that prompted a lockdown at the community college in metropolitan Detroit (The Associated Press, 2009). A Dearborn police officer I knew personally told me, "That was supposed to have happened at WCCCD, not in Dearborn." I submitted a proposal to transition to an armed police agency after a student at WCCCD was in class and a perpetrator entered and snatched his $2000.00 pair of Cazel eyeglasses off of his face and ran away.

Meanwhile, WCCCD contracted the services of the Wayne County Sheriff's deputies. The Sheriff's deputies are there to provide additional enforcement staff to patrol, investigate, and assist in the monitoring of the Wayne County Community College District campuses (District Police Authority, 2023). On March 2, 2010, WCCCD held a special Police Authority swearing-in ceremony for 17 campus safety officers at the Central Administration Building. Many were on hand to congratulate the newly-appointed police authority officers, including Trustees Charles Paddock and Alan Anderson, local law enforcement agencies, faculty, staff, and students. The officers were sworn in by Darnell Blackburn and John Steele from the Michigan State Police MCOLES division. This initiative continued the efforts throughout the district to provide training and the very best public safety for its students, faculty, staff, and visitors (Ivery, 2010). The officers were now certified under Michigan's Public Act 330, which gave them misdemeanor arrest authority equivalent to a police officer with three limitations: 1. must be on employer's property, 2. must be in uniform, and 3. must be on official duty. In 2013, approximately 13 individuals reported being robbed at gunpoint off of the campus grounds. The PA 330 certified officers did not have jurisdiction to investigate crimes off the campus grounds. Therefore, we submitted a proposal to expand the department certification to full-sworn MCOLES.

In January 2014, I made history at WCCCD by swearing in Lieutenant Pride Johnson as its first MCOLES sworn police officer. Two advantages of WCCCD moving some of its officers to Michigan Commission on Law Enforcement Standards (MCOLES) certification are an increase in police officers and training standards. The increased security measures included hiring extra police officers and expanding their area of responsibility to cover the neighborhoods around the school. Other Michigan colleges and universities, such as Wayne State University, Oakland University, University of Michigan, Michigan State University, and others, embraced the same level of authority as the MCOLES police certification (WCCCD Increases Security, 2014). We would not be recreating a wheel but conduct best practice visits to several university and college police departments. They included Wayne State University, Oakland University, University of Michigan, Michigan State University, Grand Rapids Community College, Oakland Community College, Lansing Community College, Henry Ford College, Western Michigan University, Kalamazoo County Community College, Schoolcraft College, Tarrant Community College, Dallas County Community College District, Baltimore County Community College, Northern Virginia Community College, George Washington University, University of Tennessee, Mott Community College and Virginia Tech University to name a few.

In addition to best practice visits, we intensely recruited retired police officers. Unlike candidates from pre-service academies, retired police officers have the experience and training. They weren't trying to arrest all of the students. I had the pleasure of being the chief of WCCCD police, where some of the finest semi-retired and retired officers joined our ranks, such as Eric Eaves, John Lohmeier, Lee Richardson, Darryl Bennett, Pride Johnson, Johnnie Rogers, Willy Ridley, Curtis Sanford, Raymond Batts, Wilhelmina Collier, Michael Jemison, Lisa Collins, and Ashley Miller to name a few. They and a few others played a significant part in the success of the WCCCD police department. I was also fortunate to have such an excellent leadership team, which included Bahrija Livadic, Keiara Younger, Byron Young, Brian Duneske, Tamika Townsel, Cynthia Brown, Isaac Bynum, Tamika Barton, Lamiah Rahman, Munenur Jesan, Matthew Wilds, Dwayne Page (deceased) and

Richard Mundy (deceased) to mention a few.

Under my leadership, the WCCCD Police Authority had numerous significant achievements, including:

• Recognition by the Michigan Commission on Law Enforcement Standards (MCOLES) as a certified sworn police department

• Graduated several police officers from Macomb police academy and recertified eight law enforcement officers

• Graduated several police officers from Macomb police academy and recertified several law enforcement officers

• Established a memorandum of understanding with the Wayne County Sheriff's office and the Taylor Police Department to expand police patrols to adjacent streets around each campus, including Heritage Park in Taylor, Michigan

• Expanded authority of sworn officers to carry firearms

• Creation of an umbrella organization of public safety programs under which the Police Authority, Health Science Center, Wayne County Sheriff's Office, and the Michigan Institute of Public Safety Education collaborate

• Expansion of patrol vehicle fleet to include fully marked Crown Victoria's, Chevy Tahoe's, Dodge Chargers and Ford Explorers

• Expanded and improved field training and maintenance program

• The Police Authority website provides direct access to register students for the Emergency Alert System

• Expanded the CCTV surveillance system, including the ability to view cameras on mobile iPad devices

• Creation of a Student Safety Corps

• Purchase of automatic external defibrillators

• Renovated Police Authority offices at the Downtown Campus, Northwest Campus, and Eastern Campus with upcoming plans for the Downriver Campus and Ted Scott Campus

• Centralized dispatch communication control center

• Procurement of 800 MHz radios with talk group permissions with local police departments

• Acquired access to Law Enforcement Information Network (LEIN)

• Established a background investigation unit

• Established the Campus Liaison Initiative Mission with the Federal Bureau of Investigation (FBI), which maintains an on-call FBI agent to assist in specific emergency circumstances

• Installation of anti-skateboard bollard covers in strategic locations

• Initiated Coffee with a Cop brings police officers and the community members they serve together–over coffee–to discuss issues and learn more about each other.

• Participated in National Police Week, where tens of thousands of law enforcement officers from around the world converge in Washington, DC, to participate in a number of planned events that honor those who have paid the ultimate sacrifice

• Increased safety awareness workshops throughout the district

• Established a Police Advisory Committee to improve the district's law enforcement operations

• Established and maintained professional membership with the International Association of Campus Law Enforcement Administrators, International Chief of Police Association, National Organization of Black Law Enforcement Executives, and Michigan Association of Campus Law Enforcement Administrators

• Hired a police investigator to work with the local Courts to prosecute criminal offenses

• In 2022, the District Police Authority established its first K-9 Police Unit (Annual Report, 2022, 53).

In April 2017, WCCCD established a Police Advisory Committee, which finalized its membership and had its first meeting in an effort to improve the district's law enforcement operations

(Ivery, 2017). The Police Advisory Committee represented a range of experiences, professions, interests, and concerns; their dialogue offered me valuable perspectives on the community's needs and expert law enforcement advice. The Police Advisory Committee members were James Jackson, Retired DPD Commander and CRJ Faculty Chair; George Anthony, Retired DPD, Attorney and CRJ Faculty; Anthony Holt, Chief of Police Wayne State University; Yoseph Demissie, Chief Technology Officer; James Baylor, Retired Chief of Police Dallas County Community College and WCCCD Chief; Thomas Fisher, former Security Director Briarwood Mall, Security Awareness Somerset Mall; Aracely Hernandez, Executive Project Manager Office of Chancellor; James Younger, Retired DPD Deputy Chief, and CRJ Faculty, Michael Bruggeman, Director Campus Safety College for Creative Studies; Deborah Robinson, Retired DPD Deputy Chief and CRJ Faculty (Annual Report, 2022, 56). James Gillespie, Finance from Dimmit and Owens Financial, was a previous member.

I assumed that we were successful at WCCCD Police Authority. Mr. Baylor told me, "You took this department much further than I expected." In November 2004, I was featured in the State of Michigan and Crains's Detroit Business "Hire Michigan's Best"—a special publication promoting a cross-section of exceptional students from throughout the state from both public and private higher education institutions (Kramer, 2004). In the February/March 2013 issue of Campus Safety Magazine, I was featured as a 2012 Director of the Year finalist (Gray, 2013). I was also featured in “Celebrating African American Achievement” as the Director of public safety in the “Who’s Who in Black Detroit” (Jackson, 2013). As one of my mentors, Chief Holt from Wayne State Police, stated, “Chief Muhammad is now the best practice that I go to for information; it used to be the other way around. As colleges across the country ask how to initiate a campus police department, I refer them to Chief Muhammad because he developed the blueprint” (Ivery, 2021, 3). However, I did not make the journey here alone. Numerous people have supported me along the way. And it’s the men and women of that department who made it what it is! I truly thank God for allowing me to serve! While some were congratulating me on my success, others were orchestrating my downfall. When you get to the top, people become predators, and they hunt you down like you are prey.

It was about March or April 2022; winter had ended, and the weather was getting warmer, so I decided to walk down the street coming from the WCCCD District office to the campus. All of a sudden, out of nowhere, two men came charging towards me. One with a channel 7 microphone and the other with a camera rapidly approached me. It was Ross Jones from WXYZ 7 News, an investigative reporter. He ambushed me with a series of questions regarding sexual harassment complaints, to which I responded that I could not comment on pending civil litigation. I understand that it was Mr. Jones’ job to cover a story. However, as in his title, “investigative reporter,” he neglected to investigate the background of the individual’s making complaints against me. Within a week, on April 4, 2022, Mr. Jones ran the first of three stories titled, "Accused by six women of sexual harassment, WCCCD's police chief remains on the job." On April 22, 2022, Mr. Jones did a second story titled "Ex-officers: WCCCD police bosses sent us on food runs, told us to change reports."

The media, newspaper, radio, and television news reporting have the power to manipulate the thinking of the people to mold your opinions into what they want you to believe. They can silence and control who gets to speak. Malcolm X said it best like this:

> ***The media's the most powerful entity on earth... [T]hey control the minds of the masses. The press is so powerful in its image-making role, it can make the criminal look like he's the victim and make the victim look like he's the criminal. This is the press, an irresponsible press. (Malcolm X quotes, n.d.)***

Fani Willis expressed her frustration with the news media during her investigation and prosecution of President Trump:

> ***Lies were told and printed in the media because, you know, we used to be in a date and time where***

> ***you had 60 minutes. And people did stories, and they verified information… you had this great reporting, but it seems today that a lawyer writes a lie, and then it's printed for all of the world to see. (11Alive, 2024)***

While the liars and disgruntled ex-officers were privileged with Mr. Ross Jones' aired news, I was silenced, only able to say, "I can't comment on pending litigation." Now is the first time I get to tell my story — the truth. God says in the Holy Qur'an, "And say: Truth has (now arrived, and falsehood perished for falsehood is (by nature) bound to perish" (Holy Quran 17:81).

I had become exhausted from Mr. Jones calling my phone and appearing at District meetings, reporters, and process servers camping outside my residence. I decided, in an effort to protect the college and for other reasons, that I would resign. On July 13, 2022, Mr. Jones ran his last story titled, "WCCCD police chief accused repeatedly of sexual harassment resigns from college." Now is the first time I get to tell my story — the truth.

Many sworn affidavits were filed against me, predominately by former disgruntled employees. I will not bother to address all of their numerous lies and misrepresentations. While the United States is not the most litigious nation in the world, it has a backlog of lawsuits that fill its courts every year (Friedman, 2022). However, the courts often do not appear to be interested in determining the truth but more in things that have a semblance with the 'fight' theory. This theory derives from the origin of trials as substitutes for private out-of-court brawls" (Frank, 1950, 92). The judges do not investigate the facts but instead serve as an umpire or warden of order and fair play. Judge Jerome Frank, in his brilliant and eloquent book *Courts On Trial: Myth and Reality in America Justice*, said:

> ***In short, the lawyer aims at victory, at winning the fight, not at aiding the court to discover the facts. He does not want the trial court to reach a sound, educated guess if it is likely to be contrary to his client's interests. Our present trial method is thus the equivalent of throwing pepper in the eyes of a surgeon when he is performing an operation. (Frank, 1950, 83)***

Thus, the judicial system in the US is more beneficial to the individual with the best means to fight. This is further evidenced by the many innocent people wrongfully convicted in courts and sentenced to life in prison and some on death row for crimes they did not commit (Scheck, Neufeld & Dwyer, 2000). Despite being a broken court system, I will deal with those who had the audacity to file civil lawsuits against me and WCCCD in the order of their dismissals.

The first lawsuit to be dismissed was filed on behalf of Vanessa Liddell by her attorney, Scott Batey. Ms. Liddell falsely claimed in an affidavit, civil lawsuit, and in an April 4, 2022, interview by Ross Jones of WXYZ Channel 7 news and stated that she was fired for reporting me for sexual harassment. Ms. Liddell also claimed that she met in a WCCCD Human Resources conference room with me and a WCCCD Human Resources representative. She also reported that the Human Resources representative informed her that she was being placed on administrative leave pending an investigation into her sexual harassment allegations against me. Lastly, she claimed that WCCCD and I ended her assignment because of her allegations against me. Her fabricated story is categorically untrue, without any merit whatsoever, and does not correspond to what actually happened.

On April 13, 2012, at 3:08 p.m., an agent from the Bureau of Alcohol, Tobacco, Firearms and Explosives and a police officer from the Detroit Police Department met with Dawud Muhammad (Faison) and I at the WCCCD police authority conference room. They asked us to compel Liddell to cooperate with their investigation of her boyfriend, Deshawn Blackwell, aka Rossahn Black. Liddell was served a subpoena by them, and she admitted to fraudulently issuing two fake WCCCD student ID cards. They advised us that Liddell was involved in much more serious behavior, but they would disclose it after the trial of Blackwell. On April 27, 2012, Liddell was suspended for five days without pay for conduct unbecoming an officer. On March 25, 2013, at 10:39 a.m., I spoke by telephone with the Assistant U. S. Attorney. He stated that Liddell testified after giving oath in U. S. District Court that she produced and provided two fake WCCCD identification cards to Blackwell, who was not a student at WCCCD, testified that she provided a stolen state identification card of a relative to Blackwell, testified that she purchased an AK-47 and a Glock firearm and according to a police officer, who testified that he arrested Black and confiscated the AK-47, Glock and "an arsenal of weapons in the trunk" of Liddell's vehicle. They stated that they believed that Liddell was buying guns and supplying them to Black, who was a convicted felon. The Assistant U. S. Attorney stated that Liddell was granted immunity during Black's trial. However, she committed perjury in court, and her testimony ended after she had pleaded the Fifth Amendment. The Assistant U. S. Attorney provided a copy of the transcripts from the court case 10-20225 in U. S. District Court, U.S. v. Rossahn Black, aka Deshawn Blackwell. I immediately notified WCCCD Human Resources, and they placed her on leave of absence and eventually ended her assignment.

On February 2, 2023, in the Circuit Court of Wayne County, Ms. Liddell's lawsuit was dismissed with prejudice after reviewing motions to dismiss and having heard oral arguments. In October of 2022, I filed a counterclaim in Wayne County Circuit Court through my attorney, Monica Hunt, for defamation, slander, and libel. As of this writing, the counterclaim case is still pending.

The second civil lawsuit was brought by Ms. Myke-a Littles through her attorney, Scott Batey, filed on July 13, 2022, in the U.S. District Court Eastern District of Michigan Southern Division. In my opinion, Ms. Littles erroneously thought that WCCCD would settle her lawsuit and she'd win the lottery. Ms. Littles claimed in her lawsuit that I requested her to come to my residence located on the campus. On at least one occasion, I opened the door wearing an open bathrobe, an undershirt, and underwear. Ms. Littles also claimed that I regularly asked her and other women, excluding men, to ignore their job duties to complete menial personal tasks, such as picking up my dry-cleaning, groceries, and carrying out orders Ms. Littles further alleged that I retaliated against her after she complained by assigning her to the midnight shift. She claimed that I endangered her safety by opening the locked gates for various women that I invited to my on-campus residence. All of her claims were either fabricated or misrepresented and lacked merit. While being questioned at her deposition by attorney Steven Potter, after approximately 45 minutes, Ms. Littles appeared to be having an emotional breakdown. She took a break with her attorney and never returned to her deposition. On May 9, 2023, the Court made a stipulated order of dismissal, and Ms. Littles' lawsuit was dismissed in its entirety, with prejudice, and without attorneys' fees or costs to any party.

The third lawsuit was from a lady named Anita Akbar, filed on September 6, 2022, through her attorney Scott Batey in the Circuit Court of the County of Wayne or in the U.S. District Court

Eastern District of Michigan Southern Division. Her lawsuit shocked my conscience because it was rumored that she was telling some co-workers that she wanted to marry me. I avoided her like she had Covid-19 because there was no physical chemistry between us at all. Ms. Akbar claimed in her sexual harassment lawsuit that I called her at 12:00 midnight on a Saturday and asked her to come for an interview for a campus safety officer position. She claimed that at the interview, I told her, "I need something from you," while staring at her private parts. Ms. Akbar lacked creativity in her made-up scenarios in claiming that she was dispatched to my residence on campus, and I opened the door wearing only a bathrobe with my private parts visible. Lastly, she claimed she was "constructively" discharged from the WCCCD Police Authority due to the hostile and intolerable environment.

In my opinion, and unfortunately for Ms. Akbar, she lacked a mustard seed of honesty and credibility. Ms. Akbar resigned from WCCCD police authority on June 11, 2020. In her resignation letter, she indicated that she was quitting due to WCCCD not allowing her to be off work to be available for a second job and that she was offended that her supervisor asked her, "You going to your new job," when she called off work. This was confirmed in a subsequent letter she wrote. Akbar never indicated in these two letters that she was complaining about discrimination or harassment. Additionally, Ms. Akbar's information on her employment application was falsified. She answered "no" on her employment application to the question, "Have you ever pled no contest to, pled guilty to or been convicted of a crime other than a minor traffic violation." However, this was at variance to a previous conviction for a misdemeanor charge of violation of controlled substances. On July 12, 2023, in a stipulated order of voluntary dismissal, the Court dismissed Ms. Akbar's lawsuit with prejudice and without costs or attorney fees to any party.

DaJuan Dickerson filed the fourth lawsuit. Coming from almost anyone else, it would be a preposterous, almost laughable claim. I've taken FBI Former Director J Edgar Hoover's erroneous claim against Dr. Martin Luther King Jr. in describing Dickerson. Dickerson is indeed, in my opinion, "the most notorious liar in the country." Dickerson's lawsuit through his attorney Scott Batey, filed on September 6, 2022, in the Wayne County Circuit Court, alleged that I discriminated and retaliated against him in violation of the Michigan Elliot-Larsen Civil Rights Act (Dickerson v. WCCCD, 2022).

More specifically, Dickerson claimed that I retaliated against him because he gave statements to WCCCD Human Resources that I sexually harassed multiple women and denied him opportunities to be promoted. He argued that I promoted several inexperienced females over him because of his testimony. Dickerson also claimed that he was constructively discharged on August 11, 2020, due to a hostile and intolerable work environment (Dickerson v. WCCCD, 2022). All of his claims were fabricated and misleading. The facts are to the contrary.

Dickerson emailed his supervisor on March 24, 2020, indicating that he would be out sick as per his doctor. Dickerson submitted a doctor's note dated March 21, 2020, indicating that he would remain undetermined off work. Dickerson emailed me on May 12, 2020, with a doctor's note attached. I received approved FMLA documentation for Dickerson dated May 13, 2020, for intermittent leave from March 22, 2020 – March 21, 2021. On the evening of August 10, 2020, his lieutenant informed me via telephone that he was told that Dickerson was employed at the Detroit Public School (DPS) police department.

On August 11, 2020, I gave the lieutenant a directive to confirm this information. The lieutenant gave the directive to a sergeant/investigator. The sergeant stated that he was unable to contact DPS after he attempted to telephone a former WCCCD police officer who was now a DPS officer. Approximately an hour later, Dickerson responded to the front desk of the WCCCD Curtis L Ivery's downtown police authority desk with a resignation letter and all of his uniforms and equipment. Upon further investigation, it was discovered that Dickerson was hired by the DPS police on May 20, 2020, which was confirmed through the MCOLES (Michigan Commission on Law Enforcement Standards) MITN (Information and Tracking Network) system.

Dickerson was responsible for not being promoted because he declined the entry-level supervisory position. On October 29, 2019, Dickerson was interviewed for a sergeant position. At the end of the interview, I asked him why he had not applied for a corporal position, which was the next step above an officer before a sergeant. Dickerson replied that his family was more important because he did not want to work a Corporal's afternoon shift of 3:00 p.m. – 11:00 p.m. A captain and two lieutenants witnessed his response. However, it was another lie that Dickerson's family was so important.

The everyday routines, overall stability, and routines of the family are frequently severely disrupted by adultery; the deterioration of the family is not caused by working an afternoon shift. Regina Pickett (Bonner), who we will discuss more lately during her sworn deposition testimony, said that she had a "sexual encounter" with Dickerson while they both were on duty inside one of the campus buildings. She claimed that Dickerson did not tell her he was married and found out after being confronted via social media by his wife (Bonner v. WCCCD, 2021, 85-89). Dickerson reluctantly agreed that he had sex with Pickett but claimed it was at a motel, not at the college, and that they both were off duty (DaJuan Dickerson v. WCCCD, 2023, 29-36).

Dickerson's credibility was severely damaged when he was listed in the police "liars' squads," or the "liars' list," which often refers to a police officer being placed on the Brady-Giglio list (Liars' Squads list, n.d.) A prosecutor's office or police department will typically compile a list known as the Giglio-Brady list, which includes the names and information of law enforcement officials who have been involved in incidents of dishonesty, convictions for crimes, problems with candor, or other issues that cast doubt on their credibility (Reimund, 2013). This does not mean he's a member of the Brady Bunch television show. In December 2022, Wayne County Prosecutor Kym Worthy released a list of 74 current and former police officers in Wayne County who have been deemed untrustworthy to testify in court cases. Dickerson was included on Prosecutor Worthy's 2022 Giglio-Brady list. (Neavling, 2022). Dickerson was eventually charged with the crime of making false statements (DaJuan Dickerson v. WCCCD, 2023, 19-21).

On March 27, 2024, it was widely reported in TV news channels, newspapers, and social media that DaJuan Dickerson was convicted by a jury of lying to police about being the victim of a carjacking and lying to a peace officer. Prosecutors said Dickerson called 911 and reported a carjacking of his vehicle on March 7, 2021, at 9:08 p.m. at a church in the 14100 block of Evergreen Road in Detroit. Investigators found no evidence to substantiate Dickerson's claims, according to the prosecutor's office. Dickerson was scheduled to be sentenced by Judge John Gillis on April 24, May 3, and May 13, 2023. He could be sentenced to four years in prison and a fine of up to $2,000, or both (Siwicki, 2024; Carr, 2024; Ramirez, 2024; WWJ Newsradio, 2024). "You reap what you sow" is a proverb that says future consequences are inevitably shaped by present actions.

I found this quote on a Detroit police officer's Facebook

page, "When you destroy someone's life with lies, take it as a loan; it will come back to you with interest" (Young, 2024).

Dickerson lied so much during his deposition that it caused a fiery exchange between his and WCCCD's attorneys:

> ***ATTORNEY POTTER - Why should I believe you?***
>
> ***DICKERSON - Why not?***
>
> ***ATTORNEY BATEY - Objection. Argumentative.***
>
> ***ATTORNEY POTTER - Why not? You know you're on a Brady list, correct?***
>
> ***DICKERSON - I am aware of that.***
>
> ***ATTORNEY POTTER - What does a Brady list mean?***
>
> ***DICKERSON - You can define that.***
>
> ***ATTORNEY POTTER - It means that the Wayne County prosecutor has determined that you cannot be put on a witness stand because you are not truthful. Do you understand that?***
>
> ***DICKERSON - I do understand that, but that --***

ATTORNEY POTTER - Why should I believe - why should anyone believe what you're saying in this case?

ATTORNEY BATEY - Objection. Then we can end this deposition right now if you like.

ATTORNEY POTTER - Go ahead, end it. I don't care.

ATTORNEY BATEY - Either you are going to take his testimony, and you are going to shut up or - you are going to –

DICKERSON - Let me just say this.

ATTORNEY POTTER - Off the record for a second before I freaking explode at you.

ATTORNEY BATEY - You want to go outside? Let's go.

ATTORNEY HUNT - No, no, no, no. You guys are not going to do that. Stop it. (DaJuan Dickerson v. WCCCD, 2023, 17-18)

I could not believe the lies that were coming out of Dickerson's mouth as he said that he witnessed me having sex inside my department-issued police Tahoe parked next to an administrative parking lot (Dickerson v. WCCCD, 94-105). I always say, be careful throwing mud at someone when you wear a white outfit. It's my opinion that Dickerson orchestrated and encouraged individuals to lie and file fake lawsuits against me. Now look at him; his mug shot from his arrest has appeared on several media outlets. He's now convicted as a liar, and I sat in the courtroom as Judge Gillis sentenced him to three months in the Wayne County jail and two years of probation.

On July 6, 2023, in a stipulated order of voluntary dismissal, the Court dismissed Dickerson's lawsuit with prejudice and without costs or attorney fees to any party. A counterclaim filed on behalf of WCCCD against Dickerson was also dismissed. However, none of these frivolous lawsuits affected me until Alexis Holmes filed her meritless claim.

There's a quote about loyalty that, in my opinion, describes my former captain, Alexis Holmes. Some people aren't loyal to you. They are faithful to their need of you. Once their needs change, so does their loyalty. You're weak if you let someone put something in your ear to poison your loyalty to someone who has always been loyal and real with you.

I did receive notice from an anonymous source warning me that a member of my command staff was conspiring against me:

Darrick-

You need to resign! Shit about to get real bad for you.

Who is this?

Consider me as a friend with inside knowledge! It's a number of people working together coming for you, and they have evidence. It's people that's close in your command that's in on this. Don't let your ego get in the way of the good reputation you have built for yourself.

Do not contact me any further.

That's the politically correct response as I am texting your work phone. I gave you a fair warning: if you choose to embarrass yourself, that's fine. [_____] will not be able to save you again! He will want to keep his legacy in place and have no other option but to ask for your resignation. This will be a public exposure. The news is going to soak this up. You have been careless and messy! You have incriminated yourself. All good things come to an end! Money will not save you this time (text message, March 10, 2020).

I never suspected that Alexis Holmes was the "People that are close in your command that's in on this" until she went to WCCCD Human Resources.

One day, I asked her to check on my on-campus residence after a female companion was to leave for derelict conduct. She had a key to the residence as a security backup. I thought that she left the premises. Holmes called me and said, why did you have me go to your house, and a woman opened the door. She said, "I don't want any part of this." She went to Human Resources and said that it was the last straw. In my opinion, Holmes was suffering from erotomania, and her motivation for the complaint was born of her obsession with me as the Chief of police. However, I believe Holmes is the female version of Judas, Brutus, and Benedict Arnold combined. I felt the pain of betrayal that Elijah Muhammad felt towards Malcolm X after he lifted him from obscurity and placed him in a position of national prominence and trust (Louis X, 1964, 11).

I raised Alexis Holmes from a young, inexperienced officer to a position of authority in the WCCCD police authority department. I taught her what she knew about security and policing with dignity, respect, patience, and gracious mentoring. I tutored her after she failed a psychological screening to carry a firearm and allowed her to retest successfully after a year. I guided her in leadership after a retired sheriff deputy complained that she made him carry her purse while on duty. I advised her to relax control over retired police officers who were complaining that she would not let them go to the restroom without her permission. I treated her like my daughter and little sister. However, Holmes chose to serve the "Dark Side" like in the Star Wars movie and betray the Chief and the entire WCCCD police authority department. I must admit that her reckless and malicious behavior should've devastated me. In my opinion, Holmes was manipulated to support another female who exploited the "me too" movement and filed a complaint against me.

On July 5, 2022, Alexis Holmes, joined by a police officer Bonita Carey-Powers, filed a lawsuit against WCCCD and me through their attorney Zachary Runyun in Wayne County Circuit Court on Judge Charles Hegarty's docket. Carey-Powers falsely claims that she was dispatched to my residence and I greeted her "at the front door, wearing nothing other than a revealing bathrobe...pressured [her] to come inside for a personal visit" (Powers and Holmes vs WCCCD, 2022, 3-4). Okay, Grandma, your thoughts are extremely delusional. She also claimed retaliation, which resulted in constructive demotion and putting her safety in jeopardy. Holmes claimed that I "subjected [her] to years of inappropriate text messages and comments about her breast" (Powers and Holmes vs WCCCD, 2022, 8). She also claimed that I used her to retaliate against other employees, causing her a constructed demotion from captain to officer, resulting in a $30,000.00 pay decrease. Holmes also alleged that I retaliated against her by refusing to issue her a police badge, excluding her from emails, and indirectly ordering her to stay out of the office.

Interestingly, Holmes manufactured several hours of secret audio recordings that failed to substantiate any of her frivolous claims (Powers and Holmes vs WCCCD, 2022). At the time of this writing, their lawsuit is pending, and therefore, I will make no additional comments. Holmes and Powers probably wouldn't file their meritless lawsuit except that Derrick Bonner and Regina Pickett initiated these lawsuits with their fake complaint.

On January 23, 2020, Regina Pickett (Bonner) and Derrick Bonner filed a lawsuit against WCCCD, and several officers, including me, Captain Bahrija Livadic, Lieutenant Pride Johnson, and Sergeant Byron Young, for sexual harassment, retaliation, malicious prosecution, false arrest, false imprisonment, and assault and battery. The lawsuit is currently on the court docket of Judge Qiana Lillard, case number 20-001062-CZ (Derrick Bonnor and Regina Pickett vs. WCCCD et al., 2020). The lawsuit was filed as a vindictive retaliation for the legal arrest of Derrick Bonner at WCCCD in 2019.

Regina Pickett was hired as a campus safety officer at WCCCD on April 12, 2018. Pickett, in a very short time period, developed attendance problems. On October 8, 2018, in a meeting between Pickett, her supervisors Carey-Powers, and Chris O'Harris, she became irate over being scheduled to work on Saturdays and cursed at her superiors. Carey-Powers told O'Harris to escort her out of the office due to her behavior. O'Harris escorted her to her vehicle, and she took off her uniform shirt, indicating she was quitting, but changed her mind. I recommended WCCCD Human Resources to end her assignment. In February 2019, Pickett asked me for a job reference pending a position at the Michigan Department of Corrections. I rehired her because I felt that the October 2018 incident could've been handled differently.

On March 11, 2019, at 3:00 pm, Pickett arrived at WCCCD for the platoon III shift at the Curtis L Ivery downtown campus. At approximately 4:14 pm, Sergeant Young noticed a few scratches on Pickett's face. She told him that she and their children's father (Derrick Bonner) had a physical fight before work, and he caused the visible scratches. She also said that Bonner was on his way to the Downtown Campus to drop off her children because he was still mad at her. Captain Livadic came to my office and asked for assistance with Bonner, who was at the front desk with the children. I attempted to offer Bonner and Pickett to try to resolve their problem in our conference room. Bonner became extremely irate and cursed at me, so I told him to leave the campus. As he was leaving, I saw Pickett's face and asked her what happened. She told me that Bonner had beat her up at their residence before she came to work. I advised Livadic and Young that they needed to detain and investigate Bonner for domestic violence (Young, 2019).

Bonner was escorted back inside the campus to the police authority's office. Once inside, he pushed Sergeant Young and fled on foot out the main entrance and across Fort Street, heading northbound on Fifth Street. After a brief chase, Bonner was apprehended by Lieutenant Pride Johnson with the assistance of Detroit Police and conveyed back to the WCCCD police authority detainment room. He was arrested for domestic assault and battery after admitting to having a physical altercation with Pickett earlier at their home in Detroit. Pickett became uncooperative once Bonner was in custody. Bonner stated that he couldn't breathe, and an ambulance was called, which responded and evaluated him. Bonner was conveyed to the Wayne County Sheriff's Jail Division for processing (Young, 2019)

On April 1, 2019, a preliminary examination was held at 36th District Court before Judge Michael Wagner. Pickett continued to be uncooperative, making several untrue statements in an effort to protect Bonner. However, Judge Wagner determined that WCCCD police had sufficient probable cause to arrest Bonner, bounded him over for trial, and determined Pickett's testimony to be lacking credibility. Judge Wagner said:

> ***I find her testimony to be highly suspect. I heard the testimony of a woman in love. I didn't hear the testimony of a woman that I believe to be truthful, but - and if there is any domestic violence going on, I'm afraid, because as we know, there are many, many women who endure and go back to abusers. They will say, swear up and down nothing happens in the face of***

overwhelming evidence. (People State of Michigan vs Derrick Bonner, 2019, 52)

It was also determined during the preliminary examination that Bonner had at least five other incidents of domestic violence—one of them involving his previous wife, Vivian Palmer.

On May 13, 2012, Birmingham, Michigan, police responded to the Bonner residence for a report of domestic violence. Birmingham police found Vivian after she ran out of the house into the street. The Birmingham police documented what Vivian told them about how Bonner assaulted her:

At approximately 2200hrs, an argument ensued, and Vivian tried to leave the house. She said as she was attempting to leave the residence, Derrick grabbed her by the back of her head and pulled her back toward him. She said that while she was struggling, Derrick punched her on the right side of her face and threw her to the ground. While on the ground, Derrick placed his hands over her mouth and around her neck. Vivian said Derrick also bit her on her right shoulder…Vivian said this type of behavior was not unusual for Derrick. She said he had been arrested 6 times for domestic assault in the past 6 months (Romanowski, 2012).

Bonner was convicted of domestic violence after pleading no contest in the 48th District Court on July 10, 2012 (Worthy, 2019). Unfortunately, the prosecution in the 2019 WCCCD case decided to dismiss the charges despite so much proof that Bonner and Pickett were lying.

Regina Pickett and Derrick Bonner, in my opinion, are both psychopaths and pathological liars who lie most often to themselves about their ability to fool others. During Pickett's March 10, 2021, deposition, she claimed that I asked her if she liked older men. She said that I told her that I wanted to fuck her and that I had other girls, and I wanted to have a threesome with her (Bonner v. WCCCD, 2021, 23). She claimed that I told her I wanted to fuck her every time she saw me (Bonner v. WCCCD, 2021, 29). However, she never reported it to WCCCD Human Resources; she only told her husband, Derrick. The question arises: why would she send me the following Instagram direct message in December 2018:

> ***Hi Mr. Muhammad,***
>
> ***There are somethings that have came to my attention that I said that I was going to sue you and lots of other things. I want to be the 1st to say that I was completely blindsided by that because there's no way whatsoever that I would say anything bad about you, and there's no reason for me to sue you. From my understanding, you haven't did anything wrong to me. Yes, you did fire me, but I'm grown. I'm***

going to pick myself up and move on I'm not going to try to start rumors etc.

I am aware of who told you that, and he's a very miserable, disgusting man. His wife caught him doing things that he wasn't supposed to be doing, and now he's trying making up lies, deformation my character, and trying to get the heat off of him.

I'm not one to gossip or be in drama, but I have lots of proof from Dickerson and his wife stating that I've tried to sleep with you, talking about you and your personal life etc. I would be happy to send you screenshots of everything. He has even told other officers these rumors. Sgt. Powers has also told officers stories about your personal life and how you would come outside with your robe on when she brought you food. What you do in your personal life is none of my concern. I'm not sure why he's making these false allegations. (Pickett, R. [iamreginap] Instagram direct message. December 2018)

One month after Derrick Bonner was arrested, Pickett filed an EEOC complaint against me in April 2019. Pickett also fabricated stories about Lieutenant Johnson driving past her and Bonner on 8-Mile Road, staring at them, screaming out the window, and saying fuck you (Bonner v. WCCCD, 2021, 202). Pickett also said that I had Bonner arrested so that I would have a better opportunity at getting at her if he was out of the picture (Bonner v. WCCCD, 2021, 205).

Pickett's complaint is gloriously fabricated and utterly deranged; this is hypocrisy, without a doubt, an embarrassment to the "me too" movement. Another glaringly Instagram direct message communication clearly illustrates that I did not sexually harass Pickett:

[You replied to their story]

Me: Lol (thumbs up)

Me: I'm scared of you...

Pickett: Why lol

Me: (GIF lady talking, blah, blah, blah

Pickett: Huh, lol?

Me: Don't act brand new

Pickett: Lol tell me what you're thinking, I'm confused

Me: Never mind, GN

Pickett: Ok. As you can see, I clearly don't work there anymore. You think I'm gonna talk? Is that what you mean?

Me: YEP

Pickett: I'm grown, I don't kiss and tell

Me: Ok…It's inappropriate for me to be involved with employees and/or students of WCCCD

Pickett: ok…If you say so. (sad face emoji) (Pickett, R. [iamreginap]. Instagram direct message. October 31, 2018)

Pickett's explanation of this communication is both fascinating and unbelievable. Pickett claimed that after this conversation (DM), she told me to stop commenting on her Instagram because it made her feel uncomfortable. She flips the script and later says, "I decided to play his game and feed into it, just to get him to admit his wrongdoing and what he did, the sexual harassment…During that time, I was considering filing an EEOC, and, you know, I needed proof; everything he did to me and said to me was verbal. He never put it on here besides commenting on the pictures. So, this was my way of getting him to admit to the sexual harassment" (Bonner v. WCCCD, 2021, 49-51).

Pickett would later agree that I did not take her bait and that she was trying to set me up. As to liking multiple pictures of me on Instagram, Pickett claimed, "I didn't like it. This was me having him believe that I liked it…I was trying to set him up" (Bonner v. WCCCD, 2021, 55).

According to recent research, African American women who experience domestic abuse may be more likely than Caucasian women to acquire post-traumatic stress disorder (Griffing et al., 2002), also referred to as battered woman syndrome. A common foundation for domestic abuse is fear and worry about what your abuser may do next (Heal, 2019). A fifty-year-old male (Derrick Bonner), who has a history of multiple domestic violence incidents, is no match to a young victim like Regina Pickett. Law enforcement personnel have long recognized domestic violence - Stockholm syndrome with battered women who fail to press charges, bail their battering partner out of jail, and even physically attack police officers when they arrive to rescue them (Logan, 2018). It's not uncommon for a police officer to have to fight and arrest the abusive husband and the wife/girlfriend after arresting the husband. Such was the case with Regina Pickett, after reporting being a victim of domestic violence from Bonner, later claiming that the WCCCD police fabricated the charge and accusing me of orchestrating his arrest based upon a desire to have her all to myself. She did not want to expose her attacker (Bonner) and instead became the puppet of a psychotic narcissist.

According to his own testimony, Bonner has been diagnosed with bipolar disorder and has an extensive mental illness history with Henry Ford Hospital (Bonner v. WCCCD, 2022, 131-137). While Bonner claimed that he was not taking medication for mental illness, his manic behavior manifested in Facebook postings he made toward Lieutenant Pride Johnson after his arrest. Bonner posted on Lieutenant Johnson's Facebook page, "You puck bitch, why are you on my Facebook, bitch", "People, this bitch fucks little girls. Him and that bitch pussy ass fake chief. Bitch, if you're ever around my wife, our children, I'm fucking you up," "bitch ass, pussy ass, punk, pussy, is a rapes ass punk. Let everyone in Detroit know what type of dude you are, bitch," "I think I fucked your grandmother, you puck-ass bitch. Bitch, you rape your niece, tell everybody what you did," "Dude, why do your bitch ass keep sending me shit on my Facebook?" and "You rape your niece, puck ass bitch. Your mom is a bitch. I am going to the police. Dude, fuck you and your cross-eyed niece. She had a baby by you, you pussy" on five separate occasions (Bonner v. WCCCD, 2022, 253-258). Bonner justified his use of such lewd and profane language by explaining that the officers harassed his family, arrested him, bullied and destroyed his family (261).

Bonner's narcissistic behavior of having an excessive preoccupation with himself and his own needs, often at the expense of others (Narcissism, 2021), may be illustrated in his relationship with Pickett. For example, in 2015, Bonner was in his forties when he impregnated 15-year-old Pickett with their first child, Derrick Jr.

(Bonner v. WCCCD, 2021, 145-151, 209). Under Michigan law, Bonner committed statutory rape because he had sex with Pickett, who was under the age of consent, also referred to as third-degree criminal sexual conduct CSC-III (Michigan Penal Code Act, 1931). Bonner's narcissism was further evidenced by possibly fraudulently using his son's social security number; Bonner's son and mother blamed him for using his son's identification. Bonner testified, "Someone stole my identity and…he asked me if I did it, and I was like, dude, I didn't use your ID…I never used it, but someone used it, and I was the one that was being blamed for it" (Bonner v. WCCCD, 2022, 38-39). In addition to being narcissistic, Bonner wasn't a good liar.

It would be obvious to anyone listening to Bonner's testimony that he is a compulsive and pathological liar. Bonner fabricated the initial contact between him and me. He said that I "came from out the door…He wasn't behind the counter…Regina was behind the counter…He said, 'Who the fuck are you" (Bonner v. WCCCD, 2022, 154-155). While there is no audio available, there is CCTV video. Video is the best witness, seeing is believing, and the best evidence is the CCTV video. CCTV footage revealed that I approached the counter and started talking to Bonner. The video shows that I never "came from out the door." In fact, Pickett is standing behind me, and Capt. Livadic is behind her. Bonner and Chief are gesticulating, and it is Bonner who appears agitated (WCCCD Police Authority CCTV. 2019). Bonner's integrity was further tarnished when a detective came to their residence to serve her a subpoena. Bonner claimed that Pickett was not home, and he gave the detective a false name, "Michael Johnson, landlord," and provided a forged signature (Bonner v. WCCCD, 2022, 205-206).

In my opinion, Derrick Bonner is a deranged narcissist, psychopath, and child molester. A woman beater and a coward. His attorneys knew that he had no case, so they retained deceiving private investigators, who dug up several disgruntled former employees who fabricated multiple stories against me. They used the media to create a smear campaign. I believe that I will be fully exonerated in the end. I'm sure, like most narcissists, Bonner is saying, how dare you ruin my reputation by telling the truth about the things I said and did. I understand that this introduction went off-topic. However, it was therapeutic for me, and it will give the readers a little of my Kimora. Since leaving law enforcement, I'm currently a real estate investor.

In 2014, I rented my personal residence to a tenant and was amazed at how much money I acquired in 3 years. I used some of that money to procure 7 additional single-family homes, and I eventually sold 2 of them. I purchased a single-family home from the Detroit Land Bank in 2017 for only $1,000.00. I invested approximately $20,000.00 into rehabbing the house. After getting my money back from a tenant, I sold it for a substantial profit in 2022. Many years ago, my father actually named my investment company *Black Gold Real Estate*. While speaking as a Minister, he told an audience, "I know my son Darrick gets into trouble every now and then. But once he makes his mind up, whatever he touches, he turns to gold."

In August of 2022, I read Mike Ealy's book, From Broke to Millions, and it changed the trajectory of my real estate goals. I am currently taking a Mastermind course on real estate investing under the tutelage of Mike Ealy of Nassau Investments. It looks like it will be an amazing adventure with the correct business partners and a solid support network. As Mike Ealy says, remember... You're ONE BIG DEAL away! I still have a passion for security and policing. I truly want to see police reform, and I pray that this book sheds some light on some of the corrections that are needed.

For most of us, when we complete any post assignment (Chief, Deputy Chief, Captain, Lieutenant, Sergeant, Corporal, Officer, etc.) given to us and our tour of duty in that post is over, there is no fanfare, no party and hardly even a wave goodbye. You have done your job, and it's simply time to leave. The best you can do is hold your head up high and be satisfied with what you have done and achieved during your time in that job you were designated. Don't do the work to be glorified; do the work to help create a better reality. Show and prove your sincerity through your actions and example, not lip profession (Black Muslim Culture, 2023). This is one of my inspirations for writing this book.

Police brutality and fatal police encounters with African Americans appear to be the most formidable monstrosity confronting police-community relations. Unfortunately, this issue is a recurrent policing problem for nearly every urban metropolitan city. According to Skolnick and Fyfe, the videotaped beating of Rodney King destroyed the dragnet image and vision of the police. The 2000 killing of George Floyd at the hands of Derek Chauvin and the Minneapolis police put policing on its death bed, and many are ready to take police off of life support. It may be misleading to suggest that attempting to put restraints on racism and police brutality is an appropriate or realistic issue for a metropolitan city. The task will not be completed until we provide police administration and field officers with education so they will understand the horrors of this nation's past. The role or function of the police must be re-defined to eliminate the slave-catching tactics of the past (Muhammad, D., 2002).

Chapter 2: I Can't Breathe

"Please, please, please, I can't breathe. My stomach hurts. My neck hurts. Please, please. I can't breathe," George Floyd's last words. (Madani, 2020)

Perhaps the American public and polity should've listened to Colin Kaepernick when he kneeled during the national anthem before an NFL game. Kaepernick was protesting the police being able to kill unarmed Black people without consequences. However, he was labeled anti-police, anti-military, and anti-American (Johnson, 2020). President Donald Trump called Kaepernick a "son of a bitch" and said that NFL owners should get him off the field and fire him (Gottlieb and Maske, 2017). Police brutality, misconduct, excessive use of force, and killings may appear to be the most daunting monstrosity confronting police-community relations. Unfortunately, this issue is a recurrent policing problem for nearly every major American city. The problem made its way to every American citizen with the killing of George Floyd, who had his neck knelt on by a White Minneapolis police officer for nearly nine minutes, even after pleading, "I can't breathe" (George Floyd died of asphyxia, 2020).

On Memorial Day – May 25, 2020, an employee at Cup Foods store in Minneapolis, Minnesota, called 911 and reported 46-year-old George Floyd was attempting to pass a counterfeit twenty-dollar bill to pay for a pack of cigarettes. Officers Derek Chauvin and his partner Tou Thao, along with Thomas Lane and J.A. Kueng, arrived at the scene and attempted to get Floyd into the back of a police car. Floyd complained that he was claustrophobic, refused to get in the car, and said that he couldn't breathe while he was standing up. Floyd ended up on the ground in handcuffs, and Chauvin placed his knee on Floyd's neck while he was on the street. 17-year-old Darnella Frazier recorded the incident and streamed it on Facebook. Floyd can be heard telling the officer he couldn't breathe, and onlookers can be heard pleading with Chauvin to release Floyd. Chauvin kept his knee on Floyd's neck for eight minutes and 46 seconds, including 2 minutes and 53 seconds when Floyd was unresponsive. None of the police officers even attempted to give Floyd first aid, and he was later pronounced dead at a hospital (Graves, 2020).

The day after the murder of George Floyd, protestors took to the streets in Minneapolis and quickly erupted into confrontation with police. Protests broke out in other cities across the United States and began to turn violent by the evening. On May 28, the Minneapolis third precinct police station was burned down, and nearly every major city protest turned to looting and rioting. After a week of protest and civil disobedience or riots, at least 200 cities imposed curfews, and nearly 30 states and Washington, D. C.

activated over 62,000 National Guard troops (Sergent, Loehrke, J., Padilla, R., & Hertel, 2020).

Protests escalated beyond the shores of the United States. Every continent except Antarctica had their citizens protesting against the killing of George Floyd; at least 40 countries, including Australia, Canada, China, England, France, Germany, Israel, Japan, Mexico, South Africa, and Wales, just to name a few of the entire globe (Smith, Wu, & Murphy, 2020). There is a long history in the United States of police brutality against civilians, predominantly African Americans (Carter, 2017). However, was the murder of George Floyd a catalyst for unprecedented civil unrest or just the straw that broke the camel's back?

The cumulative deaths of George Floyd, Ahmaud Arbery, and Breonna Taylor grazed a wound on African Americans who have been subjected to police abuse for several decades. On February 23, 2020, Mr. Ahmaud Arbery was on an afternoon jog in Brunswick, Georgia. A retired police detective and retired district attorney investigator, Gregory McMichael, who resides in the neighborhood, along with his son Travis McMichael, armed themselves with a pistol and a shotgun and got into a pickup truck driving through the neighborhood. They pursued Arbery, and a video shows the idle pickup truck on the road ahead of the jogging Arbery. He attempted to go around the pickup truck and began to struggle with a man with a shotgun. The other man was standing in the rear of the pickup, and three gunshots were fired. Arbery falls dead to the ground. A third man, William Bryan, videotaped the murder and claimed he "had nothing to do with it" and was in "complete shock." However, the Glynn County police indicated that Bryan was in "hot pursuit" of Arbery and that he had unsuccessfully tried to block Arbery's trail (Ahmaud Arbery: What do we know, 2020). The released video was shocking to the conscious and caused a national outcry as there appeared to be no interest on the part of law enforcement in making an arrest.

The arrest of Gregory McMichael and Travis McMichael was delayed for over two months and probably would not have happened except for the released video. The arrest of Bryan came a couple of weeks after the other two. The investigation of the case went through four prosecutors. The Brunswick District Attorney blamed the police, and two County Commissioners blamed the Brunswick District Attorney for ordering the police not to arrest. The Waycross Circuit District Attorney George Barnhill told the police that Gregory McMichael and Travis McMichael were making a citizen's arrest against Arbery and there were no grounds for the arrest of the two (Ahmaud Arbery: What do we know, 2020). While active members of the police did not kill Arbery, the lack of the administration of justice is equivalent to the perception that the Government does not value the lives of African Americans.

A 26-year-old EMT who wanted to be a nurse was doing what we all do after midnight, sleeping. Unfortunately, Breonna Taylor would not wake again after she was shot multiple times as

Louisville, Kentucky, police raided her apartment.

On March 13, 2020, at 12:30 a.m., Taylor and her boyfriend, Kenneth Walker, were awakened by "a loud bang at the door" and thought someone was breaking in. Police officers Jonathan Mattingly, Brett Hankison, and Myles Cosgrove claimed that they knocked and announced police as they were serving a no-knock search warrant for narcotics. Walker claimed that Taylor yelled several times, "Who is it?" Walker said that no one responded. Suddenly, the door appeared to explode off the hinges as it may have been hit with a battering ram by police. Walker, who was a licensed firearm carrier, claims that he fired a shot in self-defense. A police officer was shot in the leg. Police returned fire, shooting more than 20 rounds into Taylor's home, striking objects in the living room, dining room, kitchen, hallway, bathroom, and both bedrooms. Taylor was shot at least eight times and was pronounced dead at the scene (Read, 2020).

While it's understandable for police to limit their response during an ongoing investigation, the Louisville police failed miserably in terms of accountability and transparency in the killing of Breonna Taylor. Approximately three months after the police shooting of Taylor, the Louisville police department released a copy of the report, which was "almost entirely blank. The report lists the time, date, incident number, scene location, and the victim's name, but it indicates no injuries, no forced entry, and the narrative simply read, 'PIU investigation.'" Local newspaper editor Richard

A. Green asked city officials, “Are you kidding? This is what you consider being transparent to taxpayers and the public?" Louisville Mayor Greg Fischer called the report “unacceptable” and ordered an external review of the Police department (Duvall, 2020).

The murder of Breonna Taylor is a clear sign that the killing of Black victims by police does not warrant the administration of justice in the United States. One of the officers involved, Brett Hankison, has been fired for “want only and blindly fir[ing] 10 rounds into the apartment of Breonna Taylor,” lacking any facts that the deadly force was used against the person posing an immediate threat. He was accused of firing ten shots through a door and window that he was not able to see through in order to determine whether a “person [was] an immediate threat or, more importantly, any innocent persons present. However, Hankinson’s termination was merely a result of protest after the worldwide reaction to the George Floyd murder. There appeared to be no desire on the part of police and city officials to hold officers accountable for their actions, and there still has not been an arrest for her murder (Costello, 2020).

The tragic murder of George Floyd, witnessed by cell phone video, and the worldwide protest afterward sent shockwaves throughout the United States and the world, resulting in an echoed demand for police reform. The United States was still smoldering in the aftermath of the murders of all three, Floyd, Arbery, and Breonna Taylor, when all of a sudden, another police shooting erupted in Kenosha, Wisconsin, which brought reminisces of the landmark United States Supreme Court ruling in Tennessee V Garner. In Tennessee V Garner, the Supreme Court held that, under the Fourth Amendment, when a law enforcement officer is pursuing a fleeing suspect, the officer may not use deadly force to prevent escape unless "the officer has probable cause to believe that the suspect poses a significant threat of death or serious physical injury to the officer or others" (Tennessee V Garner). While the facts of the shooting are uncertain, the initial perception is that a White policeman shot a Black man several times in the back as he attempted to leave. In addition, protesters denouncing the shooting are more concerned about what happened to Jacob Blake and, more so, what it's like to be Black in America (Lockwood, 2020).

On August 23, 2020, Kenosha police responded to a 911 call of a domestic violence dispute. According to Attorney Benjamin Crump, "Blake was attempting to de-escalate a fight between two other people when officers arrived at the scene." The videotape shows that Blake walked away from police to the driver's side of his vehicle, followed by two officers with guns drawn. Officer Rusten Sheskey tried to grab Blake, and when Blake opened the door and leaned in, Officer Rusten grabbed him and fired at least seven shots into Blake's back. A witness who recorded the video of the shooting said he heard police shouting, "Drop the knife," but said that he saw no weapons in Blake's hand (Freiman & Carissimo, 2020).

In the aftermath of the Blake shooting, thousands gathered

in Washington, D. C., on August 28, 2020, in a march sponsored by Reverend Al Sharpton called the Commitment March: Get Your Knee Off Our Necks. The speakers at the rally included the family of George Floyd, Breonna Taylor, Jacob Blake, and many others (March on Washington, 2020). Indubitably, protests immediately followed Blake's shooting in the streets. On August 24, 2020, protesters damaged police cars, injured officers with bricks, set a dump truck to flames, and vandalized the local Court, museum, charter school, and post office, resulting in a state of emergency being declared (Carson & Jones, 2020).

On August 26, 2020, the Milwaukee Bucks sparked a National sports boycott or strike by refusing to come out of their locker room minutes before the scheduled start of the first-round playoff game against the Orlando Magic in protest of the Blake shooting. This had a domino effect and led to other boycotts by the National Basketball Association (NBA), Women's National Basketball Association (WNBA), Major League Baseball (MLB), the National Hockey League (NHL), and Major League Soccer (MLS) (Gregory, 2020). Unfortunately, the protest suffered an extreme twist when militias decided to patrol the streets of Kenosha.

On August 25, 2020, during a Blake protest, 17-year-old Kyle Rittenhouse was walking down a street armed with a long gun, got into a confrontation with people near a car dealership, and opened fire, allegedly killing two people and wounding a third, according to a criminal complaint. After the shooting, Rittenhouse walked towards Kenosha police officers with his hands up and still armed but was not arrested or detained. He was able to leave the crime scene and was arrested later. Kenosha police Chief Daniel Miskin defended the officer's inaction, stating that officers were driving into "a shots fired complaint, not a shooting, not a person down complaint. Unfortunately, we have had many of those over the course of this. They're responding to that; they see somebody walking towards them with their hands up, which, too, isn't out of the ordinary given how events have been going on. We have armed individuals out protesting or simply walking around exercising (their) right" (Karimi, 2020). For many African Americans, this is reminiscent of Dylann Roof, who murdered in cold blood nine Black people at a Charleston church, in which Shelby police bought the suspect food from Burger King after he was taken into custody (McCormack, 2017).

African Americans being killed by White police officers is an issue that is sending shockwaves throughout the United States, resulting in an echoed demand for police reform. The frequency with which it occurs and the role that race plays is obscured. In particular, the United States government does not require the police to report the use of lethal force. Nevertheless, it is difficult to study empirically, and often, one has to rely on media databases to track individuals killed by the police (Hehman, Flake & Calanchini, 2017). Our work reviews police shootings and killings that were reported through the newspapers and television over the years throughout history. George Floyd was not the first victim who pleaded with police that "I can't breathe."

Frederick Finley was killed on June 22, 2000, after plain clothes security officers confronted him and family members outside of Lord & Taylor at Fairlane Town Center Mall in Dearborn, Michigan. This time, the killer was not a policeman but rather a private security officer. Finley's 11-year-old stepdaughter was suspected of shoplifting after a video recording showed that she slipped a $4 bracelet on her wrist and left the store without paying for it. Three Black and one White Lord & Taylor plainclothes security officers confronted the family in the parking lot. Finley thought the men were bothering the girl and tried to defend her when a struggle ensued (Warikoo & Bailey, 2000). Finley punched one of the security officers and was restrained by the other officers. They knocked him to the ground, handcuffed him, and held down his legs. Simultaneously, one of the Black officers named Dennis Richardson placed his knee on Finley's neck as he pleaded, "Get off me, get off me." Richardson then placed Finley's neck in a chokehold; ten seconds later, Finley was dead. A Black plainclothes security officer snatched Finley off the ground and yelled, "Get the fuck up," then dropped him back down to the ground (Sternisha, 2010).

While it may appear that race was neutral in the Finley murder since Richardson and Finley both were Black, meticulous examination reveals a process of assimilation. At a subsequent protest at Fairlane Town Center of 7,000 people, Reverend Al Sharpton argued that "Whites certainly don't get choked to death" by security guards. Reverend Horace Sheffield said at the rally, “Corporations deliberately hire minority guards so that when bad incidents occur, they can wash their hands clean” (Warikoo & Bailey, 2000). Are Black security and police officers being brainwashed to attack their own people? My experience in law enforcement was that officers who engage in aggressive tactics are considered good officers and labeled as “John Wayne,” whereas officers who utilize de-escalation verbal tactics are labeled as “officer friendly” and are not viewed as good officers. It is referred to as "Blue is blue.” In other words, police work shapes the officer, not the other way around. Criminologist James Messerschmidt argues that "the police construct a White, heterosexual form of hegemonic masculinity” (Sklansky, 2006). The Honorable Elijah Muhammad said that “the Black police officer always has had to try to keep his position and promotion to higher office by how much he can mistreat his own people, beating and killing [them]” (Muhammad, Demetri, 2017). According to a former African American NYPD officer, “Black cops had to be more vicious and brutal to their own to get approval and confidence from their White counterparts. It was a type of insurance that Black cops would have a backup instead of being set up” (Abel, 2006). Thus, the unconscious Black Officer adopts a posture that he must be much more brutal on Black suspects in policing matters.

We are looking at private security in relation to brutality because while arrest authorities may differ, they are one and the same as police. Private security is the police twin cousin. A significant similarity between police and private security is that they both play a role in social control. According to a study, "43 percent of police officers have prior experience in security, and 64 percent of security professionals have prior law enforcement experience." The study also revealed that private security officers are "police officer-wannabes" and have a desire to become fully sworn police officers. However, they are poorly trained, poorly educated, and poorly compensated and are "often a hindrance to the efforts of police officers in criminal investigations, or may even be the target of an investigation themselves" (Nalla & Hummer, 1999). Thus, the brutal actions and behaviors of security officers merit tangible examples of police abuse.

On January 28, 2014, 25-year-old McKenzie Cochran was killed by Northland Mall security at the now-closed Detroit suburban mall of Southfield. Cochran allegedly told a Northland mall jewelry store employee that he wanted to kill someone. The employee called security. Northland mall security arrived and told Cochran to leave the mall. He refused, and the security officers pepper-sprayed and restrained him. Cochran struggled on the ground as three officers held him for several minutes, one with a knee in his back. Shoppers videotaped on a cell phone Cochran pleading, "I can't breathe," and asking bystanders to call the police because he was dying. The video captures a security officer telling Cochran several times to stop resisting. The Oakland County Medical Examiner's Office ruled Cochran's cause of death as "position compression asphyxia" or strangulation.

However, Oakland County Prosecutor Jessica Cooper refused to prosecute the security officers, citing that they were poorly trained and lacked criminal intent (Abbey-Lambertz, 2014). After the worldwide "Black Lives Matter" protest and the murder of George Floyd, Michigan Attorney General Dana Nessel has agreed to review the 2014 death of McKenzie Cochran (Baldas, 2020). It appears that some bad private security officers are mirroring the actions of some bad police officers.

Similar to some police officers, race can unfortunately also play a role in how security officers interact with individuals. On May 31, 2019, Lucas County Sheriff's Deputy Alan Gaston went to the office of the IRS office in Toledo, Ohio. Deputy Gaston, a Black man wore his full uniform and had his service weapon on his side. A White security guard named Seth Eklund, ordered Gaston to leave his gun in his car. Gaston refused and attempted to leave the office. The White security guard pulled his own handgun and aimed it at Deputy Gaston. Gaston turned around and walked away from Eklund, who followed the deputy pointing a gun at his back. Eklund followed Gaston to an elevator and blocked the elevator doors from closing. Another IRS office employee called 911, telling the dispatcher that there was a man in the office with a gun who was refusing to leave. The caller didn't mention that the man was a sheriff's deputy (Hutchinson, 2019). The White security guard made it abundantly clear that even a Black deputy or police officer will be subjected to hostile racial hatred. My argument assumes that this would never happen to a White policeman.

I agree with Vice President Joe Biden when he said, “I know most cops are good, decent people. I know how they risk their lives every time they put that shield on and go out the door” (Weigel, 2020). The majority of police officers I observed do not regularly engage in the excessive use of force, and many cases are extreme examples of isolated occurrences in some police departments. However, New York Governor Andrew Cuomo said, “We have a problem. Let's acknowledge it,” in reference to the failure of the criminal justice system to resolve cases of police brutality (Vielkind, 2014). One such case was the “chokehold” killing of Eric Garner by the New York Police, which President Barack Obama referred to as “an American problem and not just a Black problem” (Bobic, 2014). The American problem was a New York grand jury’s decision not to indict a NYPD officer in the chokehold death of a Black man named Eric Garner.

On July 17, 2014, Eric Garner was confronted by NYPD officers, accusing him of selling loose cigarettes. Garner denied selling cigarettes and told police that he was tired of them harassing him. In an attempt to arrest Garner, a plainclothes officer, Daniel Pantaleo, grabbed him, and Garner resisted by pulling away. Pantaleo then placed his arm around Garner's neck and wrestled him to the ground. Several officers held Garner down as he pleaded eleven times, “I can’t breathe,” as he was lying face down. Garner lost consciousness and died an hour later at a hospital. The medical examiner determined that Garner’s death was a homicide resulting from “compression of the neck, compression of chest and prone positioning during physical restraint by police" (Goldstein& Santora, 2014). "I can't breathe" has become a rallying cry in protests against alleged police brutality cases as it was the last words of Garner before he was killed. According to the video clip, Garner said:

> ***Get away [garbled] ... for what? Every time you see me, you want to mess with me. I'm tired of it. It stops today. Why would you...? Everyone standing here will tell you I didn't do nothing. I did not sell nothing. Because every time you see me, you want to harass me. You want to stop me (garbled) Selling cigarettes. I'm minding my business, officer; I'm minding my business. Please just leave me alone. I told you the last time, please just leave me alone. Please, please, don't touch me. Do not touch me. I can't breathe. I can't breathe. I can't breathe. I can't breathe. I can't breathe. I can't breathe. I can't breathe. I can't breathe. I can't breathe. (Capelouto, 2014)***

Kobe Bryant and the Los Angeles Lakers wore "I Can't Breathe" shirts during warm-ups before an NBA basketball game against the Sacramento Kings to protest the killing of Eric

Garner (Capelouto, 2014).

"I can't breathe" or asphyxiation against Black people in this country, legitimated by White lynch mobs and supported by Southern police and sheriff, was perhaps nowhere more evidently demonstrated than in the historically common practice of lynching African American males accused of a sex crime against a White female. In 1932, the National Association for the Advancement of Colored People (NAACP) released a report that inventoried "3,290 people were lynched in the South between 1889 and 1931," of which the majority were African Americans (Tolnay, Beck & Massey, 1989). Ida B Wells asserted that the cause of these lynchings was the false claim of Black men raping White women, yet obscured the actual reasons were Black economic progress and, more importantly, enforcing the oppression of Blacks to a second-class status (Wells, 1892). The cause of death should've been listed as "asphyxia due to hanging by lynching by assailants" (Zagier, 2010). Asphyxia is the lack of oxygen in exchange for carbon dioxide or interfering and stopping a person from breathing. In contemporary times, positional asphyxia is the cause of sudden death in police suspect aggressive encounters. The New York police department and the F. B. I. recommended that prone restraint techniques, which contribute to positional asphyxia, should be avoided to reduce the potential for in-custody deaths (U. S. Department of Justice, 1995). However, recent prominent cases of police in-custody deaths involving Black men suggest that the NYPD and FBI advisory are being ignored or may be perceived as a modern-day lynching at the hands of police.

It appears that George Floyd and Eric Garner are not the exclusive proprietors of the phrase "I can't breathe." Recently, USA Today released a story titled, "George Floyd is not alone. 'I can't breathe' uttered by dozens in fatal police holds across U.S." The story examined numerous in-police custody killings where the suspect died from asphyxia. USA Today boldly reported:

> ***USA TODAY examined 32 fatal police encounters since 2010 in which victims said they couldn't breathe while being restrained. The incidents, which were identified by combing through court cases and media reports, are by no means a complete account. At least 134 people have died in police custody from "asphyxia/restraint" in the past decade alone, even though many apparently did not — or could not — express difficulty breathing, according to a review of Fatal Encounters [https://fatalencounters.org/], a searchable database of people who died while interacting with police. (Wedell, Kelly, McManus & Fernando, 2020)***

The in-custody killings of Black men examined by USA Today indicate that some police departments are using restraint tactics, which is perhaps the proximate cause of asphyxia. These types of killings at the hands of police, upon which the unarmed suspects pleaded "I can't breathe," have led to protests and a tremendous outcry of "I can't breathe." Realistically, a violent struggle between police and a person will increase the potential for asphyxia or in custody death (U. S. Department of Justice, 1995). All physical force by police is not excessive force or police abuse. For example, on July 10, 2020, there was a huge community outcry after Detroit police shot and killed 20-year-old Hakim Littleton. Family and witnesses claimed that Littleton was shot in the back multiple times after surrendering. However, video footage from a police body cam showed that Littleton was armed with a handgun and firing at officers before he was shot and killed (Hermes, 2020). Ultimately, all victims of in-custody police killings by asphyxia are not of the Black race (Wedell, Kelly, McManus & Fernando, 2020). Now, we will examine other incidents where unarmed persons were killed after pleading "I can't breathe" in an encounter with police.

On January 9, 2017, a Columbus, Georgia, police officer sat on a Hispanic man named Hector Arreola for several minutes, causing his death. 30-year-old Arreola called the police after suffering a major panic attack, which was triggered by his use of methamphetamine. The police initially requested medical assistance at the scene to evaluate him for mental illness or "drug-induced mental health issues." However, police decided to arrest Arreola for disorderly conduct after he displayed erratic behavior (Wedell, Kelly, McManus & Fernando, 2020). The officer's body cam reveals the police giving Arreola commands, "Stop, stop, stop." We can hear Arreola yell, "I'm not even doing nothing, Ma; they're going to kill me." According to family members, Arreola pleaded sixteen times, "I can't breathe." Arreola's mother tells officers that he is hurting, to which a police officer tells her, "He's fine, he can breathe" (Watson, 2020). An officer, described as at least 300 pounds, sat on top of Arreola's back, and another officer held him down with his knee over his neck. Arreola was held face down for six minutes until he became unresponsive and died (Wedell, Kelly, McManus & Fernando, 2020).

47-year-old Muhammad Abdul Muhaymin Jr. loved his tiny dog Chiquita so much that he took him everywhere. Unfortunately, it cost him his life (Garcia, 2020). On January 4, 2017, Muhaymin attempted to use the restroom at the Maryvale Community Center in Phoenix, Arizona. The police were called, and an employee blocked the restroom entrance because Muhaymin was carrying his service dog, which he used for emotional support. According to a resulting lawsuit, Muhaymin was "suffering from Post-Traumatic Stress Disorder, Acute Claustrophobia, and Schizophrenia." Muhaymin was allowed to use the restroom after providing identification to arriving police officers. Upon exiting, police attempted to arrest Muhaymin due to having a warrant for his arrest. Muhaymin refused to release his dog, and a struggle between him and the police began (Garcia, 2020). Reportedly, four officers pinned Muhaymin to the ground with their knees on his neck and head. Muhaymin repeatedly said, "I can't breathe," and died after vomiting (Wedell et al., 2020). The Maricopa County Medical Examiner determined that Muhaymin's death was a homicide. The George Floyd murder has sparked protests in Phoenix, where people are demanding "transparency, accountability, and justice for the people who have been killed by police officers" (Garcia, 2020). The Muhaymin killing begs the question, did police need to be called for a man wanting to go to the restroom with his dog? To the contrary, police were called to a DeKalb County restaurant because of a non-African American woman with a service dog. However, police made no arrests, and she was certainly not killed (Alston, 2018).

White Americans witnessed on video the killing of George Floyd, which verified the racist police brutality that African Americans complained of for many years. Georgetown University professor Dr. Michael Eric Dyson said, "The reality is White people saw this dude was no harm, ain't causing no trouble even though the police later on tried to say he was resisting. I think it moved White people in a way it hadn't done before" (Lawrence, 2020). More than half, three out of four victims of police restraint tactics that heighten people's risk of death were African Americans (Wedell, Kelly, McManus & Fernando, 2020). While White Americans are less victimized by police killings, in-custody death from asphyxia is not an anomaly to the use of certain police restraint tactics. These types of police restraint tactics put all citizens in peril regardless of one's race. Such was the case of 18-year-old Nicholas Dyksma, who died after police tased him, handcuffed him, and held him down with a knee on his neck (Wedell, Kelly, McManus & Fernando, 2020). The distinction was that Dyksma was a White American.

On August 31, 2015, at around 2:00 a.m., police responded to a Circle K convenience store for a suspicious man in a pickup truck. When they arrived, they found Dyksma slumped over the steering wheel. When police awakened Dyksma, he drove away at a high rate of speed, leading to a police pursuit. Harris County sheriff's deputies stopped his speeding truck by deploying a tire-deflation device. Dyksma was pulled from his truck after a window was broken by police and refused the deputy's orders to exit the vehicle. He was tased, held down, handcuffed, and pinned to the ground. According to a lawsuit filed by his family, police "cut off his air supply so that he was unable to breathe, and [police] did not stop applying pressure on his airway until after he lost consciousness." The Georgia Bureau of Investigation listed the cause of Dyksma's death as "a combination of the stun gun, compression of the "neck and torso, and acute methamphetamine intoxication." Dyksma's father said, "It's not the police's job to be the judge, jury, and executioner on the side of the road" (Almaguer, Seward & Ortiz, 2017). Historically, the police had used full power to judge and punish African Americans unilaterally.

USA Today reviewed 32 fatal police encounters in which victims said they couldn't breathe while being restrained (Wedell, Kelly, McManus & Fernando, 2020). However, asphyxia is not the sole tactic of causing death in police and African American encounters. President Lyndon Johnson's 1968 National Advisory Commission on Civil Disorders, aka the Kerner Commission, reported that "our nation is moving toward two societies, one Black, one White—separate and unequal... What White Americans have never fully understood — but what the Negro can never forget — is that White society is deeply implicated in the ghetto. White institutions created it, White institutions maintain it, and White society condones it" (National Advisory Commission, 1968). This huge indictment of White Americans has been largely ignored while African Americans continued to become victims of police brutality and fatal encounters.

We need not waste a lot of time arguing that African Americans have been disproportionately victims of police brutality and killings. However, contemporary police beatings, shootings, and killings of African Americans compel the argument. Studies indicate that cities with a large population of African Americans have a higher rate of killings by police (Jacobs & O'Brien, 1998). Some scholars have scrutinized police reaction to African Americans, providing evidence of the perils that exist in the relationship (Holmes & Smith, 2008). Americans were shocked to witness the amateur videotaped brutal beating of Rodney King at the hands of the Los Angeles police department (LAPD).

Reverend Al Sharpton said, "The Rodney King video was the Jackie Robinson of police video (Paybarah, 2020). CCTV video evidence is perhaps the best witness because it can't be denied. However, the videotaped beating of Rodney King was not enough to get a conviction of excessive force. Half past midnight, on March 3, 1991, King and two friends were driving on a Los Angeles freeway after watching basketball and drinking. California Highway Patrol attempted to pull King over for speeding, but he refused to stop, and a pursuit ensued with speeds up to 117 mph. The LAPD joined the pursuit and cornered the speeding car, forcing a stop. Police eventually removed King from the car. The video showed LAPD officers kicking and beating King with batons for 15 minutes as other officers watched (Linder, 2001). The nearly minute-and-a-half video showed the LAPD kicking and hitting King with batons at least 56 times (Matiash & Rothman, 2016). The video was captured by George Holliday, who took it to a local news station, KTLA. The video was picked up by CNN, which "used the tape like wallpaper." Ninety-two percent of viewers believed that Rodney King was a victim of excessive force at the hands of LAPD (Linder, 2001). LAPD Chief Daryl Gates said, "We believe the officers used excessive force taking him into custody. In our review, we find that officers struck him with batons between fifty-three and fifty-six times" (Garfield, 2020). However, the charges of assault and use of excessive force against the four police officers involved in the King beating resulted in an acquittal.

On April 29, 1992, the nearly all-White and pro-law enforcement jury acquitted all four officers of assault and acquitted three of the four of using excessive force. One of the officers, Stacey

Koon, after the beating, typed on his squad car computer, “U just had a big-time use of force. Tased and beat the suspect of CHP pursuit…I haven’t beaten anyone this bad in a long time.” Perhaps, due to extensive media coverage, the trial had a change of venue and moved to Semi Valley, California, which is a predominantly White and conservative suburb of Los Angeles. After the jury acquitted the officers, within two hours, Los Angeles was set ablaze. After six days of rioting and order was restored, there were 63 deaths, 2,383 injured people, at least 7,000 fires, and property damages to over 3,000 businesses totaling approximately one billion dollars. A helicopter captured a horrifying video of a White truck driver, Reginald Denny, being pulled from his 18-wheeler tractor-trailer, kicked and beaten on the head with a hammer, and finally knocked unconscious with a block of concrete (Linder, 2001). The generosity of Black victims in the face of police violence is amazing. Rodney King, a Black man who suffered a broken facial bone, a fractured right ankle, multiple bruises, and lacerations at the hands of the LAPD, not to mention the public humiliation of being beaten on National television, held a press conference and asked, “can’t we all just get along” (Cannon, 1999).

While doctors said that King may never recover from his injuries inflicted by the LAPD (Muhammad, J., 1992), his status quo plea of “can’t we all get along” was similar to an apology of a victim of domestic violence. Blaming oneself for the violence inflicted by a perpetrator is considered a process of losing control and taking responsibility in domestic violence relationships (Sigurvinsdottir &

Ullman, 2015). King pleaded at a press conference in the midst of the LA riots:

> ***I just want to say – you know – can we all get along? Can we, can we get along? Can we stop making it horrible for the older people and the kids? And ... I mean we've got enough smog in Los Angeles let alone to deal with setting these fires and things ... It's just not right. It's not right, and it's not going to change anything. We'll get our justice. They've won the battle, but they haven't won the war. We'll get our day in court, and that's all we want. And, just, uh, I love – I'm neutral. I love every – I love people of color. I'm not like they're making me out to be. We've got to quit. We've got to quit; I mean, after all, I could understand the first – upset for the first two hours after the verdict, but to go on, to keep going on like this and to see the security guard shot on the ground – it's just not right. It's just not right, because those people will never go home to their families again. And uh, I mean, please, we can, we can get along here. We all can get along. We just gotta. We gotta. I mean, we're all stuck here for a while. Let's, you know, let's***

> ***try to work it out. Let's try to beat it, you know. Let's try to work it out. (Transcript Rodney King, 2005)***

Self-blame and taking responsibility for being attacked by an oppressive police force is inappropriate but common in the African American community. The basic tenant of nonviolence of the civil rights movement may have been perceived as "the best weapon of Whites who want to brutalize Black people" (Cone, 2001). To the contrary was the position of so-called Black militant groups.

The Nation of Islam saw the King's plea of "Can we all just get along" as a legacy of African Americans suffering at the hands of police engraved in White America's long history of oppression and subject to God's intervening justice. The Honorable Minister Louis Farrakhan passionately exclaimed:

> ***Looking at the incident of Rodney King, those four policemen should have been tried for attempted murder, yet the jury could not even reach a verdict on whether or not excessive force was used. When God decided to kill Pharaoh, he decided to kill the people right along with him. Pharaoh said, 'me and my people are wicked.' If***

> ***those jurors could not see that excessive force was used with an attempt to kill this Black man, then they are of the same mind as the police. What chance do Blacks, Hispanics, and other minorities have of justice in America? How could a jury look at that brutal beating and bring back a verdict of not guilty? The worst is yet to come. (Farrakhan, 1992)***

The Nation of Islam's perspective of the King beating is fatalistic as far as police reform. They quote the words of their "patriarch" and eternal leader, the Honorable Elijah Muhammad:

> ***Since we cannot get along with them in peace and equality, after giving them 400 years of our sweat and blood and receiving in return some of the worst treatment human beings have ever experienced, we believe our contributions to this land and the suffering forced upon us by White America, justifies our demand for complete separation in a state or territory of our own. (Final Call News, 2012)***

It's not surprising then to see the many misunderstandings

that exist about the Nation of Islam, including their realistic perception that America lacks freedom, justice, and equality to ever end police brutality. While the circumstances that exist now have deteriorated, the majority of African Americans do not desire to separate from America. King's experience with police brutality on videotape was perhaps the beginning of America becoming a witness to the police beating of a Black man. The city of Detroit, several months after the Los Angeles 1992 riots, had its own "Rodney King" incident to deal with.

On November 5, 1992, a 35-year-old Black man named Malice Green died after being assaulted by two plain clothes White Detroit police officers named Walter Budzyn and Larry Nevers. While on patrol at night in an unmarked police car, Nevers saw Green driving a bullet hole-ridden Ford Tempo pull up in front of a known "crack house." The officers stopped behind the car to investigate. Nevers requested Green's identification. Green ignored Nevers and reentered the Tempo on the passenger side. Green looked in the glove compartment and dropped a rock of crack cocaine. He picked it up off the floor, and Budzyn ordered him to release it. Green held the crack cocaine in his hand and refused to open it. Budzyn and Nevers begin to hit Green repeatedly on the hand and head with large metallic police flashlights. One witness said that police hit Green at least ten times on the head. Nevers admitted to hitting Green in the head with the flashlight in self-defense after Green allegedly grabbed his gun.

He said, "[Green] finally let go of my gun, and I did not hit him [again]."

Arriving at EMS, a medical technician saw Green lying in a "pool of blood under his head on the street," and Nevers continued to strike him with the flashlight. Green suffered a seizure, was transported to a hospital, and died. The Medical Examiner later testified that Green died from "[b]lunt force trauma to [his] head" after receiving fourteen blows to the head (People v Budzyn, 1997).

While the beating and killing of Green drew parallels to the videotaped beating of Rodney King, the aftermath and civil unrest were divergent. Nevers and Budzyn were charged and convicted of second-degree murder in the beating death of a Green. Another officer, Robert Lessnau, was charged with assault with intent to do great bodily harm. Immediately after the killing of Green, Detroit Mayor Coleman Young said on National television that Green was "literally murdered by police." Prior to the officer's trial, the city of Detroit paid a $5.25 million settlement to Green's family (Larry Nevers has died, 2013). The day after the Green killing, Detroit Police Chief Stanley Knox suspended Nevers, Budzyn, and the five backup officers from the police force without pay. An African American supervisor, Sergeant Freddie Douglas, was charged with involuntary manslaughter and willful neglect of duty for failing to stop the beating (Levin, 1992). Detroit, with a majority African American population, did not go up in flames, nor was there any looting like Los Angeles due to the prompt reaction of city officials.

However, the Malice Green incident was controversial as the city of Detroit held its breath.

Perhaps the most controversial outcome of the Malice Green beating and murder was during the court trial. During the Budzyn and Nevers trial, the predominately African American jury was shown the movie Malcolm X during deliberations. The beginning of the film illustrated the Rodney King beating videotape. The showing of the Malcolm X movie to the jury later became a significant fact during Budzyn's appeal. At issue was whether the showing of the movie to the jury resulted in them considering "extraneous facts not introduced in evidence, [and] deprives a defendant of his rights of confrontation, cross-examination, and assistance of counsel embodied in the Sixth Amendment" (People v Budzyn, 1997). The movie opens with the voice of Malcolm X's character making a provocative speech charging "the White man with being the greatest murderer on earth" while the Rodney King beating is shown:

> ***Brothers and sisters, I am here to tell you that I charge the White man, I charge the White man with being the greatest murderer on earth. I charge the White man with being the greatest kidnapper on earth.***
>
> ***There is no place in this world that man can go and say he created peace and harmony.***

Everywhere he's gone he's created havoc. Everywhere he's gone he's created destruction. So, I charge him, I charge him with being the greatest kidnapper on this earth. I charge him with being the greatest murderer on this earth. I charge him with being the greatest robber and enslaver on this earth. I charge the White man with being the greatest swine eater on this earth, the greatest drunkard on this earth. He can't deny the charges. You can't deny the charges. We're the living proof of those charges. You and I are the proof. You're not an American. You are a victim of America.

You didn't have a choice coming over here. He didn't say "black man, black woman, come on over and help me build America." He said "nigger get down in the bottom of that boat and I'm taking you over there to help me build America." Being born here does not make you an American. I'm not an American. You're not an American. You're one of the twenty-two million black people who are the victims of America…

We didn't see any democracy on the streets of Harlem, on the streets of Detroit. ... No, we've

never seen democracy. All we've seen is hypocrisy. We don't see any American dream. We've experienced only the American nightmare. (People v Nevers, 1997)

While the Malcolm X speech is indeed inflammable, yet debatable as to its factual historical merits, on July 31, 1997, the Michigan Supreme Court ordered a new trial for Walter Budzyn, predominately on the grounds of showing the Malcolm X movie. (People v Nevers, 1997). Malcolm X understood the reactive nature of African Americans, which allowed him to play a significant role in opposing police brutality.

A defining moment in Malcolm X's historical leadership and notoriety was his capacity to address American racism, including police brutality. On April 26, 1957, in Harlem, New York, two White police officers were beating an African American suspect from a street fight with their nightsticks. To intervene, twenty-two-year-old Nation of Islam, Temple number 7 member Johnson X Hinton yelled at the officers, "You're not in Alabama. This is New York." The police ordered the men and Hinton to "move on." However, Hinton and the men did not run away and continued to be bystanders. The Police turned their attention and aggression towards Hinton and two other men. The police savagely beat Hinton with their nightsticks. Hinton's scalp was split open. Hinton, along with the other men, was arrested for failure to disperse and resisting arrest and was conveyed to the 28th police precinct (Marable, 2011; Haley, 1964).

The Malcolm X and Hinton incident was pivotal in how police dealt with the barely known, at that time, Malcolm X and the Nation of Islam. Nearly thirty minutes after the Hinton beating and arrest, fifty members of the Nation of Islam men, aka the Fruit of Islam (FOI), marched and stood in military formation outside the 28th police precinct. Malcolm X demanded to see Hinton to ascertain his condition, but the police denied accommodating him. However, the crowd outside began to increase in size, and the police finally agreed and allowed Malcolm X to see Hinton. Malcolm X could barely maintain his composure after seeing Hinton's condition. Malcolm X said, "[Hinton] was only semi-conscious. Blood had bathed his head, face, and shoulders. I hope I never again have to withstand seeing another case of sheer police brutality like that."

While suffering from pain and disorientation, Hinton told Malcolm X that he tried to pray and prostrate, and police hit him again with their nightsticks on his mouth and legs. Hinton was transported and treated at Harlem Hospital and released back to the 28th police precinct. By now, the crowd outside the 28th police precinct had grown to 4,000 people. After Malcolm X was convinced that Hinton had received the proper medical care, he approached the FOI and the crowd, raised his arm, and gave a hand signal. The crowd dispersed from Malcolm X's silent command, which police officials took notice of. One high-ranking police official said, “This is too much power for one man to have.” Hinton eventually won a civil lawsuit filed against the NYPD and was awarded the largest police brutality settlement in New York City at the time of $70,000.00 (Marable, 2011; Haley, 1964). On the horizon was a new type of interaction between African Americans and the NYPD (English, 2012).

There was no mention of the police killing of Ronald X Stokes in The Autobiography of Malcolm X nor in Spike Lee’s film. However, was it a historical incident and notable for police religious persecution? One study on the Stokes incident argued that “The Nation of Islam was a targeted organization...the only rational conclusion that can be drawn is that the shooting was a case of police brutality and a religious, political, and racial attack (Knight, 1994). Innovative religious groups often attract the extremely apprehensive attention of government and police officials and often incite hostile reactive policing because the polity is structured to perceive such groups as threats to social stability and political control (Muhammad, D., 2004). While slightly off-topic, the brief analysis of “religious policing” is necessary as a background to understanding the peril of when a group is being subjected to a totality of racial and religious police brutality. Such was the case in the police shooting death of Stokes in Los Angeles.

On April 27, 1962, Muhammad’s Mosque # 27 secretary Ronald Stokes was approached by a police officer as he was handing clothing from his automobile trunk to a fellow Muslim brother. The officer, with his handgun drawn, accused Stokes of selling stolen clothing and demanded to see his business license. Stokes attempted to explain that he received a discount from the cleaners that he worked at for bringing in more business. The next words out of the officer's mouth were intended to trigger a civil disturbance: "Nigger, turn around and put your hands up against the car and spread-eagle" (Evanzz, 2001; Muhammad, D., 2004; Marable, 2011).

The officer ignored Stokes' request to check with the cleaners and that he was innocent. Several of the bystanders ran to the Mosque a block away and told the other Muslims what was happening. By the time the Muslims arrived, Stokes was lying in the street dead from a gunshot wound to the chest and a crushed back of the head as several police officers were beating the lifeless handcuffed victim. The Muslims immediately fought with police, which resulted in two of them being seriously injured from blows from nightsticks, one shot and paralyzed, and another shot in the groin (Evanzz, 2001; Muhammad, D., 2004; Marable, 2011).

Police then went to the Mosque and ransacked it by emptying files and desk drawers onto the floor as they claimed to be looking for weapons. After finding no weapons, police ordered the Muslim men to form a single-file lineup. Police attempted to escalate the event further as they yelled at the Muslims, "We shot your brother outside. Are you going to do something about it?"

Several men accused of acting belligerently were poked in the rectum with nightsticks. The police then ripped the men's pants to shreds with a sharp object and forced them to walk slowly in front of hundreds of witnesses. Fourteen Muslims, including the local Minister John Shabazz, were arrested for assaulting a police officer and a host of other charges. Malcolm X immediately planned a massive retaliatory strike against the police with a group of Muslim men from the entire country. However, Elijah Muhammad foresaw a violent police assault as he told Minister Malcolm to cool it (Evanzz, 2001; Muhammad, D., 2004; Marable, 2011). Seven African American Muslims were shot, one died, and another was paralyzed for life while a "coroner's inquest determined that Stokes's death was justifiable." Elijah Muhammad's disapproval of Malcolm X recruiting Nation of Islam "members for an assassination team to target LAPD" may have contributed to the deteriorating relationship between Malcolm X and Elijah Muhammad (Marable, 2011).

There were many conflicts between law enforcement officials and the Nation of Islam, including the FBI in 1967 officially extending its Counter-Intelligence Program [COINTELPRO] to target and put an end to the so-called "Black Muslims" (Carson, 1991). The NYPD, on two occasions in 1972 and 1994, raided the Nation of Islam Mosques, breaching agreements to refrain from such police activity in respect of a religious institution (Silverman, 1999; Muhammad, D., 2004). In March 1960, in Monroe, Louisiana, police raided a Nation of Islam

Temple and brutally beat men, women, and children. They killed one person and attempted to lynch the local Minister Troy X Cade, known today as Minister Abdul Bey Muhammad, by his necktie (Love, 2010). Finally, in 1934 in Detroit and 1935 in Chicago, police attacked Nation of Islam members and charged them with contributing to the delinquency of minors because they elected to teach their children at the University of Islam and refused to put them in public school (Muhammad, E., 1965). The Honorable Elijah Muhammad wrote about these incidents in his book, Message to the Blackman:

> ***In Chicago, Illinois, at the Police Court on 11th and State Streets, there was a complaint made against one of my followers concerning his children going to our school, the University of Islam. As the courtroom began to fill with spectators, two court deputies showed disrespect for the Muslim women. They started pushing them around, and the Muslim brothers resented this harsh handling of the women. The police officers then began beating the men, and almost within seconds, the entire courtroom was in confusion and fight.***
>
> ***When the battle was over, the Police Captain lay***

> ***dead from a heart attack, and others were wounded by their own gun fire. They opened fire upon my followers point blank in the courtroom because of their Muslims seeking justice in the charge made against us and our school, as in Detroit, Michigan, the previous year. (Muhammad, E., 1965)***

The culmination of attacks against the Nation of Islam may appear to be inspired solely on religious grounds. However, as Malcolm X explained, "We're not brutalized because we're Baptists. We're not brutalized because we're Methodists. We're not brutalized because we're Muslims. We're not brutalized because we're Catholics. We're brutalized because we are Black people in America (Malcolm X, 1962). The primary characteristic that triggers police violence and brutality is the color of one's skin.

While the "hands up, don't shoot" gesture became tantamount to Black men being shot and killed by police, the numerous contradictory mountains of evidence in the Ferguson police shooting death of Michael Brown would leave a reasonable person to be suspended in judgment as to what actually happened.

On August 9, 2014, in Ferguson, Missouri, police officer Darren Wilson shot and killed an 18-year-old Black teenager named Michael Brown. This shooting led to multiple protests and riots all across the United States. There are numerous different explanations from witnesses as to what happened during that late-morning incident. What is consistent is that Officer Wilson, while driving his police SUV, stopped Brown and his friend Dorian Johnson and ordered them to get out of the street. A physical altercation took place between Wilson and Brown while Wilson was still in the police car, and two shots were fired. Brown and Johnson ran away, and Wilson exited his police car and chased them. Brown turned towards Wilson, who then fired twelve shots, six of which hit Brown. Wilson claimed he fired in self-defense. Several witnesses alleged that Brown pleaded "don't shoot!" prior to being killed (Michael Brown is killed, 2020). What became apparent during Officer Wilson's grand jury deliberation was that the State of Missouri may allow a police officer to shoot and kill a fleeing felon.

During the Darren Wilson grand jury presentation, the prosecution gave an outdated Missouri law to the jurors, allowing police to use deadly force to prevent the escape of a person in custody. As previously mentioned, the Supreme Court in Tennessee v. Garner declared it unconstitutional for law enforcement to use deadly force against non-dangerous, fleeing felony suspects (Tennessee v. Garner). Prior to grand jury deliberation, the prosecution told the jurors to ignore a portion of the Missouri law authorizing the use of deadly force. Assistant Prosecuting Attorney Kathi Alizadeh said to jurors, "So, the statute I gave you, if you want to fold that in half just so that, you know, don't necessarily rely on that because there is a portion of that that doesn't comply with the law." Saint Louis University law professor Chad

Flanders said, "They are telling the jurors to disregard the law and telling them to heed their own 'spin' on the law" (Freivogel, 2014). This diabolical scheme made it nearly impossible for that grand jury to indict Wilson for killing a young African American man.

Does an African American man put his life in peril simply by carrying a wallet, a cell phone, or keys? On February 4, 1999, 23-year-old African American Amadou Diallo was shot and killed by four White plainclothes police officers, Sean Carroll, Richard Murphy, Edward McMellon, and Kenneth Boss. At approximately 12:40 after midnight, Diallo was standing in front of his apartment when police claimed that he was acting suspiciously. They erroneously thought that he was a serial rapist or a lookout for illegal drug activity. As the officers approached, Diallo ran and ignored their commands to stop and show his hands. Instead, in a dark hallway, Diallo reached into his pants and pulled out his wallet. Officers fired a total of 41 bullets, striking Diallo 19 times. An unarmed Diallo slumped to the floor and died, dropping his wallet (Fritsch, 2000).

A year later, all four NYPD officers were acquitted of all charges of second-degree murder, negligent homicide, and reckless endangerment in Diallo's death after three days of deliberations. The trial was moved from the largely minority Bronx population to the largely White population of Albany, New York. After the acquittal, over 300 protesters were met by a large police presence, resulting in 29 arrests for disorderly conduct. The officers admitted that they made a mistake in shooting and killing Diallo. However, they claimed that Diallo was partly to blame for ignoring their commands to stop and not keeping his hands in sight. On the contrary, Scherrie Elliot, a neighborhood eyewitness, said police fired shots with no warning (Fritsch, 2000). Was Diallo a victim of a racially motivated police shooting or a victim of police making a tragic mistake?

Police officers have to make split-second decisions regarding the use of deadly force but can't escape race as a variable influencer. Journalist, author, and public speaker Malcolm Gladwell committed an entire chapter in his book reviewing the Diallo killing by police. He studied the "psychology of a police officer's instant response to an object in an innocent Black person's hand might differ from his/her response to an object in a White person's hand." Gladwell argues that it is "wrong to say that the officers killed Diallo because they were murderous racists." Instead, he believes that the police killing of Diallo is in the "grey area between deliberate and accidental behavior" (Gladwell, 2005). In a scientific study to ascertain the police "automatic cognitive processes" in the Diallo killing, it was found that "biased error rates require two conditions: the presence of stereotypic cues, and the limited opportunity to contemplate and control one's response" (Holmes & Smith, 2008). Diallo was guilty of merely pulling out his wallet and shot dead. In other words, a Black male doesn't stand a chance when police have to make a split-second decision regarding lethal force.

It became evident that some White policemen surely would

fail a shoot/don't shoot scenario of even an African American child because of "the stereotypic association of Blacks with violence" (Holmes & Smith, 2008). On November 22, 2014, a White Cleveland police officer, Timothy Loehmann, shot 12-year-old African American Tamir Rice. Loehmann responded with his partner Frank Garmback to a male with a gun. The caller told a 911 dispatcher that the gun was probably fake and the suspect was probably a juvenile; however, that information was not given to responding officers. Within seconds of arriving on the scene, Loehmann shot Rice twice, who died the next day in a hospital. Loehmann told other officers, "He gave me no choice. He reached for the gun, and there was nothing I could do."

Loehmann, in 2012, was judged unfit for duty by the Independence, Ohio, police department. In 2014, the U. S. Justice Department determined that Cleveland police officers used excessive deadly force, including shootings unnecessary and in retaliation. The city of Cleveland settled a wrongful death lawsuit, paying $6 million to the Rice family (Lopez, 2017). Tamir's mother, Samaria Rice, said, "No parent should have to endure something like this. The day was very horrific for me. I was enraged by the way he was killed, murdered, assassinated, lynched, whatever they may call it" (Rice, 2020). The unfortunate, tragic, and horrible killing of a twelve-year-old kid by police shocks my conscience and literally takes my breath away. It's no wonder that African Americans are prone to run from the police during law enforcement encounters.

A CNN reporter described a shooting of an African American male by a White police officer as "dogs usually are not treated this badly…the man was shot like a runaway slave" (Love, 2015). On April 4, 2015, an African American named Walter Scott, a 50-year-old, was shot and killed by a 33-year-old White male police officer named Michael T. Slager. Slager pulled Scott over, who was driving a Mercedes-Benz with a broken taillight. According to the police report, Scott fled the scene and was chased by Officer Slager. A struggle occurred, and Slager fired his Taser (electronic stun gun) at Scott with negative results. Slager broadcast on his radio, "Shots fired, and the subject is down. He took my Taser." A bystander video contradicted Slager's version and showed Scott running away, Slager pulling his firearm out and firing at least eight shots from 15 to 20 feet away. Scott then falls to the ground. Slager returned back to where the traffic stop occurred, picked an object up off the ground, and placed it next to Scott's body (Schmidt & Apuzzo, 2015).

The CNN reporter asked, "What if there was no video? What if there was no witness, or hero as I call him, to come forward? Then, this wouldn't have happened because, as you can see, the initial reports stated something totally different. The officer said that Mr. Scott attacked him, pulled his Taser, and tried to use it on him. But somebody was watching" (Love, 2015). The eyewitness, Feidin Santana, who recorded the video, initially feared releasing the video but was angered after the police report falsified the incident (Eversley, 2015). Fortunately, probably due primarily to the videotaped witness on December 7, 2017, Slager was sentenced to 20 years in prison for second-degree murder. Scott was shot five times in the back and killed for running away, simply for having a broken taillight. (Edwards & Andone, 2017). In view of these most glaring incidents of how some police treat African Americans, a reasonable mind is compelled to inquire, does Black Lives Matter?

In July of 2013, the Black Lives Matter (BLM) movement was started after George Zimmerman was acquitted of shooting and killing 17-year-old Trayvon Martin on February 26, 2012. It may have been initiated by a hashtag on social media. BLM propagated in 2014 after the police killings of Michael Brown in Ferguson, Missouri, and Eric Garner in New York. While the group lacks a national leader, one of the people who emerged from BLM is 30-year-old African American activist and educator Brittany Packnett. Packnett said BLM "is about defending the humanity and the dignity of all people in this country and of people of color in particular." On December 1, 2014, she met with President Barack Obama, and that led to the formation of the President's Task Force on 21st Century Policing, which identified "best policing practices and offered recommendations to strengthen trust among law enforcement officers and the communities they serve" (Luibrand, 2015). Many of my law enforcement colleagues, along with some White Americans, believe that saying "Black Lives Matter" excludes them in that their lives are important.

In response to BLM, other phrases emerged, including "All

Lives Matter" (Chan, 2016) and "Blue Lives Matter" (BBC Trending, 2015). An erroneous assumption is that BLM means that Black lives are more important than another life. On the contrary, there does not appear to be a deficit in the valuing of other lives. A recent study by ProPublica found that young African American males are "21 times more likely to be fatally shot by police than young White males. And 67% of teens killed while fleeing or resisting arrest were Black" (Love, 2015). An empirical study found that African American "victims were substantially over-represented relative to the U.S. population, comprising 34% of victims but only 13% of Americans… were also more likely to be unarmed than Whites or Hispanics, and less likely than Whites to have evidence suggesting an immediate threat to [police]" (DeGue, Fowler & Calkins, 2018). And in Arguendo, another study found that African American police officers are often victims of police racial profiling (Barlow & Barlow, 2002). I concur that "Blue Lives Matter" and police should not be targeted for assassination in retaliation for the disproportionate killing of African Americans by police. However, killing a police officer is automatically considered first-degree murder, and acquittal is highly unlikely. Police officers, or "Blue Lives" as well as "White Lives," are already valued by American society. According to UC Berkeley professor and philosopher Judith Butler, "All Lives Matter fails to acknowledge that society doesn't consider Black lives to fall under the same umbrella as all lives — which often gets translated into just White lives" (Chan, 2016). BLM continues to challenge American society in regard to the police disproportionately killing African Americans.

BLM advocates that society needs to know the names of the African American victims killed by police in the United States. An Al Jazeera BLM website highlights, in addition to George Floyd, Breonna Taylor, Eric Garner, Tamir Rice, and Michael Brown killings, which we previously discussed, others killed that appear questionable at best. Some of those highlighted on the website are Rayshard Brooks, who fell asleep in his car at a fast-food drive-through; Brooks, who was shot in the back twice after fleeing from police and taking an officer's taser; Stephon Clark, who was shot at over 20 times in his grandmother's yard after police thought he had a gun, which turned out to be a cell phone; Botham Jean who was at his home eating ice cream when off-duty police officer Amber Cuyger entered his apartment thinking it was hers, shot and killed him as an intruder; Philando Castille who shot and killed during a traffic stop after he told police he had a legal firearm; Alton Sterling tasered, pinned to the ground and eventually shot 6 times. He was suspected of selling illegal CDs and DVDs, and Freddie Gray, who mysteriously died in police custody. He was found 45 minutes after being arrested in a police van with a severed spinal cord (Chughtai, n. d.). Do some White Americans believe that the police's role is to kill or execute African American lawbreakers?

On February 26, 2012, 17-year-old African American Trayvon Martin was shot and killed by a neighborhood watchman, George Zimmerman. Martin was on his way back home from a neighborhood store, buying Skittles and iced tea. Zimmerman telephoned Sanford police and reported Martin as suspicious. A 911 dispatcher told Zimmerman that police were on the way and to let them handle the situation. The two men had a physical altercation, and Zimmerman shot and killed Martin, claiming self-defense. A year later, Zimmerman was acquitted of second-degree murder (Lee, 2012). The irony is that Zimmerman was not even a police officer, and Martin did not appear to be breaking any law. The Zimmerman acquittal is petrifying in that the prejudice and hate that existed during slavery still exist today in creating and reinforcing stereotypes. "The Social Conflict theory is based upon the view that the fundamental causes of crime are the social and economic forces operating within society... the Criminal Justice System and criminal law are thought to be operating on behalf of rich and powerful social elites, with resulting policies aimed at controlling the poor" (Robinson, 2016). Thus, Zimmerman was justified in shooting Martin because society viewed him as a criminal, subject to "police," in this case a substitute, to eliminate the perceived danger. Would the jury have convicted Zimmerman if the killing of Martin was recorded on videotape?

A Chicago police officer was charged with first-degree murder after a court ordered the police department to release a dashcam video contradicting the officer's fabricated version of a shooting. On October 20, 2014, 17-year-old African American Laquan McDonald was shot and killed by White police officer Jason Van Dyke. Police were responding to a trucking yard of McDonald's breaking into vehicles and carrying a knife. Initially, police reported that McDonald ignored their commands to drop the knife, lunged at them, and Van Dyke shot him in self-defense. Van Dyke opened fire, firing 16 shots at McDonald. The shooting at the time was ruled justified. However, the court-ordered released video of the shooting showed Van Dyke pursuing McDonald as he was walking away and then firing a shot. After McDonald fell to the ground, Van Dyke fired more shots into his lifeless body. Cook County prosecutor Anita Alvarez described the videotaped shooting as “graphic,” “violent,” and “chilling.” She said she had never seen anything like the McDonald killing in her 30-year career in law enforcement. Alvarez said, “To watch a 17-year-old young man die in such a violent manner is deeply disturbing” (DeGue, Fowler & Calkins, 2018). On January 18, 2019, Van Dyke was given a lenient sentence of just over six and a half years in prison for the fatal shooting of McDonald (Crepeau, Gutowski, Meisner & St. Clair, 2019). The police dashcam video was a better witness than the actual police officers, and it served as their condemnation.

Apparently, some police regret the use of video cameras capturing their law enforcement activities. Police officers throughout the United States, mostly through their unions, are fighting to prevent the use of bystander’s smartphones as well as police-worn body cams to record their interactions with the community they serve (Bruinius, 2016).

On November 23, 2017, 33-year-old African American

Marcus Smith arrived at a train station to meet his awaiting mother, Jacquelyn Smith, who was sitting in a parked car behind a Chicago police car. As Marcus Smith approached his mother, White police officer Eric Puszkiewicz pointed his firearm at him. Jacqueline Smith told Puszkiewicz that Marcus Smith was her son, and he holstered his weapon. Puszkiewicz claimed that Marcus Smith was walking suspiciously, and there were several robberies reported near the train stop with African American teenage suspects. Jacqueline and Marcus Smith complained to Chicago police officials of having a gun pointed at him for "walking while Black."

To their amazement, after Puszkiewicz told them the incident was recorded on dash and body cam, no such video recording of the handgun brandishing existed. A Chicago CBS news station found that Chicago police are less likely to record encounters in African American and Hispanic communities but often do exclusively in predominately White communities (Assad, Hacker & Savini, 2020). The lack of the use of body cams in African American communities is extremely suspicious and reprehensible, where police-citizen encounters are significant.

Crime and disorder do appear to be problematic in African American communities. Criminologists consistently acknowledged that crime is much higher in African American communities. African American areas of major cities "have as much as 35 times as much serious crime per 100,000 residents as does a... White district." An African American resident is 75 percent more likely to be a victim of a major crime (Coffey, Eldefonso & Hartinger, 1982). African American neighborhoods are overwhelmed by crime, with homicide rates for African American males having been reported at 67.5 percent compared to White males at just 9.1 percent for White males per 100,000 citizens (Walker, 2001). While African Americans make up approximately 13 percent of the United States population, the arrest rate for crime stands at nearly 50 percent (Hacker, 1992). Thus, there continues to be a non-negotiable need for the police in African American communities regardless of the recent outcries for police defunding. However, the police's role is to bring criminals to the Courts, not to exercise police use of force as "judge and jurors."

The viciousness of racist police attacks involved more than someone selling cigarettes or attempting to pass a counterfeit 20-dollar bill. The attack by the Alabama State Police and the sheriff posse upon a group of civil rights protestors on the Edmund Pettus Bridge shocked the conscience and literally took everyone's breath away. In response to the Alabama State Police beating, shooting, and murder of protestor Jimmy Lee Jackson, Civil Rights protestors initiated the Selma to Montgomery marches (Fleming, 2005).

On February 18, 1965, nearly 500 Civil rights protestors marched from Zion United Methodist Church to the city jail to sing freedom songs to protest a Civil Rights worker's arrest. They were met by city and Alabama State police and sheriff's deputies. All of a sudden, the streetlights were turned off, and the police attacked the protestors with nightsticks. Police chased a group of protestors into Mack's Café. The police beat an 82-year-old Cager Lee and his daughter Viola Jackson. Jimmie Lee was shot by police when he tried to help protect his family. He died in the hospital eight days later, on February 26, 1965 (Fleming, 2005).

On March 7, 1965, John Lewis of the Student Non-Violent Coordinating Committee SNCC and Reverend Hosea Williams of the Southern Christian Leadership Conference SCLC led nearly 600 protestors across the Edmund Pettus Bridge. They were met by a wall of Alabama State Troopers and Dallas County Sheriff Deputies. The troopers and sheriffs pushed the peaceful protestors to the ground, beat them with nightsticks, fired tear gas at them, and charged them with police horses. The day would become known as "Bloody Sunday," as 17 protestors were hospitalized and 50 were injured (Reed, 1966). Congressman John Lewis described the horrific events of how police turned violent against a group of 1st Amendment protestors:

> ***[I]t was the Edmund Pettus Bridge, crossing the Alabama River. We were on our way from Selma to Montgomery to dramatize to the nation and to the world that the black people and the black belt of Alabama wanted to register to vote, to participate in the democratic process... We had to walk across that bridge... We got on the other***

side of the bridge. There was a group of state troopers standing, and the major said — the Alabama State Police, "This is an unlawful march; it would not be allowed to continue. I'll give you three minutes to disburse and return to your homes or to your church." And one of the guys walking with me, leading the march, by the name of Hosea Williams, said, "Major, give us a moment to kneel and pray," and the major said again, "Troopers, advance." And I said, "Major, may I have a word?" He said, "There will be no word. Troopers, advance." You saw these guys putting on their gas masks. They came toward us, beating us with nightsticks, tramping us with horses... I was hit in the head by a state trooper with a nightstick. My legs went from under me; I thought I saw death; I thought I was going to die. And to this day, I don't know how I made it back across that bridge to the streets of Selma, back to the little church where we had left from. But I do remember being back at the church. They asked me to say something, and I stood up and said, "I don't understand it, that President Johnson can send troops to Vietnam, but cannot send troops to Selma, Alabama, to protect people who only desires to register to vote." And I was

hospitalized with 16 other people, and a group of nuns took care of us. (Capehart, 2019)

After the "Bloody Sunday" incident, Dr. Martin Luther King Jr. successfully led thousands of protesters from Selma to Montgomery, President Lyndon Johnson signed the Civil Rights Act, and President Obama gave a speech marking the 50th anniversary of the Selma to Montgomery marches (White House, n.d.).

Selma, Alabama, has made tremendous progress in race relations since "Bloody Sunday" in 1965. Selma appointed Earnest L. Tate as its first African American police chief in 1997 (First Black police chief, 1997). However, over 50 years after "Bloody Sunday," the police may continue to kill innocent African Americans who are not even accused of a crime, which is evidenced by some White police officers' hostilities towards their own co-workers, African American police officers.

Being an African American police officer doesn't exempt him or her from being a "Black Nigger" in the eyes of some White American police officers. A White NYPD officer conducting a study on the work environment of African American police was asked by a White detective co-worker, "What are you, a nigger lover or something?" (Leinen, 1984, 2). In the 1930s, throughout the South, White police officers would routinely arrest African American police officers outside their patrol jurisdiction for carrying their handgun while off duty and charging them with carrying a concealed weapon (Dulaney, 1984). On January 28, 1959, Detroit police Commissioner Herbert W. Hart issued a departmental order that patrol cars are to be integrated with African American and White officers. As a result, the majority of White officers participated in the “largest ‘Blue Flu’ campaign” in the department’s history. The White Detroit police officers resisted by neglecting to write tickets, delaying response time to police calls for service, and neglecting the safety and security of the citizens of Detroit (Lawrence, 2017, 31).

Former Detroit police Chief McKinnon describes what policing looked like from the inside for African Americans in the 60’s:

> ***My very first night as a Detroit police officer, and the supervisors, the sergeant and lieutenant came into the room, and they announced roll call. And as they announced the assignments, they announced this one officer's name, and they gave the assignment. Then they said, McKinnon, scout 27. And this officer said Jesus effing Christ. I'm working with the [Nigger] and he said the racial derogatory term. (Shapiro, 2020)***

Young officer McKinnon was introduced to a police culture

with a legacy of prejudice and racism. In 1889, a White sergeant fired two African American police officers for neglect of duty and told them, “Niggers were not wanted on the force anyhow” (Dulaney, 1984, 14). An African American Columbus, Ohio police officer, Benjamin Eddings, while working a Ku Klux Klan parade, was surprised at how many Klansmen were White police officers (Dulaney, 1984). These examples illustrate the deep hatred that some White police officers had towards African American police officers, yet this hostility at times leads to a phrase I created, “being a cop while Black” encounters.

Are African American police officers victims of “driving while Black” or tasting the resentment of some White police officers experiencing their worst nightmare, a “Nigger” with a badge? I drove an unmarked Chevy Tahoe police vehicle, which is easily identifiable to police, and still, I’ve been pulled over at least a half dozen times in five years. I was shocked and amazed at a particular stop when a White Dearborn Heights officer gave me his reason for the traffic stop, saying to me, “I just wanted to see who was driving this car.” When McKinnon was the Detroit chief of police, he was pulled over while driving his unmarked police car by a subordinate White Detroit police officer. After the officer recognized him as chief, McKinnon asked, “Why did you stop me?” The White officer replied, "I thought it was a stolen car” (McKinnon, 2020). It got even worse in 1997 when African American off-duty Metro-Dade police major Aaron Campbell was pulled over for allegedly making an illegal lane change by White Orange County sheriff's deputies. The minor traffic offense escalated to Campbell being tackled to the ground, pepper sprayed, and arrested. Campbell described his frustration by saying, "The majority of people they are searching and humiliating are Black people. That's why I was so angry. I went from being an ordinary citizen and decorated officer to a criminal in a matter of minutes" (Harris, 1999). Being a cop while Black shows how easily African American police can easily be cast to the other side of the law when stopped by White police officers.

There were incidents when "Being a cop while Black" evolved into extreme prejudice, resulting in serious violence and sometimes near fatalities. Chief McKinnon described an incident with White Detroit police officers as a new African American officer when he came close to death:

> ***I felt the sting of betrayal as an officer during the 1967 rebellion. One night, after a grueling shift, two White DPD officers pulled me over. I was still in uniform, badge affixed to my chest and a #2 pin on my collar, indicating that I worked in the 2nd Precinct. I identified myself as a fellow officer, thinking they would see me as an equal. Instead, one pointed his gun at me and said, 'Tonight you're going to die, [Nigger!],' before discharging his weapon. I dove back into my vehicle and miraculously managed to***

> ***escape. I realized then that not even our shared uniform could save me from their racism. And I wondered that if they were willing to shoot and kill a black police officer, what were they willing to do to black civilians? (McKinnon, 2020)***

Chief McKinnon was lucky or blessed that he did not lose his life or was seriously injured that evening in Detroit. In 1974, near the United States Federal Court, after a hearing on affirmative action, several White Detroit police officers attacked an African American officer who had to be rescued by courthouse security. All of the police officers were assigned to the same 12th precinct (Lawrence, 2017). Detroit police chief James Craig remembers his first scout car partner, a 25-year veteran White officer, telling him, "I don't want you here. You do one thing. You just sit over there on that passenger side and be Black. Don't touch the radio. You're not going to drive this car" (Monacelli, 2021). There were many other African American police who were not so fortuitous.

Was the "friendly-fire" shooting of an African American plainclothes policeman by two White undercover officers due to reacting to the "Black male" stereotype or "being a cop while Black"? On November 17, 1992, an African American plainclothes transit officer, Derwin Pannell, was shot by two White plainclothes transit officers, John Napolitano, and Robert Green, after they saw him and his White plainclothes partner, Kenneth Donnelly, detaining a White female fare skipper suspect. Pannell was pointing his handgun at the suspect while his partner was searching her purse. They fired 21 rounds at Pannell while a third female officer, Barbara Jesberger, never fired a shot. Donnelly recognized Jesberger and yelled, “Barbara, it's me, 3/8," and "What are you doing? We're cops!" after the other two officers began shooting. Pannell survived due to his bulletproof vest but was seriously injured. An organization representing Black police officers called for African American officers to refuse undercover assignments until the NYPD retrained its White officers, citing those White officers needed to know "that the Black guy wearing Adidas sneakers and a backward baseball cap might be a cop” (Davis & Graham, 1995; Associated Press, 1992). While the National Law Enforcement Officers Memorial indicates that friendly fire does not discriminate and that police officers of all races appear to be at risk (Floyd, 2000), Transit police Chief Michael O’Connor said that a contributing factor in the Pannell shooting may be that he was an African American (Associated Press, 1992).

A toxic work environment with racial animosity between African American and White officers undoubtedly led to a White officer shooting an African American colleague in St Louis. On June 21, 2017, off-duty African American St. Louis police officer Milton Green was holding out his badge when he was shot in his arm by a White police officer, Christopher Tanner.

A high pursuit police chase ended in front of Green’s house

when the suspect crashed while Green was helping a neighbor repair a car in his driveway. As the armed suspect attempted to flee, Green pulled out his badge and service weapon and told him, "Police! Put the gun down!" Within seconds, the pursuing officers pulled up, and an officer ordered Green to put down his weapon and get on the ground. As Green complied, a White detective recognized him and told officers that he was a police officer as well. Green got up and walked towards the detective, his weapon pointed down, and held out his badge. Another officer repeated for him to drop his weapon, and Green was simultaneously shot in the right arm by Tanner. Green said to Tanner, "Man, you done shot me," before collapsing to his knees. Green said that Tanner never gave him a chance because he was Black with a gun. Green said of Tanner. "You wouldn't have walked up to a White guy and just shot him like that." Ironically, Green was one of the few officers who complained of racial discrimination within the St Louis police department (Eligon, 2019).

While African American and White officers wore the same blue uniform and carried the same badge, it could not shield them from the "bad blood" from the racial animosity within the ranks. In addition to hearing racially derogatory comments while on duty, Green filed a lawsuit against the department for racial discrimination. Another African American officer, Luther Hall, while working undercover at a St. Louis protest, was beaten by four White officers. Hall describes the attack as a "Rodney King" beating. His White undercover partner was spared, and the beating launched a federal investigation.

An African American female officer, Leviya Graham, requested the transfer of a White officer, Michael J. Calcaterra, out of her unit due to him making racial and religious posts on social media. Graham considered Calcaterra a threat to her safety. Three months later, Graham accused Calcaterra of hitting her with a police car while on duty. White officers defeated an affirmative action program, two White officers won thousands of dollars in a reverse discrimination lawsuit, and an African American captain received 1.1 million dollars in a racial discrimination termination lawsuit. St. Louis police Colonel John Hayden said, "You hate to believe that it only happened because they were African-American" (Eligon, 2019).

Retired African American police officer Reginald Miller watched the George Floyd video, and it brought back recollections of when he was a victim of police brutality (Gibbs, 2020). On December 14, 1992, Miller was on-duty undercover in a Nashville undercover police blue pick-truck investigating prostitution. A White officer, Jeb D. Johnston, activated his police car flashing lights, attempting a traffic stop after observing Miller's car had an expired license plate. Miller did not want to blow his cover in front of the prostitutes and drove two blocks before stopping. In all, five White uniformed Nashville police officers pulled Miller from the truck, put a gun to his head, beat him, and kicked him in the groin. A White woman, Cindy Donnelly, witnessed the incident and said,

"I wish I had a camera like they did for Rodney King...I'll never forget it as long as I live" (Davis & Graham, 1995, 405). Police Chief Robert Kirchner denied that the beating was motivated by race. However, Miller said the beating was motivated by race, "if I were White, it never would have happened" (Davis & Graham, 1995, 405). Miller said, "I still feel that I was a piece of meat thrown to a pack of dogs, and everybody got a bite out of me" (Davis & Graham, 1995; Smothers, 1992). Miller contests that racism in policing is a very serious problem and pleads, "How can you not see this. America has to wake up" (Gibbs, 2020).

While some African Americans, particularly youth, refer to African American police as "Uncle Toms" and "White niggers" (Dulaney, 1984, 43), some of these officers are unsung heroes in trying to protect them from racist police. One such person is former African American police detective Don Jackson, aka Diop Kamau, who has been on a mission to investigate and resolve police brutality in the United States. In January 1989, Jackson (in his experimental test of racial profiling) was pulled over by the Long Beach police department for a traffic violation by two White officers. After a heated argument, Jackson was beaten, thrown face-first into a plate glass window, and arrested. The arresting officers were charged later with falsifying the police report (Associated Press, 1989; Stone, 1989; Jackson, 2020).

Unfortunately, unknown to the Long Beach police officers, a film crew followed Jackson, videotaped the incident, and broadcasted it on the NBC Today News (Associated Press, 1989). Former LAPD Chief Darryl Gates referred to Jackson's acts as "crazy, crazy, stupid, idiotic act," and there was a picture of "Jackson with a bloody arrow through his head on a police bulletin board." However, Jackson argues, "We don't do this for money. We didn't even want to do this. It was shoved down our throats by our lives." Congresswoman Maxine Waters referred to Jackson as a hero who was one of the first to document police racism (Stone, 1989).

Watching the videotaped incident of the Jackson and Long Beach Police encounter presents a question. Why would an African American police officer cross the "thin blue line" and risk his life to expose racial police brutality? In 1994, Jackson and his wife Tyra Ferrell started Policeabuse.com, where victims of police brutality can report such incidents (Jackson, n.d.). Jackson claims to have witnessed police brutality and heard racial comments like, "Black women liked being raped" by White officers throughout his police career. However, it was an April 1987 incident when his father, Woodrow Jackson, a retired 28-year L.A. County Sheriff's Office veteran, was allegedly stopped and beaten by Pomona police, even while carrying his deputy sheriff's badge. Jackson said, "It broke me for good. I couldn't stay on the force anymore" (Stone, 1989). Unfortunately, "the police, of course, were not unaffected by the racism permeating American society" (Dulaney, 1984, 21). What are the consequences when an African American female police officer crosses the thin blue line or the code of silence and interferes or reports improper and unlawful conduct by a fellow White officer?

An African American city of Buffalo female police officer named Cariol Horne was terminated and charged with obstruction after she stopped a fellow White police officer, Gregory Kwiatkowski, from punching and choking an African American arrestee named Neal Mack. On November 1, 2006, approximately ten officers, including Horne and Kwiatkowski, responded to the residence of Mack and his girlfriend on a report of domestic violence. According to Horne, after Mack was handcuffed, Kwiatkowski started to choke him. She said to Kwiatkowski, "Greg! You're choking him." She assumed that something had happened inside the residence that Kwiatkowski was still upset about. When Kwiatkowski refused to stop choking Mack, she grabbed his arm from around Mack's neck. Kwiatkowski retaliated and punched Horne in the face; her injury required the bridge of her nose to need a replacement. Horne was fired two months before retiring and charged with obstruction for "jumping on Officer Kwiatkowski's back and/or striking him with her hands" (Mendoza Lao, 2021).

It would be fifteen years later before Horne would win a lawsuit and receive her pension. In a 2021 New York State Supreme Court ruling, Judge Dennis Ward opinionated, "The City of Buffalo has recognized the error and has acknowledged the need to undo an injustice from the past. The legal system can at the very least be the mechanism to help justice prevail, even if belatedly" (Siese, 2021). Unfortunately, "[t]he blue wall [of silence] is not crumbling" (Johnson, 2005, 77) and is still alive and well. Today, officers who manage to seep through the cracks are retaliated against and may be severely punished.

Whistleblower punishments and or interference can be severe. It can be a life sentence. Some officers faced death threats and resigned after exposing police corruption (Carroll, 2021). Had it not been such an outcry from the public after the George Floyd murder by former officer Derek Chauvin, a new Black female Pasadena police officer named Taisyn Crutchfield would have suffered tremendous torture and retaliation.

On February 20, 2023, Officer Crutchfield attempted to push a White police officer, Ralph Palacios, away after a Black teenager "was thrown face-first into a cactus." Crutchfield receives warnings from Palacios not to "do that." They are ordered to separate by a supervisor, who also gives them orders to return to the police station. Crutchfield was placed on paid administrative leave for six months without any explanation, and she eventually filed a lawsuit. Later, another Black police officer, Jarvis Shelby, filed a lawsuit alleging that "a police commander placed [him] in a headlock …resulting in serious injuries." Shelby's complaint also includes that he was the victim of numerous racial slurs from fellow White officers (Noel, 2023; Second police officer, 2023). Can "being a cop while Black" and breaking the blue wall of silence push a police officer over the edge of no return?

Did "being a cop while Black" contribute to former LAPD officer Christopher Dormer going insane and becoming a serial cop killer? The following analysis is provided for informational purposes only. All the information about Dormer is provided in good faith as to research and study. However, I do not condone his murderous behavior of any kind or anyone killing individuals as acts of retaliation to resolve grievances of any nature. On February 3, 2013, Dormer began a series of shootings in four counties in the Los Angeles area, targeting police officers and their families. In all, Dormer killed four people, including two police officers, wounded another three people, and pledged to kill dozens of police and their families (Goldman, 2013). Dormer's victims included the daughter of an LAPD captain and her fiancé, who defended him against the LAPD fabrication charges (Smith, 2013). According to Dormer, he was victimized by racial abuse, and the LAPD had gotten worse after the Rodney King beating (Kelly, 2013).

In August 2007, Dorner filed an official complaint against his White field training officer, Teresa Evans, that she used excessive force and kicked a mentally ill African American suspect, Christopher Gettler, in his head during an arrest. Dorner and Evans were dispatched to a Double Tree hotel for a disturbance, and it appeared that they physically struggled with Gettler. The LAPD internal affairs unit investigated the complaint and concluded that Evans did not commit excessive force and that Dorner made a false accusation. However, Gettler's father testified during a hearing that his son told him that a police officer had kicked him. Yet, Gettler did not report the assault to a doctor who examined him after arrest, and three hotel employee witnesses testified that they did not see an officer kicking him. Evans claimed that Dorner fabricated the assault due to her criticizing his performance in his field training report. The LAPD disciplinary board ruled that Dorner had lied and fired him. After years in court to get exonerated and maybe to get his job back, in 2010, a judge ruled in favor of the LAPD (Goldman, 2013; Kelly, 2013; Smith, 2013). LAPD Chief Charlie Beck later announced that they would examine Dorner's termination. Beck said, "I do this not to appease a murderer; I do it to reassure the public that their police department is transparent and fair in all the things we do" (Kelly, 2013).

While the LAPD internal re-examination concluded that Dorner's termination was justified and his allegations of excessive force unfounded, they also found that it still has problems with racism (Abdollah, 2013). Dorner died during a standoff with the San Bernardino County Sheriff after a shootout at a mountain cabin, maybe from a self-inflicted gunshot to the head and law enforcement firing pyrotechnic tear gas canisters into the cabin, which resulted in the cabin catching fire and burning to the ground (Rubin & Blankstein, 2013). Did the LAPD transform Dorner into a martyr? Bruno 2016 argues that people are defending Dorner because he's a modern-day Nat Turner figure against a racist LAPD:

> ***Maybe it was in order to make sense of Dorner's difficult violence that many came to read him as a black folk hero 'rebelling' against the 'slavery' of the LAPD. On Facebook, groups appeared***

such as 'We Stand With Chris Dorner,' 'We Are All Chris Dorner,' and 'Chris Dorner and the Revolution,' with these three alone having a combined 33,881 followers in April 2013. The latter group, in particular, describes Dorner's actions as 'his revolt.' Others went so far as to draw comparisons between Dorner and Nat Turner himself. One Twitter user writes, 'Chris Dorner considered armed and dangerous and extremely black . . . this is the Nat Turner of our time' (sic). Another writes that 'Chris Dorner went Nat Turner . . .,' and another that 'Chris Dorner is officially the Nat Turner re-incarnate of 2013. Way to kick off [Black History Month] by righting the wrongs of the system.' Still another writes that 'Chris Dorner our modern age Nat turner. Masta gonna be scare now you hear?' (sic).

Of course, Chris Dorner was never an actual slave, and his retaliation against the LAPD and its loose associates was by no means a slave revolt, just as the militant White supremacy of the LAPD could never constitute actual slavery. Yet as one of the most recent cultural recollections of the rebel slave, the popular

> ***discourse surrounding Chris Dorner belongs in the living archive on Nat Turner (Bruno, 2016, 948).***

Comedian Dave Chappelle, in his standup comedy special titled "8:46," which was the amount of time that former police officer Chauvin held his knee on Floyd's neck as he screamed, "I can't breathe," made reference that Dorner did what he was trained to do. Chappelle said Dorner was trained by the military and LAPD "to fight acts of terror." He suggested that police represent terror to African Americans (Ryzik, 2020). While Dorner chose insanity and violence to clear his name, what we can learn is that racism within the ranks of police is a peril and must be rooted out.

Police officers, like anyone else in a dangerous job, typically expect to face life threatening risks, but the idea that they would be at risk from another police officer is unsettling. Such was the case on April 9, 1962 of a 27-year-old Black military police officer named Cpl. Roman Ducksworth Jr. Ducksworth was on his way home to Mississippi by bus. Due to complications, his wife Melva, who was expecting their sixth child, was currently in the hospital. He was asleep by the time he got home to Taylorsville, Mississippi. To wake him up, the driver summoned white police officer William Kelly aboard the vehicle. Instead, Kelly arrested the serviceman on the grounds that he was mistaken for a "freedom rider," that was intoxicated. As the two fought off the bus, the officer fired twice, hitting Ducksworth in the chest. Unaware that his wife had just given birth to a healthy baby daughter, he passed away. Kelly was never charged because he said he shot Ducksworth in self-defense (Mitchell, 2024).

The above incidents of racial animosity toward African American police officers may appear pessimistic. "The problem is not a "few bad apples," but rather an organizational climate that molds new officers into thinking and doing as the organization wishes" (Johnson, 2006, 5). However, I disagree that "defunding police" is not the solution. What about the good police officers, who are, at most times, unsung heroes when it comes to saving lives and keeping the cities of America safe and secure?

For example, on March 5, 2021, in Carroll, Iowa, police officer Patrick McCarty risked his life when he stepped in front of a fleeing suspect from a traffic stop. Officer McCarty yelled, "Stop the car, man. Stop the car," after jumping on the hood and hanging on during a brief chase in a gravel lot. McCarty fell off the car and broke his back (CNN Wire, 2023). There is no doubt that there are police officers throughout this nation who put their lives on the line and are dedicated to protecting and serving all people. However, despite the heroic deeds of these officers, racism in police units has existed for over 400 years.

According to Michigan State University criminal justice professor Jennifer Cobbina, "Law enforcement officials across the U. S. have a much longer history of killing Black people." Cobbina explains:

> ***Too often, people look at the contemporary issue that is going on right now but not understanding that all that is happening is seeped in 400 years of legacy of injustice. These past grievances past harms by law enforcement, need to be addressed before even attempting to move forward. (Philimon, 2020)***

As USA Today indicated, "There is truly no place to hide, no place to truly be safe" (Philimon, 2020) for Black people in the U. S. Just when the country starts to talk about reform, 5 Black Memphis police officers step out of the sewer of humanity and commits ferocious acts against another Black man which simply shocks the conscience.

On January 7, 2023, Memphis police made an alleged reckless driving traffic stop of a 29-year-old Black man named Tyre Nichols. The officers immediately attacked Nichols by snatching him out of the car; they maced and tasered him. Nichols escaped and attempted to run to his mother's house, which was approximately a mile and a half away. The five police officers re-captured Nichols, where he was severely beaten by a baton; he was kicked and punched numerous times. Nichols called out to his mother as police were beating him to death. As Nichols was nearly limped and propped against a police car, the officers fist-bumped and boasted about their brutal attack. Nichols was delayed first aid by medics and was transported to a hospital, where he died three days later. However, the strange twist in this story was that all five of the police officers were African American (Sainz, 2023).

Nearly every person with a conscience must've asked, how could this happen after hearing Nichols say, "You guys are really doing a lot right now; I'm just trying to go home" (Sainz, 2023). Wasn't diversity the solution to poor relations between the police and the African American communities? Reverend Al Sharpton, while giving Nichol's eulogy, zealously proclaimed:

> ***And the reason why…what happened to Tyre is so personal to me is that five Black men that wouldn't have had a job in the police department - would not ever be thought of to be in the elite squad - in the city that Dr. King lost his life, not far away from that balcony, you beat a brother to death.***
>
> ***There's nothing more insulting and offensive to those of us that fight to open doors, that you walk through those doors and act like the folks we had to fight to get you through them doors.***

> ***You didn't get on the police department by yourself. The police chief didn't get there by herself. People had to march and go to jail, and some lost their lives to open the doors for you, and how dare you act like that sacrifice was for nothing? (ABC 24 Staff, 2023)***

When I heard the news story of Nichols's beating and death at the hands of the five Memphis Black police officers, I was struck to the core. Dr. Martin Luther King would be rolling over in his grave.

Dr. Martin Luther King led a march in support of the Memphis sanitation workers in March of 1968, and a sixteen-year-old Black teenager protestor named Larry Payne was killed by a White police officer named Leslie Dean Jones. According to witnesses, Jones shot Payne in the stomach with a shotgun while he had his hands raised in the air (Watts, 2019). Dr. King had planned to visit Payne's mother during his next visit to Memphis but was assassinated prior (Larry Payne, 2015). The hiring and promotion of Black police officers in Memphis was contentious and discriminatory and resulted in a 1974 Civil Rights lawsuit by the United States Department of Justice and a dissent decree. The city of Memphis acknowledged "that certain of its past practices may have given rise to an inference that it had engaged in unlawful discrimination" (Miller & Allen, 2008). In Arguendo, historian W.

Marvin Dulaney commented that a former 1920's Memphis mayor said that keeping Blacks off the police force "was integral to the preservation of "White supremacy" (Lartey & Cooper, 2023).

Shouldn't the presence of Black officers reduce police brutality and police killings during police encounters with African Americans? "The public tends to associate racially mixed policing with impartiality, fairness, and trustworthiness in the delivery of police services" (Gustafson, 2013). The argument appears plausible that increasing the number of Black officers on the police force would solve the shootings and killings of Black citizens, particularly after the Ferguson incident. However, an empirical study suggests that more Black officers "is not an effective policy solution (Nicholson-Crotty, Nicholson-Crotty & Fernandez, 2017). Black police officers may have "same-race" prejudice and may over-police Black persons in an effort to fit in with departmental cultural standards (Carbado & Richardson, 2018).

The Honorable Elijah Muhammad offered to the American public the Nation of Islam's answer to the problem of police brutality and the problem of Black officers policing the Black community:

> ***The Black man, who has been a servitude slave and now a free slave of White America, can never hope to enjoy peace, freedom, justice and***

equality under the control of a mixed law enforcement agency (Black and White) …

In the past and maybe present, the White officer chooses from among us the "uncle-tom-like" men to serve as law enforcement officers over us.

This type of Black officer makes more trouble in the community than the trouble that is made by the community because he wants to be loved and honored by the White officer at the expense of mistreating his Black Brother. Surely, he does not want to place, on the force, a Black Man who loves his Black people and wants to see them at peace with each other…

[The White officer] rides with the Black officer over the Black section or community of the Black people to see to it that the Black officer mistreats his people, as he would do himself.

The Black policeman, hoping that he will keep his job as policeman, follows the instructions of his White officer, which causes him to lose all love and respect of his people for him as their peace officer. (Muhammad, E. 1968)

Any similarity between Elijah Muhammad's depiction of the Black policeman and Samuel Jackson's role in Django Unchained, who played Stephen Warren, the head house slave for the villainous Calvin Candie (Leonardo DiCaprio), is not a coincidence. By studying and modifying the enemy's methods of survival, Stephen redefines the fight against slavery through the theory of anthropophagy. Stephen's combination of ferocity toward his fellow Black people and subservience to his master was disconcerting (Mukwara & Mongosho, 2016).

These generalizations should not suggest that all Black police officers will sell out their race for the sake of loyalty to "blue" and engage in brutality. I personally know many Black police officers who abhor racist practices within their department and some who defended suspects who were being victimized by their fellow White officers. However, police departments are very selective in choosing candidates. In addition to a comprehensive background check, interviews conducted by seasoned staff, evaluations from training academies, oral interviews, and the customary one-year probationary/field training period, pre-employment psychological testing of police officers has become a common practice (Simmons, Bowers & Ruiz, 2003).

According to an article published in the Harvard Law Review titled Policing Our Own, Black policemen may exhibit "same-race" prejudice and may over police Black people in an effort to fit in with departmental cultural norms. According to the authors of that article, racial diversity without significant reallocations or redistributions of power "might not only limit the possibilities for social transformation but also potentially reproduce and legitimize the very forms of inequality the pursuit of racial diversity was intended to address" (Lartey & Cooper, 2023). According to a criminologist, "Blue is blue: the job shapes the officer, not the other way around. Police officers of all kinds are assumed to make peace with the "White," masculine, heterosexual ethos' of policing, or to have difficulty lasting." Negative, rebellious police officers will display traits that support the "we versus them" mindset. When African American police officers participate in a bad police subculture, their White peers view them as "clever policemen," but the African American community views them as "dirty cops" (Dukes, 2014). However, this topic drifts into an area that one can write an entire book about.

Lionel Kimble, a history professor at Chicago State University whose research focuses on Black civil rights, argues, "[t]he country is going to have to take a hard look in the mirror and talk about how we police people, in what role the police play in supporting inequality in our society" (Philimon, 2020).

The main objective and goal of police in society is to provide a safe and secure community and a reduction of crime. Many times, police are left with this responsibility with limited funding and resources. An annoying crime problem is often associated with the African American urban communities. For the most part, police and

African American encounters in dealing with poverty, drug use, mental illness, domestic violence, murders, robberies, and hostilities are what to be expected. With the increase of volatile incidents in urban America and the police's ability to use force to stop force, lethal encounters are inevitable.

In Michigan, the Michigan Commission on Law Enforcement Standards (MCOLES) outlines police use of force as a "decision to deploy any less-lethal device." This decision, when used to physically control a subject, should be based on the subject's actions, the totality of the circumstances, and be consistent with the objectively reasonable standard that governs the application of force by law enforcement officers" (MCOLES, 2008). In other words, all police use of force is not brutality and sometimes necessary. However, a reasonable person, in view of the overwhelming evidence, would conclude that there exists a problem with the use of force by police in African American communities.

The list of incidents of police brutality and murdering of African Americans was long but not exhaustive. After years of research and dedication, I could've wrote an entire book about the history of police mistreatment of Black people in the United States. It's evident that there is a deep hostility between the police and the African American community. For example, it's worth mentioning how the FBI and the Chicago Police assassinated Black Panther Fred Hampton. As Hampton lay unconscious on a bed, one officer say, He's still alive. Two shots are fired by police and a second officer said, He's good and dead now (Hass, 2010). Tragically, we must remember in 1985, the Philadelphia police dropped two explosive devices from a helicopter onto the roof of the headquarters of the Black liberation group MOVE. The bombing destroyed 61 homes over two city blocks, killing six adults and five children (Wahrhaftig, and Assefa, 1992).

The police-community problem in African American communities is enormous. One who denies this fact is either in denial or in support of unaccountable police brutality and misconduct in African American communities. Police leaders and administrators must be willing to break rank, get off the fence, and address this monstrosity, or the integrity of law enforcement will perish. The recent global protest against police brutality, including many young Caucasians declaring "Black Lives Matter," has transformed my pessimism into optimism.

The perils that result from unaccounted police brutality may be devastating. The number of innocent lives lost from police use of force, along with outrage and protest, leading to multiple injuries and deaths, rioting, and millions of dollars in property damage, must compel this Nation to take action toward police reform. The oppressive government imposed by the King and Parliament of England led to the American Revolution. It is long overdue for America to change the perception of police as described by the Kerner Commission:

> ***The police are not merely a spark factor. To some Blacks, police have come to symbolize White power, White racism, and White repression. And the fact is that many police do reflect and express these White attitudes. The atmosphere of hostility and cynicism is reinforced by a widespread belief among Negroes in the existence of police brutality and in a double standard of justice and protection — one for Blacks and one for Whites. (Radelet, 1986)***

For African Americans to be truly merged in American society, they must be able to warrant protection and service by the police as well as protection from the police. If racist police brutality and the use of lethal force are not eliminated, nobody in America can be safe. The United States must truly practice what's written in the Pledge of Allegiance, "liberty and justice for all."

Chapter 3: Police Brutality and Race: A Literature Review

> ***Even in literature and art, no man who bothers about originality will ever be original, whereas if you simply try to tell the truth (without caring two pence how often it has been told before), you will, nine times out of ten, become original without ever having noticed it. – C. S. Lewis***

In 1944, Swedish economist and sociologist Gunner Myrdal conducted a study on race relations in American society. Myrdal described the policeman as "The personification of White authority in the Negro community" (Myrdal, 1944, 535), which often results in racial police brutality. Myrdal argued:

> ***The beating of arrested Negroes — frequently in the wagon on the way to jail or later when they are already safely locked up — often serves as vengeance for the fears and perils the policemen***

are subjected to while pursuing their duties in the Negro community (Skolnick & Fyfe, 1993, 23).

In urban communities, research data suggest that African Americans are disproportionately stopped by police and victims of aggressive force far more than other racial groups. While some estimates vary slightly, the overall rate of African American men being killed by police in their life span is 2.5 times greater than White men, which includes African American men being twice as likely to be unarmed when compared to White people (Peeples 2020).

The President's Task Force on 21st Century Policing reported that "a number of law enforcement agencies have taken the step of acknowledging past law enforcement involvement in discrimination and injustice" (Office of Community Oriented Policing Services, 2015, 5), and Texas A&M University in College Station economist Mark Hoekstra conducted a study that "concluded that White officers dispatched to Black neighborhoods fired their guns five times as often as Black officers dispatched for similar calls to the same neighborhoods" (Peeples, 2020).

The increased use of police lethal force in recent years has been associated with a higher perception of racial inequality and lack of police accountability. A group of scholars have all "scrutinized police reactions to racial and ethnic minorities, offering ample evidence of minority disadvantage at the hands of police"

(Holmes & Smith, 2008, 1). It is suggested that police brutality against African Americans and other minority groups in the United States is the most serious domestic problem, significantly contributing to civil disorder and resulting in civil lawsuits costing American taxpayers hundreds of millions of dollars (Nelson, 2000). The goal of this literature review is to compare three scholarly theories to ascertain the root cause of police brutality against African Americans.

Emotional and Cognitive Theory on Police Brutality

Social psychology was refined in the 1940s and 1950s by Kurt Lewin and Leon Festinger and has been beneficial in the study of human behavior. Examples include how social psychology attempted to understand whether the brutality reported among guards in American prisons was due to the sadistic personalities of the guards (Haney, Banks & Zimbardo, 1973). Social psychology, to a few, is the theory of choice for understanding police brutality because "humans' category-based responses to others are deeply rooted in the structures and processes of the brain" (Holmes & Smith, 2008, 37). While modifications in police organization may provide some change, stereotyping by police and African Americans is a "generic human quality" that causes people to subconsciously form opinions of potential perils and react to these perceived dangers by "fleeing or by employing aggression" (Holmes & Smith, 2008; Adler, 2010). These emotional and cognitive processes in police and African Americans formulate stereotypes against each other.

Police officers, due to their frequent exposure to complex incidents and problems of citizens, are vulnerable to developing stereotypes, and this is profoundly documented (Holmes & Smith, 2008). Police officers' cognitive functions are dominated by their perceptions of dangerous people:

> ***The policeman, because his work requires him to be occupied continually with potential violence, develops a perceptual shorthand to identify certain kinds of people as symbolic assailants, that is, as persons who use gesture, language, and attire that the policeman has come to recognize as a prelude to violence. This does not mean that violence by the assailant is necessarily predictable. On the contrary, the policeman responds to the vague indication of danger suggested by appearance. (Skolnick, 1975, 45; Holmes & Smith, 2008, 72)***

Black males in the United States have a disproportionately high rate of homicide and non-fatal violence (Oliver, 2009). Therefore, African American males are stereotyped as extremely dangerous by the police and the entire criminal justice system (Holmes & Smith, 2008).

African Americans bring their own stereotypes or "cultural baggage" to the table in police encounters. Tensions between police and African Americans are a common topic of discussion in the community. "These stories reinforce pejorative stereotypes that portray the police as dangerous" (Holmes & Smith, 2008, 75). While the "big four" or "STRESS" were a notorious, dangerous Detroit police squad from the 1960s and '70s, they are still talked about in the African American community. African Americans hold negative views about the police and see them as an occupying army. "These stereotypes may become self-fulfilling prophecies that reinforce the mutual antagonism between them and police" (Holmes & Smith, 2008, 76). The community-police relationship is shattered due to the negative stereotypes they have of one another.

The police stereotypes connect African American males to crime within society. Stories told of police brutality, hostility, and misconduct against African Americans become a big picture of the "Black" community narrative. Often, these actual events inflame and distort what really happened. The atmosphere of mutual hate, distrust, and danger becomes a realistic "self-fulfilling prophecy" and results in police brutality. Police brutality "constitutes a normal, albeit highly unfortunate, manifestation of human psychological functioning" (Holmes & Smith, 2008, 102).

Conflict Theory of Policing

The conflict theory of policing asserts that crime control is a pretext for the powerful segment of society to prevent threats to their power and interests. "Privileged members of society benefit greatly from the existing social and economic order, whereas many other citizens, especially poor and racial/ethnic minorities, experience profound disadvantages" (Holmes & Smith, 2008, 17). The African American communities exemplify a separate society with a dividing line between White dominance and Black subordinates. Empirical studies confirm that "the resources and the coercive strategies of policing are linked to the racial and ethnic makeup of communities" (Holmes & Smith, 2008, 17). White Americans perceive African Americans and their association with crime as a threat to the social order. Thus, police brutality is the means to which to control the threat to the social order (Holmes & Smith, 2008). While Sir Robert Peel of England is credited with developing the United States' organized policing model (Lawrence, 2017), meticulous studies contend that the police have a contradictory function in society.

The police may be the agent of the people it polices and, at the same time, the agent of a powerful class that uses it to control those people (Muhammad, D 2002). Robinson and Scaglion (1987) contend that the police developed simultaneously with the development of the state. Society uses the police to dominate based on class status while pretending to support the entire society. Police history and foundation were traced from pre-state to State societies and consist of four interdependent propositions:

> ***(1) The origin of a specialized police function depends upon the division of society into dominant and subordinate classes with antagonistic interests;***
>
> ***(2) specialized police agencies are generally characteristic only of societies politically organized as states;***
>
> ***(3) in a period of transition, the crucial factor in delineating the modern specialized police function is an ongoing attempt at the conversion of the social control (policing) mechanism from an integral part of the community structure to an agent of an emerging dominant class; and***
>
> ***(4) the police institution is created by the emerging dominant class as an instrument for the preservation of its control over restricted access to basic resources, over the political apparatus governing this access, and over the labor force necessary to provide the surplus upon which the dominant class lives. (Robinson and Scaglion, 1987, 113).***

Their argument is that the police were designed by the dominant of society to preserve their status and maintain control over the subordinate class so that they may continue to live off of their resources.

For the conflict theory, an idealized picture from Paul Chevigny's 1969 book, Police Power: Police Abuses in New York City, gives the best answer to the charge that the police represent the dominant segment of society:

> ***The routine denials of due process of law' by false arrest, framing suspects, unlawful search and seizure, systematic harassment, violence, and 'summary punishment' were a routine feature of street encounters between police officers and citizens. Chevigny argued that police abuse was not just patterned and normal but political. For the powerful, the police are vital because they need an agency to keep society running smoothly and, as a result, are willing to turn a blind eye to police criminality. The police have been given the mandate to construct a criminal class and criminal threat that justifies the use of existing legislation and new legislation. However, police***

> *practices are also counterproductive and create contempt for authority. The criminal justice system within which the police work 'is evil for the simplest of reasons: because it injures people and destroys their respect for the legal process. It is not for nothing that ghetto people have chosen police abuses as symbols of oppression; it is because they actually are acts of oppression. (McLaughlin, 2006, 59)*

Consistent with conflict theory, the analyses suggest that the racial and economic composition of states has a significant impact on the average rate of police killings.

Bad Apple Theory of Policing

The bad apple metaphor may be claimed by those who choose to protect the police image when officers engage in misconduct or brutality. The argument is that the actions of a few bad officers do not reflect upon the values and performance of the entire department. On its face, it may appear plausible that there are bad lawyers, bad doctors, bad politicians, and even bad Indian chiefs, yet the bad ones do not make the entire profession bad. "The bad apple theory of policing argues that the vast majority of police officers are good and that it is a few bad cops (or bad apples) that cause the majority of the problems" (Greenwald, 2017). The bad apple theory suggests that police are independent and are solely responsible for their street behavior of brutality. "Police are not mere minions of the powerful" (Holmes & Smith, 2008, 20).

To support the bad apple theory is to support that the entire police system is fair and justified and police brutality is the result of a lone rouge police officer. "System justification theory proposes that people are motivated to hold positive views about existing social, economic, and political arrangements" (Jolley, Douglas & Sutton, 2018, 4). It is proposed that a justified system with police brutality would result in a conspiracy theory formation:

> ***Conspiracy [theory] beliefs satisfy important psychological needs, allowing people to make sense of events, avoid feelings of uncertainty, avoid existential anxiety, help make sense of a chaotic world, address feelings of powerlessness, deal with a lack of control, protect the image of the ingroup, and cope with disadvantage. Conspiracy theorizing may represent a substitute route to these needs when system justification is untenable...Conspiracy theories may paradoxically bolster support for the status quo when its legitimacy is threatened. (Jolley, Douglas & Sutton, 2018, 4)***

In other words, the blame for police brutality is on the police officer because the police department and criminal justice system are legitimate. Pointing fingers at the bad police officer– even groups of individual officers charged with police brutality may exonerate the police system, just as "blaming a driver for a car crash shifts blame from the car" (Jolley, Douglas & Sutton, 2018 21).

Shifting the blame from the entire police system onto the officer puts the "bad apple officer" outside of society and its history of racism and the American infrastructure, which negatively affects all the apples in the barrel. The "bad apple officer" is a part of the barrel; he is a part of the bad apple tree. Perhaps the entire tree is rotten. In his book "The Tears We Cannot Stop: A Sermon to White America," Michael Eric Dyson argues:

> ***That metaphor of a few bad apples doesn't begin to get at the root of the problem. Police violence may be more like a poisoned water stream that pollutes the entire system. To argue that only a few bad cops cause police terror is like relegating racism to a few bigots. Bigots are surely a problem, but they are sustained by systems of belief and perception, by widely held stereotypes and social practices. (May & Yancy, 2020)***

As long as the bad officer is a part of the department, the entire agency is viewed as bad. Bad apple policing is an oxymoron in comparison to the structural make-up of police departments.

Simply making the baseless claim that brutality is the result of the actions of a bad police officer ignores the basic foundation of the administration of the American police. The structure and functioning of police departments has a hierarchical and autocratic command structure:

> ***Police departments are hierarchical, with a chain of command as in the military and a sharp division between the leadership and the rank-and-file. Under the prevailing quasi-military style of police department organization, management seeks to maintain a high level of internal discipline and strict rank-and-file obedience to rules and policies…The prevailing belief is that the rank-and-file must be strictly controlled and monitored in order to ensure compliance (Fisk & Richardson, 2017, 722-723).***

Additionally, within the police system are police unions that are obligated to "protect cops who appear to have engaged in clear misconduct rather than protecting the interests of 'good' ones by allowing 'bad' ones to be disciplined, fired, or prosecuted" (Fisk & Richardson, 2017, 714). Thus, the bad apple police officer can't be dissected from the police agency.

Discussion

A thorough review of the literature revealed that police are human beings and are subject to emotional and cognitive variables. A plausible analysis is that police and African Americans are engaging each other with criminal and racist stereotypes. This point raises an important question: where historically did these stereotypes come from? The answer to this question may lie in a historical review of American slavery. Dr. Joy DeGruy presents an alternative perspective called Post Traumatic Slave Syndrome (PTSS), which she describes as "a condition that exists when a population has experienced multigenerational trauma resulting from centuries of slavery and continues to experience oppression and institutionalized racism today. Added to this condition is a belief (real or imagined) that the benefits of the society in which they live are not accessible to them" (DeGruy, 2005, 109). PTSS connects violent acts and aggression during chattel slavery against African Americans with law enforcement practices (DeGruy, 2005). Southern White slave patrollers had a law enforcement duty to watch, catch, or beat African American slaves. "The most dangerous people who were thought to need watching were slaves — they were the prime targets of patrol observation and capture" (Hadden, 2001, 4). My assumption is that the slave patroller's violence resulted in the formulation of emotional and cognitive stereotypes, which results in police and African American violent confrontations today.

According to the literature evidence base, there is an advantage to the dominant Whites in society to use law enforcement to maintain their status and to protect their resources from the subordinate African Americans. Once again, we review the economic gain from American slavery. Dr. Claude Anderson described this "conflict theory" in his book *Black Labor, White Wealth*:

> ***The profitability of Black slaves as a wealth-producing commodity was so great that anything short of a civil war would have had little, if any, effect on the slavery system...After the slaves were emancipated, those who had founded their livelihood in exploiting free Black labor feared the potential financial consequences... [Whites] had a vested financial interest in maintaining a large and cheap supply of labor" (Anderson, 1994, 134-5).***

Laws were passed to allow Whites "to brand, whip, or

actually kill enslaved Blacks" (Anderson, 1994, 158). The slave patrol was established to enforce these laws to protect their wealth and resources (Hadden, 2001).

An additional dialogue of a "bad apple officer" offers a significant advantage for the polity in preserving their trust in society. The research literature, along with my personal law enforcement experience, leaves me suspended in judgment regarding the "bad apple" theory. Former President Barack Obama said it best regarding the George Floyd killing, "The majority of men and women in law enforcement who take pride in doing their tough job the right way, every day" (May & Yancy, 2020). President Obama's statement clearly confirms that former Minneapolis officer Derek Chauvin was indeed a "bad apple" cop. However, a study conducted on the presence of bias-based policing in the Virginia police department revealed that 12 percent of Virginia police officers agree that it exists. This finding casts doubt on the "rotten apple" theory and provides support for the "systems failure" theory (Gottschalk, Dean & Glomseth, 2011). Additionally, Chicago police administrators watched the 2014 video of Laquan McDonald being shot while walking away by Officer Van Dyke, and they all agreed that the shooting was justified (Greenwald, 2017). Perhaps many officers want to protect the integrity of policing yet remain silent when witnessing fellow officers committing acts of brutality, which may suggest "systems failure" as opposed to "rotten apple."

We conclude, based on the current evidence, that the

emotional and cognitive theory and the conflict theory of policing are strongly associated with the incidence of racial police brutality and that the bad apple theory of policing may not be significantly supported. In the current literature review, a major limitation discovered was that bad-apple policing did not outweigh the probability of the entire police system's failures. However, according to Holmes and Smith (2008), there is "considerable value in the insights of micro-level perspectives that identify human mental characteristics implicated in the production of aggression (37). Robinson & Scaglion (1987) offers an interesting theory of the origin and evolution of the police function, using both historical and cross-cultural analysis. They argued that changes in the police function are associated with the formation of the state and a transition to a class-dominated society. Future studies should use similar assessment models considering the history of race relations during American slavery, which could yield results that are easier to compare and strengthen.

Conclusion

Police use of lethal force and brutality against African Americans has increased in occurrence and has galvanized the media and the public's attention. The goal of this literature review was to compare three general theories as the root cause of excessive force and police brutality against African Americans. The three theories were ***(a) emotional and cognitive theory, (b) conflict***

theory of policing, and (c) bad apple theory of policing. The reviewed literature suggests that there are advantages in the study of racial police brutality with a review from the perspectives of both the emotional and cognitive theory and the conflict theory of policing. The contradiction between bad apple theory and police system failure has been widely documented throughout literature studies (May & Yancy, 2020; Gottschalk, Dean & Glomseth, 2011). Current research supports the use of the emotional and cognitive theory and the conflict theory of policing, as discussed above. However, a continuation of current research with the review of post-traumatic slave syndrome and the evolution of slave patrollers with consistent and strengthened research will help to understand this monstrosity of race and police brutality. (Key, Rich, DeCristofaro & Collins, 2010).

As a sidebar, social psychology studied "The most notorious genocidal and democidal instigator of the twentieth century, Adolf Hitler" (Mandel, 2002) and in understanding the Holocaust. In a 2017 speech to law enforcement, President Donald Trump encouraged police to be more violent against criminal suspects:

> ***When you see these thugs being thrown into the back of a paddy wagon, you just seen them thrown in, rough. I said, please don't be too nice.***

> ***When you guys put somebody in the car, and you're protecting their head, you know, the way you put their hand over [their head]. Like, don't hit their head, and they've just killed somebody, don't hit their head. I said, you can take the hand away, OK?***
>
> ***I have to tell you, you know, the laws are so horrendously stacked against us because, for years and years, they've been made to protect the criminal. Totally made to protect the criminal. Not the officers. You do something wrong, you're in more jeopardy than they are. (Keneally, 2017)***

President Trump has also suggested that police shoot rioting protestors by saying, "When the looting starts, the shooting starts," which was a racist phrase used by former Miami police chief Walter E. Headley in 1967 (Sprunt, 2020). What can social psychology tell us about President Trump and his significant number of supporters in the United States in 2020?

Chapter 4: The Civil War was about Slavery

> ***"It was about slavery – Ask what caused the Civil War; Nikki Haley refuses to mention slavery: 'What do you want me to say about slavery? Next question.'" – President Joe Biden***

> ***"If you want to understand any problem in America, you need to focus on who profits from that problem, not who suffers from that problem." – Dr. Amos Wilson.***

The last words of the pledge of allegiance, "With liberty and justice for all," are perhaps one of the biggest fallacies in American culture and society. Nearly from its beginning, America, particularly in the South, was extremely dependent on the free labor of African Americans as slaves (Kolchin, 1993). Peter Kolchin, in his book American Slavery, described how the "Founding Fathers" were intertwined with slavery in the United States:

> ***Most of the Founding Fathers were large-scale slave owners, including George Washington, 'the father of his country,' Patrick Henry, author of a stirring cry 'Give me liberty or death,' and Thomas Jefferson, who proclaimed in the Declaration of Independence that 'all men are created equal.' Indeed, eight of the United States' first twelve Presidents, in office for forty-nine of the new nation's first sixty-one years, were slaveholders. (Kolchin, 1993, 3)***

The primary reason for slaves being brought to America was for their ability to work and generate wealth for the slave owners despite their moral disparity. Thomas Jefferson knew that slavery was morally and politically wrong. He argued that God abhorred the evil of holding another man in slavery:

> ***God, who gave us life, gave us liberty. Can the liberties of a nation be secure when we have removed a conviction that these liberties are the gift of God? Indeed, I tremble for my country when I reflect that God is just and that his justice cannot sleep forever. Commerce between master and slave is despotism. Nothing is more certainly***

> ***written in the book of Fate than that these people are to be free. (The Jefferson Monticello)***

However, there's a substantial difference between Jefferson's thoughts and his actions. He continued to own slaves while believing it was evil to keep another man in bondage (Cohen, 1969).

Jefferson stated in reference to African Americans in southern slavery, "We have the wolf by the ears and can neither hold him, nor safely let him go. Justice is in the one scale, and self-preservation in the other" (Cohen, 1969, 524). However, he could not resist the financial benefits of chattel slavery. He made a fortune from the American slave trade. While he often articulated his displeasure for human commerce, he sold slaves when he needed cash, and Jefferson appeared to have only freed two slaves in his lifetime. Jefferson's land acquisitions and slaves "made him the second wealthiest man in Albemarle County and one of the richest men in Virginia" (Cohen, 1969, 507). "Slavery [in America] constituted, first and foremost, a system of labor" (Kolchin, 1993, 6). African American slavery was a significant part of the New World, the "Americas," and provided a major source of free labor and economic advantage.

American capitalism and the rise of the British Empire can be credited to the economic gains from the brutal African American slavery in the New World (Williams, 1944). Dr. Claud Anderson argued, "Slaves were walking credit cards. Any White who owned a slave could always earn money by either selling the slave's labor or selling the slave. Both the slave and his labor carried value" (Anderson, 1994, 134). Frederick Douglas described the benefits of free labor as:

> ***The American slave trade... is especially prosperous... the price of men was never higher... This trade is one of the peculiarities of American institutions. It is carried on in all the large towns and cities in one-half of this confederacy, and millions are pocketed every year by dealers in this horrid traffic. In several states, this trade is a chief source of wealth. It is called (in contradistinction to the foreign slave trade) the internal slave trade. (Douglas, 1852)***

The prospect of free slave labor raises a question: Whether slavery was profitable in the United States to the extent of protecting it as an institution?

Historians and scholars have debated the profitability of the American slave trade. Some scholars and historians argued in their writings that slave labor was more costly and not profitable overall (Fogel, 1989; Sutch, 2018; Phillips, 1905). However, other scholars contended that slavery was profitable in the southern United States, "The continuing demand for labor in the Cotton Belt ensuring returns to the breeding operation on the less productive land in the seaboard and border states" (Conrad and Meyer 1958, 121). Slave owners were capitalists who profited from their competitive decisions to buy or sell African American slaves (Sutch, 2018). Buying or selling slaves was considered an investment (Conrad and Meyer 1958). While those in denial continue to debate American slavery profitability, the facts and historical evidence are overwhelming and undeniable from a deductive reasoning perspective.

In his book, American Slavery, which may be the best overview of slavery in the United States, author Peter Kolchin argued that slavery spread like malignant cancer because of the colonists' desire for capital gain. Between 1680 and 1750, as a result of importing slaves, the population of African Americans in South Carolina increased from 17 to 61 percent. It was so profitable that a conservatively estimated 10 to 11 million Africans were brought to the United States over the Atlantic Ocean on slave ships. Rice, the South's most profitable crop, soared from 12,000 pounds in 1698 to 83 million pounds in 1770 (Kolchin, 1993). "U.S. slave plantations were highly efficient. Productivity increased even faster than in industry, thanks to the technology of the bullwhip and pistol, and the efficient practice of brutal torture" (Olmstead & Rhode, 2018,22). Slavery made White men wealthy. For example, upon the death of a slave owner, Robert "King" Carter, he was considered the wealthiest man residing in Virginia. He owned 390 slaves (Kolchin, 1993). White slave owners had no intention of allowing this free labor and enormous wealth to escape their control (Anderson, 1994).

There was nothing less than the American Civil War that could've put an end to chattel slavery in the United States. The American Civil War was one of the deadliest and bloodiest battles in the history of the United States. Overall, 2 percent of the population, an estimated 620,000 men, lost their lives on the battlefield between the North and the South. Nearly a million and a half Americans suffered casualties of either being killed, wounded, captured, or missing. Nearly one in four soldiers never returned home after going off to battle. Fifty-one thousand soldier casualties at the Battle of Gettysburg were more than the Revolutionary War and War of 1812 combined. The Civil War had nearly as many deaths as the Vietnam War (Civil War Casualties, n.d.). In arguendo, on April 14, 1865, John Wilkes Booth killed President Abraham Lincoln because he thought Lincoln was a despot who posed a threat to the Confederacy and the system of slavery (Wilkes, 2024). What led to the outbreak of the bloodiest conflict in the history of North America?

The new nation was divided between the Federalist and Democratic-Republican parties during the American Revolution and before the United States declared independence from Britain. They had their own ideas about how the government should function, with the Federalists believing in a strong central government while the Democratic-Republicans believed in a strong state government (Skaflestad, 2021). According to political scientist James A. Reichley, "The issue that most sharply divided the [Democratic Republicans] from the Federalists was not states' rights, nor the national debt, nor the national Bank... but the question of social equality" (Reichley, 2000, 52). The root cause of the divide between the Federalists and the Democratic-Republicans was American slavery.

The Democratic-Republicans were led by Thomas Jefferson, who wrote in the initial draft of the Declaration of Independence that King George III "has waged cruel war against nature itself, violating its most sacred rights of life and liberty in the persons of a distant people who never offended him, captivating and carrying them into slavery in another hemisphere or to incur miserable death in their transportation thither...Determined to keep open a market where Men should be bought and sold, he has prostituted his negative for suppressing every legislative attempt to prohibit or restrain this execrable commerce." This passage was omitted to please colonists and southern slave owners (Skaflestad, 2021). Make no mistakes—the split between the North and South were about slavery.

After the American Revolution where thirteen states (Connecticut, Delaware, Georgia, Maryland, Massachusetts, New Hampshire, New York, New Jersey, Virginia, North Carolina, Pennsylvania, Rhode Island, and South Carolina) took on and defeated the British Empire for independence and land, the North began to ban, reduce, limit or abolish slavery. The strength of the North's economy was manufacturing and the stock market, whereas the South economy relied on agriculture, farming, and slavery. With the expansion of the United States, laws were passed, with the central focus being either anti or pro-slavery (Skaflestad, 2021).

As the expansion moved west, the Northwest Ordinance of 1787 outlawed slavery in any newly formed state. The Northwest Ordinance outlined the process for admitting a new state to the Union and guaranteed that newly created states would equal the original thirteen states (Primary Documents, 2022). Under the ordinance, slavery was banned from the lands of the Northwest Territory. Another law that illustrates the division over slavery was the Missouri Compromise. In 1820, due to amid tensions over the issue of slavery, the U.S. Congress passed a law that admitted Missouri to the Union as a slave state and Maine as a free state while banning slavery from the remaining Louisiana Purchase lands located north of the 36º 30' parallel (Robinson, 1990).

As the United States grew rapacious for more land with the idea of Manifest Destiny, a belief that the U.S. was destined to stretch from the Atlantic Ocean to the Pacific Ocean, so did the slavery conflict. Slavery played a significant role in the tensions that led to the Mexican-American War. R&B singer and actor Tyrese Gibson shared a post on Instagram about the slavery dilemma:

Most Americans don't know that the United

States practically stole Texas from Mexico. Texas along with these whole areas stretching up to California used to belong to Mexico. In the mid 1800's, as the United States was busy expanding its territory westward, they started bumping into the recently independent country of Mexico, which at the time wanted a way for their country to become more economically productive. So they started renting out huge plots of land to American settlers in the region you might have heard of called Texas. As American settled the land, they brought slaves with them, which were totally illegal in Mexico at the time.

As the Mexican government tried to crack down on these settlers for breaking the law, these people responded by fighting a war with the Mexican government which they won. And then declared themselves as their own independent country as the Republic of Texas. Mexico acknowledged Texas as independent but the United States government disputed where the location of the border was. In 1848, the U S Congress passed a joint resolution for annexing Texas. Texas was offered the option to join the United States and they accepted the offer in July

> ***1845 and officially became the twenty eighth state on the United States.***
>
> ***President James K Polk was obsessed with acquiring California from Mexico. He sent Mexico an offer of $20 million to buy the territory. Mexico refused this offer. So he came up with a pretty dubious plan. He sent American soldiers to the disputed region in Texas who were then shot at and captured by the Mexican army. He used this event as a rallying cry for the United States congress to declare war on Mexico. The United States being the stronger power of the two easily won the war and they paid $15 million to Mexico, who reluctantly receded all the territory to the United States. In less than twenty years, Mexico lost more than half of its territory to the United States. (Gibson, 2025)***

The treaty of Guadalupe Hidalgo ended the Mexican-American War in 1848. As a result of the conflict that partially started over slavery, the United States acquired California, Nevada, Utah, Arizona, New Mexico, Texas, parts of Colorado, parts of Wyoming, parts of Kansas and parts of Oregon.

Slavery remained a controversial issue after the Mexican–

American War, which brought about the Compromise of 1850. It was several laws passed during the ferocious battle between anti and pro-slavery groups. The Compromise was intended to accommodate both sides by admitting California to the United States as a free state but allowed some newly acquired territories to decide on slavery for their selves. A section of the Compromise of 1850 was the Fugitive Slave Act, which caused animosity among the Northern states (Holder, 1936).

The Fugitive Slave Act preceded the year 1850; the Fugitive Slave Act of 1793 was an Act of the United States Congress (Article 4, Section 2, Clause 3) approved on February 12, 1793 (Annals of Congress, 1875). However, the Fugitive Slave Act of 1850 differed in that the new revision required citizens to help capture runaway slaves, denied accused runaways the right to a jury trial, and criminal penalties for anyone interfering with the recapture a $1,000.00 fine and six months in jail. The Fugitive Slave Act may have contributed to the kidnapping of Solomon Northup, a free African American and author of 12 Years a Slave who was sold into slavery in the pre-Civil War South (History.com, 2009).

Historian and college professor Matthew Pinsker, who writes about Abraham Lincoln and the Civil War era and directs the House Divided Project, brings clarity to the Fugitive Slave Act as a prelude to the Civil War:

[The Fugitive Slave Act] goes back to the

Constitution, article 4. The Constitution has a clause that we call the Fugitive Slave Clause, which orders states to deliver up fugitives from labor. The euphemism for runaway slaves when they are requested by slaveholders. The Clause gets translated into the first 1793 statute, which is a civil statute about the returning of these fugitives from labor. That was a law that wasn't well enforced according to southern slaveholders. They complained about it bitterly, especially in the 1840s, and that's what led to the creation of the 1850 Fugitive Slaves Act. That was part of the Compromise of 1850. This 1850 statute this was much tougher than the earlier one. They punish people who harbored Runaways, members of the Underground Railroad, with civil penalties and criminal penalties, including up to six months imprisonment if they were caught and prosecuted successfully. This is a controversial measure was draconian in theory, but in practice, it wasn't well enforced. The Underground Railroad was alive and well in the North in the 1850s. There are more documented escapes than renditions hearings in the years before the Civil War. There were dozens and dozens of people who were

> ***tortured and imprisoned in the South because of helping fugitives. But not under Federal law, under state slave stealing statutes. The lack of enforcement of this Federal law is what led many southern states to complain in their secession ordinance. For example, in 1860 and 61, what they were complaining about was northern state laws that they thought interfered with the Federal system. These are called personal liberty laws, anti-kidnapping statutes that many northern states passed to try to protect Black people from being unfairly accused of being Runaways. Ultimately, the fugitive crisis is one of the major causes of the coming of the Civil War (History.com, 2009).***

Pinsker's analysis suggests that an African American was subjected to being classified as a runaway slave, which required the intervention of the law, thus being a major factor in the most divisive and brutal American Civil War. While the Thirteenth Amendment outlawed the Fugitive Slave Acts, its effects may have contributed to how present-day law enforcement subconsciously treats African Americans.

Other contributing factors initiated the American Civil War. Among them was the fighting between pro and anti-slavery at

Pottawatomie Creek, known as "Bleeding Kansas." The Dred Scott decision by the United States Supreme Court ruled that Dred Scott— after living in a free state and territory— was not entitled to his freedom and was not considered a citizen under the Constitution of the United States. A White abolitionist, John Brown, led a slave rebellion attack on the army arsenal at Harpers Ferry, Virginia. This event, along with the November 1860 election of Abraham Lincoln as the 16th President— who opposed the expansion of slavery— and the secession of eleven states (South Carolina, Mississippi, Florida, Alabama, Georgia, Louisiana, Texas, Virginia, Arkansas, Tennessee, and North Carolina) forming the Confederate States of America (Skaflestad, 2021), marked key moments in history. However, I argue that the Fugitive Slave Act significantly contributed to the subconscious mindset of modern-day police officers.

President Millard Fillmore signed the Fugitive Slave Act of 1850, precipitating thousands of African Americans to migrate to Northern states and eventually Canada, evading slave catchers, some armed with pistols and knives, being obstinate to die rather than be captured (Landon, 1920). Slave patrollers carried guns and often used them against runaway slaves. Former slave Sabe Rutledge said that slave catchers shot his uncle Andrew's eye out (Hadden, 2001). Another former slave described the shooting of runaway slaves in a narrative:

I have been hunted by the hounds a great many times. The only way to do when I heard them coming was to go across water, and put them off the scent, and then climb a high tree in the thickest part of the swamp where the overseer can't come. If the hunters could see us, they would shoot us. --They don't think any more about shooting a nigger than a dog. It's all one thing. I have seen several shot. One evening about dusk when I lived with Mallard, I was going into the fields to do something, and I saw a runaway named Jack, belonging to Mr. Finkley at Four Hole Swamp. He was crossing the field with a bag on his back. Tom Galloway, our overseer, had been out hunting squirrels and was just coming back with his gun. When he saw Jack, he squatted behind a tree and waited till he got near. He hailed him and told him to stop. He did not stop but run, and just as he was jumping the fence, overseer fired, and he fell about twenty yards from the fence. He said "O'we," three or four times and died. When the overseer came home, he said he met somebody's runaway nigger, and let him have what there was in his gun. The black people that night made a hole, and lined it with boards, and buried him. (Prince,

2003)

Thus, these examples illustrate that runaway slaves were subjected to random shootings at the hands of slave catchers and without penalty in part due to the Fugitive Slave Act.

It is important to recognize that police in the modern-day United States are homogeneous to the slaughter, shooting, and killing of African Americans, as to the brutal killings by slave catchers. On October 3, 1974, at nearly 11:00 at night, Memphis police officers Leslie Wright and Elton Hyman responded to a house burglary in progress. Officer Hyman went to the rear of the house and saw a 15-year-old African American, Edward Garner, running across the yard to a 6-foot chain link fence, attempting to climb it. Officer Hyman ordered Garner to stop, and he continued climbing the fence. Officer Hyman shot Garner in the back of the head, and he died at a hospital. Garner had stolen ten dollars and a purse from the house (Tennessee v. Garner, 1985).

While the United States Supreme Court did rule that the shooting violated Garner's 4th Amendment right and placed constitutional limits on police use of deadly force, shootings and killings at the hands of police continue, as in the shooting of Michael Brown by a White police officer in Ferguson, Missouri in 2014. In Arguendo, a 2012 study indicated that young African American males are 21 times more likely to be killed by police than young White males (Grabiner, 2016). As Minister Louis Farrakhan would say, "If the Side Angle Side of Triangle A is equal to the Side Angle Side of Triangle B, the two are said to be Congruent" (Farrakhan, 2011). Thus, the runaway Slave and the fleeing Black male are subject to the same lethal force or, at minimum, excessive force and brutality. We will discuss beating at the hands of police and slave catchers in the next chapter.

As controversial as it is, my premise is that the origin of the modern-day American police evolved from and can be traced back to the slave patrol, particularly police in southern states. No scholarly person could deny this. The research and evidence are overwhelming today. "A century of studies by Howell Henry (1914), Sheldon Bacon (1939), Richard Wade (1964), Harrison Trexler (1969), Stanley Campbell (1970), Samuel Walker (1977), Hubert Williams and Patrick Murphy (1990), Sally E. Hadden (2003), and Phillip Reichel (2013) advanced the thesis that slave patrols, the colonial and antebellum law enforcement network organized to control slaves' activities were the precursors to contemporary patterns of Southern policing" (Spruill, 2016). Yet, there are some scholars and journalists who refuse to accept these historical facts as if they were Governor Ron DeSantis and it was "critical race theory."

Some scholars, journalists, and elite politicians' reluctance to tell the American public the truth about the horrors of American slavery suggests a certain amount of denial about the problem. One writer argues, "In America, the first constables were created in the

1630s in what came to be known as New England. Boston has the oldest 'modern' police department. It was created in 1838. New York and Philadelphia soon followed. They were not created to search for runaway slaves" (Goldberg, 2020). Another journalist contends, "[m]ost of the 18,000 US police agencies were founded after abolition, and many were explicitly modeled on modern concepts of policing invented by the British. And the officers in many major cities — including LA, Houston, and Atlanta — are mainly minorities" (Meyers, 2021). Yet, they both acknowledged that police in southern states may have had a foundation in slavery patrols. However, meticulous research may explain how northern cities adopted a slave patrol style of policing, primarily toward African Americans.

A brief overview of police history may be helpful in fully comprehending police malpractice in the United States. The origins of both criminal law and the United States' police forces can be traced back to early English society. England had no common police force, but any person residing in the villages scattered all over the countryside was responsible for shielding the settlement from thieves and robbers. In the thirteenth century, the watch system was established to protect property in England's bigger cities and towns. As the eighteenth century began, crime rates increased, producing the need for a new form of policing. The London Metropolitan Police came from the Metropolitan Police Act, which was Sir Robert Peel's legislation that formed the 1st systematic police force in London.

Law enforcement in colonial America paralleled the British system in the colonies. The county sheriff transformed into one of the most significant law enforcement agents; his responsibilities included keeping the peace, fighting crime, collecting taxes, supervising elections, and handling a great deal of other legal business. The contemporary police department was born out of the urban mob violence that wracked the nation's cities in the 19th century. Boston created the 1st formal United States police department in 1838. New York formed its police department in 1844. Philadelphia did so in 1854. The newly created police departments replaced the night watchmen system and relegated constables and sheriffs to serving court orders and running jails. "In rural areas in the south, 'slave patrols' charged with recapturing escaped slaves were an early, if loathsome, form of law enforcement" (Siegel & Worrall, 2014).

As the opposing author noted, Northern cities adopted Peel's police model, whereas Southern cities evolved from slave patrols. However, in the 1920s, race became a central political issue in those northern cities during the great migration of southern Blacks into Detroit, Michigan, and other cities in the North. Starting in the 1910s, Blacks from the South came to Detroit in droves, lured by Henry Ford's $5.00-a-day wage in auto jobs and the desire to escape southern oppression and hostilities. The city's small Black population increased from 5,741 in 1910 (or 1% of Detroit's population) to 40,838 in 1920, to finally around 120,000 people in 1929. The growth of the Black population in Detroit created extreme racial tensions, especially in the case of Ossian Sweet, which was highly profiled (Carlson, 2011).

The details of the Ossian Sweet incident in 1925 drew national attention to the racial tensions in northern cities following the Great Migration of Blacks. Ossian Sweet was an African-American physician in Detroit, Michigan. He is known for being charged with murder in 1925 after he and his friends used armed self-defense against a hostile White mob protesting after Sweet moved into their White neighborhood. Stones were thrown at his house, breaking windows. Shots were fired, and one White man was killed and another wounded. Sweet, his wife, and nine associates at the house (including two brothers) were all arrested and charged with murder (Bragg, 2007; Carlson, 2011).

In an attempt to solve the new problem of race, Detroit police began to actively recruit White southerners (presumable White police officers or former slave patrollers) who understood how to deal with Southern Black people. A Black Detroit police officer from 1952 clarified:

> ***From a historical background, when the five-dollar-a-day started right after World War I, after the Model A Ford, the police officers of the metropolitan cities were more or less oriented to ethnicity. The behavior of blacks was seemingly so much different. So, the first thing they did was***

> ***go to the South to recruit police officers who 'understood them' as they called it. This is the vernacular of police thinking at the time. The South had a different value system. The southern policeman's method of operation was explained very explicitly by WEB DuBois in The Soul of Black Folks. He said the Southern police system was set up to replace slavery. It was to control blacks. It had nothing to do with justice. (Carlson, 2011)***

In addition to the recruitment of Southern White policemen (former slave patrollers), the Detroit police had a significant number of Ku Klux Klan within its ranks. "Historian Kevin Boyle argues that the racist, xenophobic brutality of Detroit cops combined with gangster violence gave rise to a growing penchant for solving problems with brutish [police] force" (Carlson, 2011).

In June of 1963, The Reverend Dr. Martin Luther King Jr. led the historic "Walk for Freedom" march in Detroit down Woodward Avenue and compared the Detroit police with the Southern style of policing, which defended segregation (Lassiter, 2021). Thirteen days after the march, Detroit police murdered a 24-year-old unarmed African American prostitute named Cynthia Scott by shooting her in the back as she was walking away, according to witnesses. The shooting appeared to have been covered up by police, and the Wayne County prosecutor declared it to be a justifiable homicide (Lassiter, 2021). Another controversial, violent Detroit police initiative reminiscent of "Southern style" policing was S.T.R.E.S.S.

S.T.R.E.S.S. is an acronym for Stop the Robberies, Enjoy Safe Streets, which was a Detroit police undercover unit that operated from 1971 to 1974. Inspector James Bannon created the STRESS unit under DPD Commissioner John Nichols. STRESS used undercover, mostly White officers posing as decoys supposedly to target robbers and muggers. However, it led to the deaths of twenty-four men, twenty-two of them African-American, within three and a half years. Anti-S.T.R.E.S.S. rallies occurred after September 17, 1971, when a White officer, Richard Worobec, fatally shot two unarmed Black teenagers, 15-year-old Ricardo Buck and 16-year-old Craig Mitchell, according to witnesses, in cold blood.

Additionally, "On March 9, 1972, three African American STRESS officers and two White DPD officers fired more than forty shots into a private apartment where six Black men had gathered for a poker game. Five of the people inside the apartment were deputies in the Wayne County Sheriff's Department, and the sixth was a civilian friend of the group. Deputy Henry Henderson died in a hail of bullets as he tried to surrender with his hands up." This incident may have contributed to the dissension that still exists today between Wayne County sheriff deputies and Detroit police officers.

In 1973, Detroit's first Black mayor, Coleman A. Young promised voters that if he was elected, he would eliminate the S.T.R.E.S.S. unit, terminate Commissioner Nichols, and transition the police to "law and order, with justice" (Lassiter, 2021).

Beginning in the 1910s, Northern cities experienced migration issues similar to those in the city of Detroit. Black immigrants from the South settled in essentially every region of the North and West. The "Great Migration" attracted Blacks to large cities throughout the North and Midwest, thus increasing the Black population in cities like "Chicago, Detroit, New York, and Philadelphia." However, in virtually every city, the native Northerners were both suspicious and hostile towards them as they arrived. Southern immigrants have been blamed for many of the social problems plaguing urban communities, including crime, alcoholism, venereal disease, and illegitimacy (Tolnay, 2003). "The Great Migration brought many freedmen [Blacks] to the North, and the reaction to that brought the Southern Mind to northern police officers as well" (Temin, 2020).

Additionally, "the passage of federal fugitive slave acts from 1793 to 1850 conscripted local and state law enforcement agents throughout the northern…territories to participate in the capture and confinement of self-emancipated Black Americans" (Cook, n.d.). It's debatable whether the northern police ever searched for runaway slaves, they were modeled after Peel's police, they may have been extremely influenced by southern police "slave patrols." Arguably, large northern cities' police departments that had many minorities were subjected to a process of southern police assimilation. Yale law professor Stephen Carter argued that after the Civil War, Northern police departments progressively embraced the Southern model of proactively brutalizing Blacks (Carter, 2015).

University of Georgia's Professor Michael Robinson contended, "The first deaths in America of Black men at the hands of law enforcement can be traced back as early as 1619 when the first slave ship, a Dutch Man-of-War vessel landed in Point Comfort, Virginia" (Hassett-Walker, 2021). Fast forward to today, and the latest police shootings and killings of Black men are too numerous to keep pace with. It must be reiterated that not all White police officers are racist and waiting to pull the trigger on Black men. However, the subconscious seduction of American racism and law enforcement compels this discussion. The inquiry must be having the institution of policing moved far enough from its inception to earn the trust of Black communities. Undoubtedly, American policing, in its evolution from slave patrols, had a disastrous beginning in certain areas, for which there has never been an accounting (Hassett-Walker, 2021). Before getting to where and how far policing has to go, we must discuss the similarities between modern-day policing and slavery patrollers. Though the difference between religion and morality is as narrow as a hairsbreadth, there are striking similarities in policing tactics and procedures between modern police and slave patrollers, providing substantial support for our remonstrance.

Chapter 5: The Congruence between Modern-Day Police and the Slave Patrol

If it looks like a duck, swims like a duck, and quacks like a duck, then it probably is a duck. – Walter Reuther.

Then the paddyrollers they keep close watch on the pore niggers, so they have no chance to do anything or go anywhere. They jes' like policemen, only worser. 'Cause they never let the niggers go anywhere without a pass from his master. If you wasn't in your proper place when the paddyrollers come they lash you til' you was black and blue. The women got 15 lashes and the men 30. That is for jes bein' out without a pass. If the nigger done anything worse, he was taken to the jail and put in the whippin' post. (Hadden, 2001, 71)

A hundred years ago, they used to put on white

> ***sheets and sic bloodhounds on us. Well, nowadays they've traded in the sheets — well, some of them traded in sheets — . . . they have traded in those white sheets for police uniforms. They've traded in the bloodhounds for the police dogs. – Malcolm X***

My treatment of the similarities between modern-day police and the slave patrol is chiefly influenced by Sally E. Hadden, whose work is monumental in its very essence. However, Hadden argues that "[t]o blames the 1991 beating of Rodney King by police in Los Angeles on slave patrollers…is to miss the point" (Hadden, 2001, 5). Her analysis is simply from a historical perspective. The history of police work in the South grows out of this early fascination, by white patrollers, with what African American slaves were doing. Most law enforcement was, by definition, white patrolmen watching, catching, or beating black slaves (Hadden, 2001). As professor Brucato quotes during his class lecture on the history of U.S. policing:

> ***Policing in the southeastern states where slavery existed had a distinctive institution: the slave patrol. Because the white majority was so concerned about slave revolts (of which there***

> ***were many) and runaway slaves, they created this new form of law enforcement. The slave patrols, in fact, were the first modern police forces in the United States. The Charleston, South Carolina, slave patrol, for example, had about 100 officers in 1837 and was far larger than any northern city police force at that time. (Brucato, 2020, 115)***

Such a statement shocks the conscience, yet scholars and academia have overlooked it for so long. Throughout this chapter, we have extensively criticized the slave-patrol characteristics present in modern American police forces.

Violence against African Americans, Slave Patrols, and Modern-Day Policing are both law enforcement and share some unique similarities. Not only are these forces of law and order similar, but the only differences appear to be the time period and, as a pretext, the laws and statutes. Slave patrols and modern-day policing share a similarity in the constabulary, which includes duties, official authority, fears, equipment, and, last but not least, malfeasance.

When comparing the two slave patrols and modern-day policing to each other, similarities were found between their duties and responsibilities. First off, these duties include beating those that run or flee, stopping and searching, confiscating weapons, patrolling areas or beating, and using discretion in performing their duties and stake out. Historians, scholars, and the media introduce us to the police as well as the slave patrol as brutal, vicious, and hostile inflictors of severe punishment to African Americans.

In his hilarious comedy skit— sad but true, I'm afraid, comedian Chris Rock articulated,

> ***"We all know what happened to Rodney King. But Rodney King wouldn't have gotten his ass kicked if he had just followed this simple tip. When you see flashing police lights in your mirror, stop immediately. Everybody knows if the police have to come and get you, they're bringing an ass-kicking with them." (Rock, 2014)***

Research in the 1990s showed that using excessive force was inevitable during motor vehicle pursuits and might be dangerous; when pursuits came to an end, cops frequently overreacted out of fear, adrenaline, and exhilaration (Stroshine & Brandl, 2021). According to the majority of officers in a study on police pursuit-excessive force, approximately half of the arrests following a pursuit involve the use of force. After a chase, most officers said that some arrests were made with too much force. After being caught and apprehended, fifty-seven percent of suspects claimed that they had been beaten by the police (Alpert, Kenny & Dunham, 1997). I recall, as a security-police officer at Fairlane Town Center, where pursuing suspects in a vehicle was strictly prohibited, a shoplifter fleeing and clipped my patrol vehicle with their vehicle. My lieutenant ordered me not to pursue over the radio; however, due to the adrenaline and the exhilaration of capturing the fleeing shoplifter, I turned off my radio, chased and captured the shoplifter after a brief chase for approximately two or three miles with the help of the Dearborn police. However, no excessive force was used against the suspect.

There is something about police pursuits that clearly drives police officers out of control, which the Nation saw in the 1991 beating of Rodney King. President George H. W. Bush said after watching the King beating and verdict: "What you saw and what I saw on the TV video was revolting. I felt anger. I felt pain. I thought: How can I explain this to my grandchildren?" (Bush, 1992).

In November 2022, an innocent bystander (Adrian Cruz) claimed that after ending a 100-mph pursuit with the suspect (Johnny Anchondo), "deputies suddenly tackled and violently began to punch [him] in his head while simultaneously grabbing his head and smashing it to the ground." Cruz was never involved in the chase and claimed that Los Angeles County sheriff's deputies fired several gunshots toward him, his wife, and his child (City News Service, 2023). Lastly, on January 27, 2022, Akron police attempted to pull over a 25-year-old Black male named Jayland Walker for minor traffic offenses, who was known to have previously fled from police in a vehicle. After reaching speeds of over 50 mph, Walker pulled over and fled on foot, unarmed. Police fired 90 rounds at Walker, hitting him 60 times, killing him instantly (Bork, 2023).

Skolnick and Fyfe, in their book, "Above the Law," explain how a person who flees the police triggers such an aggressive and hostile response from the police as it is viewed as a direct challenge to their authority:

> ***One veteran Los Angeles officer [said] that he had never seen a police chase that did not end with at least a black eye delivered to the subject of the chase. What is it about these events that seem to generate such police rage? Regardless of how relatively minor the violations that lead to their flight, fleeing motorist commits cardinal sin against the police: instead of submitting immediately, they challenge the police and attempt to escape their pursuer's authority. In so doing, in the eyes of police officers accustomed to motorists and other citizens who not only submit immediately to police authority but even check their speedometers in the mere presence of police cars, fleeing motorists become prime candidates for painful lessons at the ends of police nightsticks. (Skolnick & Fyfe, 1993)***

Running or fleeing from the police can lead to serious physical injury to the person being pursued. Running from the police may lead to putting their life in peril.

Homogeneously, the runaway slave engendered the identical rage in the slave patroller. Running away was one of the most effective ways an enslaved person could resist. Risks were high if you fled. Runaways would be physically punished if they were caught, typically by whipping them, and they might be forced to wear chains or handcuffs to stop them from running away again (Runaway Slave, (n.d.)).

Solomon Northup's based on a true story, *Twelve Years a Slave*, demonstrated the occupation of the slave patroller and the brutal tactics that they used:

> ***Patrollers, whose business it is to seize and whip any slave they may find wandering from plantation…ride on horseback, headed by a captain, armed, and accompanied by dogs. They have the right, either by law or by general consent, to inflict discretionary chastisement upon a Black man caught beyond the boundaries of his master's estate without a pass and even shoot him if he attempts to escape. Each***

> ***company has a certain distance to ride up and down the bayou… (one Slave) fled before one of these companies, thinking he could reach his cabin before they could overtake him, but one of their dogs, a great ravenous hound, gripped him by the leg and held him fast. The patrollers whipped him severely. (Spruill, 2016)***

Slave patrollers used force to return slaves to their owners; they were frequently armed with firearms and whips.

Today, a Black person is guaranteed to get a beating from the police if they attempt to flee and escape arrest. As proof, in a group text, Louisiana State Police troopers joked about beating a Black man following a high-speed pursuit in 2020, saying that the victim (Antonio Harris) would have "nightmares for a long time" from the "whoopin'" (Al Jazeera and News agencies, 2021). During slavery days, a runaway slave was likely to get beaten by the slave patrollers if he was captured. Modern-day police and slave patrollers may be considered analogous. In Arguendo, there was a 1696 South Carolina law that stipulated, "All whites [slave patrollers] were required to apprehend bondsmen and give them a moderate whipping if they had no pass" (Hadden, 2001, 18). We also assume that all whites were authorized to stop and search slaves away from their plantations.

Stopping and searching slaves was mostly demonstrated

when the North Carolina legislators granted slave patrollers the authority to stop them on the road. According to Sally Hadden,

> ***"Slave patrols frequently looked at slave passes while making their rounds. Laws required the slave to carry a pass, or ticket, from her master, which permitted the slave to leave the plantation. A specific pass stated the slave's name, where she had permission to go, on what date, and how long the pass was good for, and bore the owner's signature. Owners thought that regularly giving passes kept slaves content and made them less likely to run away." (Hadden, 2001, 110)***

The police practice of "stop and frisk" proves that the same tactics may be used today by modern police. Tens of millions of people have been arrested and searched by police as a result of stop-and-frisk abuse by officers. The New York City Police Department (NYPD) stopped and searched 685,724 people in 2011 alone. Since 2002, there have been over 4 million stop-and-frisk events in New York City. This tactic has disproportionately ensnared African Americans. Stop and frisk still mostly targets Latino and Black populations. In New York City, almost nine out of 10 victims of the practice are wholly innocent (Browne-Marshall, 2013).

Nat Turner, an African preacher who was a slave, organized a slave insurrection in Jerusalem, Virginia, in 1831. A total of 55 white slave-owning households' men, women, and children were slaughtered—there was a nationwide panic. More stringent regulations were placed on how both free and enslaved Africans might move. Numerous regulations were passed due to the widespread paranoia stoked by the threat of further uprisings. A white individual was now compelled to attend African religious services (Browne-Marshall, 2013). “In Raleigh, North Carolina, news of the Turner revolt put the patrol of that city ‘on guard around the clock for several weeks’” (Hadden, 2001, 145).

In 1968, the United States Supreme Court ruled that it is constitutional for American police to "stop-and-frisk" a person they reasonably suspect to be armed and involved in a crime without probable cause or a warrant (Terry v Ohio, 1968). I am not totally opposed to the “Terry” pat down so long as the officer refrains from getting reasonable suspicion after he or she initiates a stop on a person. However, as a result of Terry v Ohio, African Americans are subjected to humiliating police tactics:

> ***At a town hall meeting on stop and frisk held at John Jay College (City University of New York), a black man in his late sixties, dressed in a jacket and tie, rose to speak. It was late in the day. The room was hot and crowded. He walked slowly,***

> ***head high, to the microphone and spoke about how the New York City police officers approached him and asked for identification. His questions about why the police stopped him were met with impatient remarks about 'fitting the description.' Seconds later, he recounted, police turned him around, kicked his legs open wide, and began patting him down. [The] room grew quiet. Trembling with the memory of this humiliation, the man's voice caught with emotion. He said, 'they treated me like they were saying, You. ain't nothing but a nigger.' Then, they let him go. (Browne-Marshall, 2013, 116)***

The "stop-and-frisk" procedures used today are a result of America's history of slave patrollers enforcing the pass system for African Americans to be off the slave master's plantation. There was, and still today, a fear for African Americans to carry firearms.

Writer and editor Jason Diamond describes a Dave Chappelle skit titled, "Chappelle's Show - The Time Haters - Great Misses - Uncensored" to justify Jewish justice is served through the subjugation of the Nazi:

> ***There's a Chappelle Show sketch that I love from***

> ***the 'Greatest Misses' episode. The characters known as the 'Player Haters' go back in time and talk trash to a slave owner before Dave Chappelle's character pulls out a gun and aims it at the slave master. The sketch cuts away to Chapelle in front of a live studio audience explaining that what comes next is why the bit never aired on an actual episode of the show. It resumes the sketch with a slave asking Chapelle's character when they will be free. Chappelle answers, 'How 'bout now?' and shoots the master right in the heart. The moment of the bullet hitting the white slave owner is played on loop three more times before cutting to Chappelle in front of the audience again, barreled over laughing. 'Apparently, shooting a slave master isn't funny to anybody but me and Neal.' (Diamond, 2020)***

While this satire comedy was fabricated, it could've been based on historical fiction.

White slave owners had a significant fear of allowing slaves to be armed because they may use guns against them during an uprising. We have Bacon's Rebellion, which occurred in Virginia in 1676. Because Black slaves and White indentured servants joined forces, it was a particularly captivating uprising. Basically, they seized a bunch of guns and started killing settlers, burning houses and fields, and slaughtering livestock. In reaction, the government implemented slave laws.

Additionally, a goal of that anti-slavery legislation was to prevent Black people from obtaining firearms, whether they were free or enslaved. Throughout history, you can observe several instances. When these uprisings took place, the government would quickly dissolve itself in order to further ethnically stratify the legal system (Demby & Escobar, 2020).

After such aborted rebellions, laws were passed to outlaw slaves from possessing firearms. For example, "[a] patrol man finding arms in a slave's house was allowed to appropriate them to his own use by making oath before a magistrate as to the manner of their seizure after the owner of the slave had had an opportunity to be heard" (Henry, 1914, 36). The plantation overseer and the slave patroller were obligated to enforce these laws prohibiting slaves from owning guns (Hadden, 2001).

The prohibition of Blacks possessing firearms, either freemen or slaves, was mostly demonstrated upon the drafting of the Second Amendment. The Second Amendment states, "A well-regulated Militia, being necessary to the security of a free State, the right of the people to keep and bear Arms, shall not be infringed" (U.S. Const. amend. II). Why is the word "militia" included in the Second Amendment? President George Washington, Secretary of

State Thomas Jefferson, and James Madison all owned slaves in Virginia. Their greatest concern was a disastrous slave insurrection that would result in the deaths of their families and the destruction of their property, a concern shared by all other Virginia landowners and prominent figures. This anxiety became extremely intense when Virginia ratified the Bill of Rights on December 15, 1791. Because only white people could join militias in the South, James Madison, the principal drafter of the amendment, purposefully linked the right to bear weapons to militia participation (Picadio, 2019). The militia and slave patrollers were interwoven. "It was in 1704 when the colony of South Carolina created the first slave patrol from the pool of men assigned militia duty" (Brand, 2020, 8). The mandatory state militias had a close relationship with the slave patrols in South Carolina and Virginia. Slave patrollers would be chosen by militia authorities from the rolls of each district to serve for specific durations (Hadden, 2001). The Second Amendment's wording was chosen to enable slave owners to put down any uprising or resistance from the people they had held in captivity. Black people have consistently been denied the constitutionally protected right to possess guns (Davies, 2021).

The Second Amendment was to protect White men's rights to carry guns, not Blacks. This was evident in a 2016 traffic stop when Minnesota police fatally shot Philando Castile, a Black man with a permit to carry a gun. In her new book, The Second: Race and Guns in a Fatally Unequal America, Carol Anderson argues: "Here was a Black man who was pulled over by the police, and the police officer asked to see his identification. Philando Castile, using the NRA guidelines, alerts the officer that he has a licensed weapon with him, and the police officer began shooting" (Davies, 2021).

I recall one day sitting in the sauna at the fitness center when a couple of young African American men entered excitedly, bragging about their plan to open carry. I advised them while it may be legal, it's not advisable. I told them *a White police officer might shoot you and say*, "I thought he was reaching for his weapon, and I feared for my safety."

In some states, open carry is legal for a person to carry a firearm in public as long as the person is carrying the firearm with lawful intent and the firearm is not concealed. "Advocates strap handguns to their hips, sling AK-47s and AR-15s to their backs, and stroll the streets with cameras in hand to catch unwitting cops violating their Second Amendment rights by asking for Identification or trying to ascertain if the heavily armed man walking toward a school might be a threat" (Zadrozny, 2015). There is a YouTube video showing the difference in how the police react when it's a White man versus a Black man doing open carry:

> ***In the clips, two men—one white, one black—walk down the street strapped with AR-15s. The white man, Warren Drouin, is a well-known fixture in the open-carry movement. In fact, he and police in his small Oregon town are on a***

> ***first-name basis because of the scores of complaints from scared neighbors over Drouin's exercises.***
>
> ***The camera shows Drouin being approached by a police officer and a polite exchange about his right to carry a gun in public. The end.***
>
> ***The next clip follows an unnamed black man as he carries the same weapon strapped across his back. A police car approaches, and outjumps a white officer who pulls his gun and orders the man, 'Get down on the street. Now!' The officer also orders the man's wife, who is recording the incident, to get on the ground. 'I'm seven months pregnant,' she replies.***
>
> ***'I am being held at gunpoint,' the man says from the ground. 'I am merely open carrying.' (Zadrozny, 2015)***

The YouTube video goes on to prove that White men in America have a monopoly on carrying and or possessing firearms, and it is a "white privilege" just as they had the right to bear arms during American slavery days.

According to historians and legal experts, as well as the Supreme Court's ruling in the McDonald versus Chicago case from

2010, the concealed permit system that was adopted throughout the South in the late 1800s was designed to make it practically impossible for Black people to carry firearms on their person, establishing a white monopoly on firearms carried outside of one's home. This is true even today when it is frequently perceived as "pro-gun" legislation (Carlson, 2011).

Adding to this, according to data analyzed in January 2022 by the Neighborhood Defender Service, a community-based, holistic public defense practice found that in Detroit, Michigan, “the number of arrests on CCW [carrying a concealed weapon] charges has quadrupled since March 2020, and 97 percent of those with the crime charged are Black” (New data show, n.d.). Black people could not be citizens under the Constitution, according to United States Supreme Chief Justice Roger Taney, because doing so "would give to persons of the negro race" the right "to keep and carry arms wherever they went."

Dr. Martin Luther King Jr. was refused a concealed carry permit despite having his home firebombed; even regulations that appeared to be neutral on the surface were applied in a racially discriminatory manner (Winkler, 2022). There was a clear correlation between the slave patrol and modern-day police in reference to the prohibition of Blacks to carry or possess firearms. The verbiage describing their patrol jurisdictions is identical as well.

The slave patrol and the modern-day police would pass the abductive reasoning, old duck test, which we all know: "If it looks like a duck, swims like a duck, and quacks like a duck, then it probably is a duck." As I reflect on my teaching Introduction to Criminal Justice class at Wayne County Community College District, I would instruct students that the criminal justice system as a whole has police officers as its most prominent and visible members. In addition to using a police car, they may also patrol designated regions of their jurisdiction known as "beats" on foot, a motorcycle, a horse, a helicopter, or another vehicle (Siegel & Worrall, 2014). Similarly situated, in 1734, a Provincial Assembly Act stipulated that the slave patrol be known as:

> ***The beat company — by which is meant the group of five men who rode over the plantations and looked after the correction of disorders — was to be composed of a captain and four other men of the regular militia appointed from time to time. The patrolmen were to receive compensation…and exemption from all other military service. For each district there were to be appointed three commissioners as supervisors of the patrol. The duties of this patrol were to visit each plantation in its beat at least once per month, chastising any slave found absenting himself from home without a pass, administering twenty lashes as a maximum, to search the negro***

> ***dwellings, confiscating any firearms that might be in the home or any goods that they might have good reason to believe have been stolen; to enter any tippling house or any other house whatever, where any one of them might have seen a slave enter. (Henry, 1914, 32)***

Sally Hadden, in her book "Slave Patrols: Law and Violence in Virginia and the Carolinas," described the history of the word "beat" in law enforcement:

> ***The language used to describe slave patrols also permeated police activities long after patrols were gone. The 'beat,' originally used as a geographic means of organizing slave patrol groups in South Carolina and other states, became the basic area that police supervised. The policeman's beat has become a common phrase in American parlance, much the same way that Americans expect a policeman to 'patrol' his rounds. The origins of both words predate the creation of slave patrols, but their use in the context of law enforcement today owes much to their application in the slaveholding South. (Hadden, 2001, 219)***

It can be implied that a person can identify the modern police by observing the slave patrol's habitual characteristics. "Beat" is not the only jargon used by slave patrol and police; they both also used the word discretion in their lexicon.

The phrase "discretion" goes to prove that the slave patrol and modern police share other similar characteristics. I also taught my class that police officers exercise discretion when deciding whether to detain one suspect for disruptive behavior while escorting a different defendant home (Siegel & Worrall, 2014). According to H. M. Henry in his 1914 dissertation "The police control of the slave in South Carolina," the slave patrol was also granted discretion in performing their duties:

> ***The following quotation from a case occurring in Newberry district, to which reference will again be made, shows the very large discretionary latitude allowed to the patrol, even to the extent of ignoring legal provisions to carry out the spirit of the law: 'Let the patrol always act in the spirit that should guide the discreet, sedate, intelligent and humane owner of slaves and they will find the judicial arm of the government nerved to sustain them, indeed if it could be presumed that in such case they would ever need it. Thus,***

guided they may often find occasion — no doubt they will - to overlook a harmless violation, a venial transgression of the strict letter.' (Henry, 1914, 40)

Suppose these assessments of the terms "beat" and "discretion" used by the slave patrol and the police are accurate. In that case, the reasoning behind the evolution into the modern-day police is indeed plausible. If the slave patroller beat required stealth and less attention, they performed surveillance like modern police do.

If the slave patrol believed that slaves were selling illegally obtained goods, they would place that home under surveillance, a practice known as "stationary patrolling." If they suspected that free Blacks or Whites had connections to slaves through illegal trade or the sale of alcohol, patrollers kept an eye on their residences and places of business. Instead of trying to keep track of every slave in the area who might be considering planning a meeting with a potential suspect, patrollers found it easier to keep the suspicious free person under surveillance through stationary patrolling (Hadden, 2001).

Modern-day police have an advanced means of surveillance through modern technology, such as cameras, GPS tracking devises, data-gathering apps on smartphones, and facial recognition software, just to name a few I'm familiar with. However, "the stakeout is an honored police tradition and the setting for any number of television and movie scenes. Stakeouts most quickly come to mind when cops talk about surveillance, and most stakeouts are pretty low-tech. A pair of binoculars, a car or van, and a steady supply of bad coffee is all the hero requires to get his (or her) man" (Dees, 2010).

When we research, compare, and study the slave patrol and modern-day police dealing with those who run or flee, stopping and searching individuals, confiscating weapons, patrol areas or beat, and the use of discretion in performing their duties and the stake out, we can conclude that there was an evolving relationship between the two. Therefore, we see the similarities here between modern-day police and slave patrol, with both these two having characteristics of being oppressive and extremely violent towards African Americans. These two also show similarities in how they obtain authority.

Secondly, in comparing official authority in slave patrols and modern-day police, there were some similar ones that both law enforcement agents shared. A predominance that stood out the most when comparing these two law men was their oath of office. When I was the police chief at Wayne County Community College District Police Authority, I had sworn many officers into their official duty. I used the same oath that most Michigan municipal police agencies used:

> ***I ________________ do solemnly swear that I will observe and support the Constitutions of the United States of America and of the State of Michigan, that I will enforce the general criminal laws of the United States of America and of the State of Michigan, that I will prevent and detect crime to the best of my ability, and that I will faithfully discharge the duties as a Law Enforcement Officer. (WCCCD oath, n.d.)***

Additionally, police officers in the city of Muskegon, Michigan, are sworn in similarly:

> ***I do solemnly swear (or affirm) that I will support the Constitution of the United States and the constitution of this state and that I will faithfully discharge the duties of the office of Police Officer according to the best of my ability. (Oath of office, n.d.)***

The slave patroller's oath of office was both similar to and different from the modern-day police oath of office. Yet they both confirm that either enforcing the law or catching or searching slaves was an official duty sanctioned by the state. In North Carolina, white men selected to serve on slave patrols had to appear before a justice of the peace and be sworn in or otherwise qualified. "The Justice of the peace recited the oath for patrollers, and the patroller either swore or affirmed that he would uphold the law" (Hadden, 2001, 78). The North Carolina Slave Patrol Oath:

> ***I, [patroller's name], do swear that I will, as a searcher for guns, swords, and other weapons among the slaves in my district, faithfully and as privately as I can, discharge the trust reposed in me as the law directs, to the best of my power. So, help me, God. (Hadden, 2001, 78)***

The primary function of these oaths of office during slavery, post-slavery, and even the modern day was the social control of African Americans utilizing policing methods. According to Jerry Brand in his Master thesis on Police Brutality and Social Control:

> ***Former slave patrols and contemporary police pledge their allegiance to overlook discrimination, justice, and fairness to accomplish their jobs. It is the Oath of slave patrollers in colonial times, antebellum era, and police of today that transforms ordinary citizens***

into power and agents to enforce discriminatory laws. It is the historical link and contemporary connection that, once sworn to, provided slave patrollers and modern police officers indemnity from civil and criminal lawsuits. (Brand, 2020, 15)

Again, we backtrack to the slave patrol and modern-day police transformational relationship as it is today. I assume that the rookie police officer just graduating from the academy has no idea of the subconscious role he is taking on. They take their oath of office in order to protect and serve. I sarcastically inquire, to protect and serve who?

In the 1982 movie 48 hours, starring Eddie Murphy and Nick Nolte in the bar scene, Eddie Murphy's character (Hammond) highly demonstrates the power, authority, and ability to brutalize someone with a police badge:

COUNTRY MAN

What the hell kind of cop are you?

HAMMOND

> ***You know what I am? I am your worst fu_ _ing nightmare, man. I'm a nigger with a badge that means I got fu _ _ing permission to kick your ass whenever I feel like it. (48 hours, 2020)***

What the police badge actually means is that he or she may use force, including deadly force, to overcome force in the execution of his or her legal duties.

What does the police badge symbolize? Perhaps the most noticeable and well-known representation of policing worldwide is a police badge. Many see it as a symbol of power, selflessness, integrity, and duty. However, in the past, police officers didn't want to wear badges because they already had a bad reputation and didn't want to be associated with people that other people didn't like (Waxmen, 2017). Yet, the slave patroller wore a badge quite identical to some modern-day police officer badge.

On June 16, 2017, Colin Kaepernick posted on Twitter an image illustrating the similarities between the two badges, the only difference being the wording "Run Away Slave Patrol" and "Police Officer." Kaepernick emphasized, "You can't ignore your history" and "Always remember who they are" (Kaepernick, 2017). Slave patrol badges gave the wearer the freedom and authority to go pretty much wherever and do whatever they wanted as long as they were on the trail of an escaped slave. Similar to the way the police use probable cause today, they could enter any home that they pleased if they suspected the occupant of hiding an escapee" (Shelton, 2020). While Eddie Murphy reversed the role of brutality in 48 hours to a Black man, the slave patroller, with his badge, was indeed the slave's worst nightmare. "Most [slave patrollers] were, by definition, white patrolmen watching, catching, or beating Black slaves" (Hadden, 2001, 4). As the badge is the symbol of authority, a police certificate or license is his or her proof that they are a bona fide law enforcement officer.

As the former chief of police at Wayne County Commissioner College District, upon an officer's completion of the police academy (approximately 590 hours) or in Michigan completion of the Recognition of Prior Basic Training and Experience (RPTE) program, I would receive a certificate from MCOLES (Michigan Commission on Law Enforcement Standards) for that particular officer.

In addition, I could log into the MITN (MCOLES Information and Tracking Network), which is an internet-based application used by law enforcement agencies around the state of Michigan to confirm the status of a law enforcement officer. Modern technology is the major distinction in comparison to how the slave patroller received his certified authority. "New [slave] patrol members received a certificate or warrant of appointment which they retained while on duty; in case they were challenged about their authority to enter a person's land" (Hadden, 2001, 45). A huge difference is that the slave patroller was poorly trained in "their inability to follow orders, shoot well, or turn out with the required equipment" Hadden, 2001, 45). Perhaps these derelictions of slave patrol duties accounted for the creation of a "patrol committee."

In the city of Detroit, there is a "Board of Police of Commissioners [which] was created in 1974 by City Charter, which was adopted by the vote of the people. The Charter vests broad supervisory authority over the Police Department in the eleven-member civilian Board of Police Commissioners." According to their website, they received 13,204 complaints between 2012 and 2022. (Board of police commissioners, n.d.). Likewise, in 2017, while I was chief of police, Wayne County Community College District adopted a Police Advisory Committee. The WCCCD Police Advisory Committee offers a discussion forum for the college community to discuss the effectiveness of law enforcement, makes suggestions for law enforcement enhancements, and offers guidance to the police chief on various law enforcement programs (Police advisory committee, n.d.).

The similarity was highly demonstrated when creating the North Carolina Patrol Committee. The North Carolina patrol committee was established by the courts to select, oversee, discharge, and consider grievances against slave patrollers, making it a perfect comparison. The police organization that is charged hears and decides on allegations against its own misconduct in these committees, which are remarkably similar to internal affairs in modern law enforcement (Brand, 2020, 8; Hadden, 2001, 48).

Coincidentally, the courts had jurisdiction over most of the slave patrol activities.

While the U.S. Supreme Court in Dred Scott v. Sanford, stated that enslaved people were not citizens of the United States and, therefore, could not expect any protection from the federal government or the courts (Dred Scott v. Sanford, 1856), the slave patrol was under the court's control. We all remember from our government high school class that the Constitution of the United States divides the federal government into three branches: legislative, executive, and judicial. This ensures that no individual or group will have too much power. I dissent! The scales of power have tilted in favor of the judicial branch ever since the U.S. Supreme Court declared in Marbury v. Madison that judicial review of the legislative and executive branch acts may be declared as unconstitutional (Marbury v. Madison, 1803). The judicial branch consistently established police procedures to be followed by law enforcement in the United States. For example, as previously mentioned, Terry v. Ohio allowed police to stop and frisk, and Tennessee v. Gardner made it unconstitutional for police to use deadly force against a fleeing felon. Additionally, Miranda v. Arizona grants an arrestee protection against self-incrimination and the right to an attorney (Miranda v. Arizona, 1966), just to mention a few.

On March 13, 1963, Ernesto Miranda was arrested in his house and brought to the police station, where police officers questioned him in connection with a kidnapping and rape. After two hours of interrogation, the police obtained a written confession from Miranda. The written confession was admitted into evidence at trial despite the objection of the defense attorney and the fact that the police officers admitted that they had not advised Miranda of his right to have an attorney present during the interrogation. The jury found Miranda guilty. On appeal, the Supreme Court of Arizona affirmed and held that Miranda's constitutional rights were not violated because he did not specifically request counsel. The U.S. Supreme Court ruled that the Fifth Amendment requires that law enforcement officials advise suspects of their right to remain silent and to obtain an attorney during interrogations while in police custody (Miranda v. Arizona, 1966).

The Miranda decision established the "Miranda Warning," which we often see in cop's motion pictures. The Miranda warning reads:

> ***You have the right to remain silent. Anything you say can and will be used against you in a court of law. You have the right to an attorney. If you cannot afford an attorney, one will be provided for you. Do you understand the rights I have just read to you? With these rights in mind, do you wish to speak to me? (History.com editors, 2022)***

Most police agencies provide small index cards with the Miranda warning printed on them and provide them to their officers, who are expected to read them to the person they arrest prior to questioning the suspect. When I was a security-police sergeant at Fairlane Town Center, I carried my index card inside of my peaked cap. Any evidence that police obtain without a clear reading of these rights would be excluded from trial, particularly a confession. Thus, the judicial branch of government established police procedures based on the Miranda court decision.

By the same token, the North Carolina Supreme Court in 1817 was a driving force in establishing that men who were not appointed and voluntarily joined the slave patrol were not shielded from civil penalties of slave owners if they abused slaves:

> ***In Richardson v. Saltar, the defendant, a patroller, took three of his friends (Allen, Bryan, and Singletary, none of them official patroller) out one night on patrol. At Major Owen's farm, they found a slave belonging to Mr. Richardson, Owen's neighbor. When the bondsman produced an invalid pass, Saltar and his friends beat Richardson's slave so severely that he could not work for days. Richardson then sued the four men for whipping his bondsman without***

> ***authority; Richardson claimed they were not an authorized slave patrols. The trial court acquitted the four men, but on appeal, the North Carolina Supreme Court remanded the case for retrial. Their reason: a 1794 North Carolina patrol law stated that a patrol must have at least two members to be active, and at least two members to be active, and at least two patrol members must be present when a slave received punishment. The justices deduced that three of the men were not patrollers, and Saltar could not act as a patrol by himself. (Hadden, 2001, 78)***

In addition to deciding legal issues regarding the behavior of the slave patrol, from the early beginning and up until the Civil War, the county court in North Carolina had the ability to select slave patrollers. Lastly, the courts in North and South Carolina and Virginia "had the authority to order [slave] patrols to search particular areas or hunt for specific slaves" (Hadden, 2001, 50). Therefore, the judicial branch has the power and authority to dictate modern-day police procedures, just as the courts had this same power during slave patrol days. The courts have the authority to interpret the law, decide if it is constitutional, and apply it to specific situations. I premise that religious belief and practice fundamentally have more persuasion than the judicial branch.

In 1960, the Honorable Minister Louis Farrakhan (Louis X) released a song titled "A White Man's Heaven Is a Black Man's Hell." The song criticized White America's history of ill-treatment and slavery of Black people and included these lyrics:

He needed someone to work the land

His back was too weak; he needed you, black man

So, he commissioned Sir John Hawkins

To commit the worst, most grievous sin

To take a man who's born to be free

And bring him down to slavery

To sell a man as merchandise

On his body, put a price

So, my friend, it's easy to tell

That a white man's heaven is a black man's hell.
(Louis X, 2021)

Perhaps it's songs like this that many Black people admire

and feel that Minister Farrakhan is verbalizing their thoughts, yet some Whites are extremely resentful and even in fear.

The Southern Poverty Law Center claims that Minister Farrakhan leads a group that is “based on a somewhat bizarre and fundamentally anti-white theology.” They state that Minister “Farrakhan is an anti-Semite who routinely accuses Jews of manipulating the U.S. government and controlling the levers of world power” (SPLC, n.d.). In 1994, Time Magazine featured Minister Farrakhan on its cover, and the article was titled “Ministry of Rage.” The cover comments and asks the question, “Louis Farrakhan spews racist venom at Jews and all of white America. Why do so many blacks say he speaks for them?” (Ministry of Rage, 1994). Minister Farrakhan represents freedom, justice, and equality to members of the Nation of Islam. Minister Farrakhan humorously asked an audience of thousands, “What’s a matter? You not free, why not?” He also boldly exclaims, “I’m a free Black man!”

Whenever the police or law enforcement “believe themselves to be seriously threatened within their jurisdiction, all available resources will be directed into maximizing the control effort" (Turk, 1982, 117). Does the fear of civil disorder, protest, or modern-day insurrection in the Black community seriously threaten the police? Yes, indeed! For example, the Million Man March peacefully displayed Black male unity. While many attendees disagreed with Minister Louis Farrakhan, they admired his ability to amass such a sizeable crowd. Perhaps Minister Farrakhan is viewed as one to start a modern-day civil disorder revolution that requires police intervention. I attended the March and observed that all of the politicians left Washington, D.C., on October 16, 1995, and there were tanks, police, and the military on the perimeter of the mall (Muhammad, D., 2004). Analogously, slave owners and White society resented and feared the freedom of the slaves, slave insurrections, and slave rebellions.

Slave owners believed that Christianity would turn their slaves into ungovernable, rebellious, and not just proud people (Akinyela, 2003). The literate Christian preacher was a threat to the slavery system:

> ***[The] influence [of] the preacher was a potentially dangerous person in the eyes of the slavocracy, particularly if he could read. The preacher was the one who could reveal the meaning and relationship between the world of the Spirit and the visible world. If the preacher could read, he was even more able to plumb the depths of the scripture to find those same liberating passages that Europeans had used to forge concepts of their own freedom. (Akinyela, 2003, 13)***

Thus, the slave preacher may have been the most perilous next to the Civil War.

The overt slave rebellions that frequently broke out in blood and were left unchecked were the most dreadful effects of slavery in America. Herbert Apthecker supplied the most thorough analysis of American slave uprisings. The history of American Negro slavery had accounts of some 250 revolts and plots, according to him (Shapiro, 2004). The major and most notorious slave revolts in the United States were: "Gabriel Prosser in Henrico County, Virginia, 1800; Charles Deslondes in St. Charles and St. John the Baptist parishes, Louisiana, 1811; Denmark Vesey in Charleston, South Carolina, 1822; Nat Turner in Southampton County, Vir-ginia, 1831; John Murrell in Madison County, Mississippi, 1835; and John Brown's Raid in Harper's Ferry, West Virginia, 1859" (Shapiro, 2004, 20). After careful analysis, we decided to discuss Nat Turner and John Brown's insurrections.

Nat Turner's was one of the deadliest and most successful uprisings in American history. It is believed to have sped up the outbreak of the Civil War by igniting a culture of dread in Virginia that later spread to the rest of the South. Norman Shapiro summarized Turner's rebellion:

Nat Turner was born in Southampton, Virginia,

on October 2, 1800. Nat, the son of slaves, was the property of Benjamin Turner, a prosperous plantation owner. He was taught to read by Benjamin's oldest son, Samuel, who became his master after Benjamin's death about 1810. Nat apparently developed deep religious beliefs and, encouraged by his parents, gradually began to believe that God had chosen him to lead his people out of slavery. Turner was sold to Joseph Travis in 1831, and in February of that year, he took an eclipse of the sun as a supernatural sign from God to start an insurrection. It wasn't until August 21, 1831, however, that Turner and about seven other slaves killed Travis and his family to launch his rebellion. In all, about 50 whites were killed, including Elizabeth, the widow of his former master, Samuel Turner. Nat had hoped that his action would cause a massive slave uprising, but only 75 joined his rebellion. Over 3,000 members of the state militia were sent to deal with Turner's rebellion, which was put down in a few days. In retaliation, perhaps more than a hundred innocent slaves were killed. Turner went into hiding but was captured six weeks later. His subsequent trial featured his now well-known confession, and he was executed

on November 11, 1831. (Shapiro, 2004, 21)

John Brown considered himself a soldier in the army of the Lord against slavery and saw slavery as a system of torture, rape, persecution, and murder. What was so unique about Brown was that he was White, not Black. Norman Shapiro summarized John Brown's raid:

> ***John Brown, on October 16, 1859, led eighteen men, thirteen whites and five blacks, into Harpers Ferry, Virginia. Three other members of his force formed a rearguard at a nearby Maryland farm. A veteran of the violent struggles between pro- and anti-slavery forces in Kansas, Brown intended to provoke a general uprising of blacks that would lead to a war against slavery. The raiders seized the federal buildings and cut the tele-graph wires. Expecting local slaves to join them, Brown and his men waited in the armory while the townspeople surrounded the building. The raiders and the civilians exchanged gunfire, and eight of Brown's men were killed or captured. By daybreak on October 18, U.S. Marines under the com-mand of Brevet***

> ***Colonel Robert E. Lee stormed Brown's position in the arsenal's engine house and captured or killed most of his force. Five of the conspirators, including Brown's son Owen, escaped to safety in Canada and the North. Severely wounded and taken to the jail in Charles Town, Virginia, John Brown stood trial for treason against the commonwealth of Virginia, for murder, and for conspiring with slaves to rebel. On November 2, 1859, a jury convicted him and sentenced him to death. Brown readily accepted the sentence and declared that he had acted in accordance with God's commandments. Responding to persistent rumors and written threats, Henry A. Wise, governor of Virginia, called out state militia companies to guard against a possible rescue of Brown and his followers. John Brown was hanged in Charles Town on December 2, 1859. (Shapiro, 2004, 24)***

Did God really call Nat Turner and John Brown to destroy American slavery? Nat Turner, who led a deadly slave uprising in Virginia, claimed to have received a heavenly inspiration. John Brown was certain that God had chosen him to lead an uprising in America that would free the slaves. Malcolm X wrote, "I read about the slave preacher Nat Turner, who put the fear of God into the white slave master. Nat Turner wasn't going around preaching pie-in-the-sky and 'non-violent' freedom for the black man" (Shapiro, 2004, 41). His master gave him permission to visit various religious meetings in the area, where he delivered sermons and exhortations from the Bible (Akinyela, 2003). Nat Turner gave his calls for independence a voice of authority by using passages from the Bible:

> ***In recounting visions and mystical events in his life, Nat Turner exhibits an ability to take the stories and images of the Bible, particularly the apocalyptic, messianic, and prophetic freedom themes, and manipulates them to give meaning to his own experiences as an enslaved African seeking freedom. (Akinyela, 2003, 17)***

For the sake of argument, the Holy Bible in the New Testament, exodus 9 says, "Then the LORD said to Moses, "Go into Pharaoh and tell him, 'Thus says the LORD God of the Hebrews: "Let My people go, that they may serve Me…" John Brown and Nat Turner took a perilous position to fight against southern slavery, with an emphasis of "Let the Black slaves go!"

As a result of the Nat Turner insurrection, Southern Whites harbored a deep-seated hatred toward all slaves, especially Turner himself. After Turner's trial and conviction, it was demonstrated "in the magistrate's words as he pronounced the sentence, perhaps suggesting his body's fate when ordering him to be hung until he was, 'Dead! Dead! Dead!'" (Spivey, 2022). After the trial, Turner was hung until he died. However, the ordeal of what his body would encounter did not stop there:

> ***His body was given over to the surgeons for dissection. He was skinned to supply such souvenirs as purses, his flesh made into grease, and his bones divided as trophies to be handed down as heirlooms. It is said that there still lives a Virginian who has a piece of his skin that was tanned, that another Virginian possesses one of his ears, and that the skull graces the collection of a physician in the city of Norfolk. (Spivey, 2022)***

They desired to use Nat Turner as an example to stop such uprisings. However, upon the realization of his death sentence for his insurrection, Turner replied, "was not Christ crucified" (Akinyela, 2003, 24).

John Brown was a man of great faith who sincerely embraced the gospel's principles. While being the worst nightmare of the southern slave states, Brown declared "that his actions against slavery were consistent with God's commandments" (Fenkelman, 1995, 3). Brown also said in an electrifying speech:

> ***I believe…that to have interfered as I have done in behalf of His despised poor, is no wrong but right. Now, if it is deemed necessary that I should forfeit my life for the furtherance of the ends of justice and mingle my blood with the blood of millions in this slave country whose rights are disregarded by wicked, cruel, and unjust enactments, I say let it be done. (Fenkelman, 1995, 3)***

As a youth, Brown saw a "white man beating a Black child with an iron shovel. He said he could not help but ask himself if God was not also the father of the victim of that atrocious violence. His answer was yes, and that shaped the rest of his life." Brown was called "A Prisoner of Jesus Christ" by a New York religious publication. Northern soldiers and slaves sang the famous song after Brown's demise, "John Brown's body lies moldering in the clay, but his soul goes marching on." Lastly, one of Brown's most notable sayings was, "Wherever there is a right thing to be done, there is a 'thus saith the Lord' that it shall be done" (Decaro, 2022). Thus,

John Brown was a White man who, through religion, inspired slave insurrection with extreme violence.

In response to these slave revolts and insurrections, Virginia, South Carolina, North Carolina, and other southern states established "slave patrols form[ing] the first line of defense against a slave rebellion, with the militia expected to take action should a revolt become large-scale" (Hadden, 2001, 42). These "town guards, city patrol, or night police… [job was] to prevent slave gatherings" (Hadden, 2001, 54). In light of Nat Turner's claim from his so-called confession that he was motivated from his childhood, inducing him to start an insurrection, thus causing the slave states to overreact. He said, "I surely would be a prophet, as the Lord had shown me things that had happened before my birth…I was intended for some great purpose…particularly among negroes" (Gray, Turner & Royster, 1831, 7).

One of the slave patrol's main duties "was the dispersion of slave gatherings of any kind. Independent religious meetings run by slaves alone were a special target. James Smith, an escaped slave, claimed that when patrollers heard hymns and religious music sung by bondsmen, they would follow the music to the slave gatherings, then break up the meetings…[Bondsmen] caught at a [religious] slave meeting was likely to be beaten by patrollers, especially if the gathering happened at night (Hadden, 2001, 108). If a slave was caught "dressing tidily to go to a place of worship, he would be seized" by the slave patrol and beaten (Hadden, 2001, 113). It appears that modern-day law enforcement lacks restraint while investigating, searching, or seizing individuals or organizations when race and religion are substantial or motivating factors.

Malcolm X spoke to a Los Angeles audience in 1962 after the LAPD killed Muhammad's Temple number 27 secretary Ronald Stokes, and said, "we are not brutalized because we are Baptist. We are not brutalized because we are Methodist. We are not brutalized because we are Muslim. We are not brutalized because we are Catholic. We are brutalized because we are Black people in America" (Hayes, 2012). For Black people during and after slavery, his words were reminiscent. There is compelling evidence that slave patrols harassed religious leaders and congregations by engaging in abusive behavior. According to Sally Hadden:

> ***Slave patrollers closely scrutinized Baptists and Methodists, whose ministers encouraged African American attendance and participation in worship…Patrollers descended upon the Baptist meeting and 'were let loose upon them, being urged thereto by the enemies and opposers of religion'…the poor negroes [were] flying in every direction, the patrollers seizing and whipping them, whilst others were carrying them off prisoners, in order, perhaps, to subject them to more severe punishment. Like their Baptist***

brethren, Methodists also suffered from [the] slave patrol. (Hadden, 2001, 126)

If discovered attending covert prayer meetings, slaves were subject to severe punishment. "[A] slave preacher 'was flogged, and his back pickled' for preaching at a clandestine service in the woods. His listeners were flogged and 'forced to tell who else was there'" (Raboteau, 1992). Yet, the Muslim slave was considered more troublesome in having no allegiance to the slave master and forever seeking his freedom from oppression.

In 1831, a captured Muslim named Omar ibn Said wrote a 15-page autobiography in Arabic. Said described his slave master as "a small, weak, and wicked man called Johnson, a complete infidel, who had no fear of God at all." He escaped in 1810 and was later "captured as he prayed in a church and thrown in jail as a runaway. With pieces of coal, he covered the walls with pleas, in Arabic, to be released." Said, "denounced his enslavement… [declaring] that God has the power over all; in effect refuting his 'owner's' supremacy" (Diouf, 2021). To impose their own understanding of freedom, justice, equality, and social relations, the Muslim slaves battled valiantly and with all available tools, including the ultimate confrontation of insurrection (Genovese, 1979).

For example, while research on Muslim slave revolts in the United States is limited, the 1835 uprising of Muslim slaves in Brazil is a significant epitome. On January 25, 1835, after midnight, a group of African-born Muslim slaves subjugated "the justice of the peace and a police lieutenant," stormed the night, fighting and destroying municipal buildings, leading "some historians [to] characterize [their] revolt as a jihad" (Hatch, 1993). To a Muslim slave, as a closed companion of the Islamic Prophet Muhammad (May Allah's peace and blessing be upon him), Hazrat Ali said, "Don't be a slave of others when Allah has created you free" (Umar, 2021).

Thus, in order to avoid the possible risks that slave religion created, a moral critique of the institution of slavery, and a pretext for slaves to gather for insurrectionary reasons, white Southern states regulated it and attacked slave religions with the slave patrol. Institutions like law and religion significantly impact the individual and societal well-being of Americans (Muhammad, D., 2004). But why was religion viewed as such a threat to White slavery society?

Religious influence has a significant impact on how people think and behave in society (Muhammad, 2004). University of Oregon School of Law Professor Tom Lininger contends, "[m]any people believe that religion is the most urgent of human affairs because it implicates one's everlasting salvation or damnation, while political and social meetings only implicate the affairs of the world" (Lininger, 2004, 1210). A fundamental objective of any polity is to maintain its position of power and to suppress any competing revolutionary or dissident group (Muhammad, D., 2004). When authorities, the state, or law enforcement perceive themselves seriously threatened by a non-traditional religious group, they commit all available resources to control the religious peril (Turk, 1982). Christianity, in its infancy, was considered new and controversial to the Roman Empire. The Romans mocked and scorned the notion that Jesus was actually the Jewish Messiah and was historically responsible for his crucifixion (Davis & Hankins, 2002; Hopfe, 1994). White society, slave owners, and the slave patrol were just as disdainful towards the slave's practice of religion for fear of slave freedom and slave rebellions. In the same way, modern-day law enforcement was used to suppress and maintain a level of control over revolutionary religious groups, particularly of Reverend Dr. Martin Luther King, Jr.

The F.B.I. was reminiscent of the slave patrol in its investigations, surveillance, and harassment of Dr. King. The FBI's five-year attempt to destroy Martin Luther King Jr. and "neutralize" him as a powerful civil rights leader and preacher is widely regarded as the most notorious instance of FBI overreach. A cassette recording that was collected from microphone surveillance of possible infidelity was sent to Dr. King's wife, Coretta, as part of these efforts, along with a note that many have interpreted as an attempt to persuade him to commit suicide (Fisher, 2004). Professor Lininger describes how the F. B. I. harassed Dr. King using electronic eavesdropping and paid informants:

The F.B.I. conducted extensive surveillance of

> ***Dr. King, including surveillance of his sermons in churches throughout the South. For example, in April 2003, a transcript was finally published of a speech that Dr. King had delivered behind closed doors at a church in Selma, Alabama, during the winter of 1965. The FBI had bugged the church and recorded this speech, and a local law enforcement officer held the tapes for three decades before releasing them. At one point, the F.B.I. was using at least fifteen different hidden microphones in its surveillance of Dr. King. Not only did the F.B.I. monitor Dr. King's activities with concealed recording devices, but the F.B.I. also arranged for at least one informant to infiltrate the [Southern Christian Leadership Conference. (Lininger, 2004, 1211)***

Fear and suspicion appear to have been the motivational factor in modern-day law enforcement pursuit of Dr. Martin Luther King.

The F.B.I. appeared to have no evidence of criminal activity or intent to pursue a criminal prosecution against Dr. King but was more interested in discrediting him personally and tarnishing the civil rights movement. Lininger argued that "the F. B. I. sought to [destroy Dr. King] who could unify and electrify the militant Black

Nationalist movement. Thus, the investigation of King had more to do with politics than with a legitimate law enforcement purpose" (Lininger, 2004, 1212). This attempt to disrupt Dr. King's movement is similar to the intent of the slave patrol efforts to disrupt the religious services of slaves. With the possibility of Dr. King and Elijah Muhammad collaborating, the "Racial Matters" section of the F.B.I. went into a frenzy, and slave patrol policing escalated (Evanzz, 1999, 313).

In February 1966, Dr. King and Elijah Muhammad met at the Muslim leader's residence in Chicago (Evanzz, 1999, 313). The Muhammad Speaks newspaper reported that Dr. King and Elijah Muhammad were united in agreement that "the world of White rule over Blacks is at an end" (Evanzz, 1999, 330). The F. B. I. sought to portray Dr. King as having "some degree of adherence to the teachings of Elijah Muhammad" (Evanzz, 1999, 334). Thus, the F.B.I. feared that Dr. King was planning a revolution or a rebellion in the streets of Washington, D. C., and the United States. The F. B. I. wrote in a memorandum:

> ***King has met with Black Nationalists and attempted to solicit their support…The combined forces of the communist's influence and the black nationalists advocating violence give [it] a potential to be an extremely explosive situation. (Evanzz, 1999, 334-335)***

Ironically, two years later, Dr. King was assassinated on April 4, 1968, as he stood on the balcony of the Lorraine Motel in Memphis, Tennessee. Elijah Muhammad concluded that Dr. King was assassinated due to the potential of the two of them working together:

> ***The devil acts as though he's worshipping Martin Luther King. After Martin Luther King visited my house, he [white agents] sat out there in his car and tuned in on what we were talking about. I guess he heard [King] say that he agreed with me, that he is the devil. He saw that Elijah was winning their disciple over, so they shoot him. (Evanzz, 1999, 364)***

Whether at the hands of the F. B. I., Memphis police, White hate groups, or violence-prone individuals, Dr. King knew that he would not live much longer. On April 3, 1968, during a tornado warning, Dr. King delivered his last speech at Mason Temple Church. His speech concluded with a reference to his very own demise:

> ***Well, I don't know what will happen now. We've got some difficult days ahead. But it doesn't matter to me now. Because I've been to the mountaintop. And I don't mind. Like anybody, I would like to live a long life. Longevity has its place. But I'm not concerned about that now. I just want to do God's will. And He's allowed me to go up to the mountain. And I've looked over. And I've seen the promised land. I may not get there with you. But I want you to know tonight that we, as a people, will get to the promised land. And I'm happy tonight. I'm not worried about anything. I'm not fearing any man. Mine eyes have seen the glory of the coming of the Lord. (Melanson, 1991, 2)***

In 1969, James Earl Ray pleaded guilty to murdering Dr. King and was sentenced to 99 years of imprisonment. However, three days later, Ray recanted his confession, saying he was set up and seeking a new trial until his death in 1998 (Douglass, 2000). There appears to be much more to the official story that James Earl Ray shot and killed Dr. King.

Over 32 years after the assassination, a Memphis jury reached the verdict in a civil trial that Loyd Jowers and "others, including governmental agencies," conspired to kill Martin Luther

King Jr. A court expanded the scope of blame for King's killing beyond James Earl Ray (Douglass, 2000). Only a mere $100.00 in damages were awarded to the King family by the jury (Jury backs King, 1999). Testimony by way of a two-hour-long tape-recorded confession of Jowers was presented to the jury. Jowers said to Dexter King and Andrew Young that law enforcement was involved:

> ***[T]he meetings to plan the assassination occurred at Jim's Grill…the planners included undercover Memphis Police Department officer Marrell McCollough (who now works for the Central Intelligence Agency), Memphis Police Department Lieutenant Earl Clark (who died in 1987), a third police officer, and two men…thought [to be] federal agents. (Douglass, 2000)***

While the U. S. Department of Justice's investigation into the Jowers conspiracy and the civil jury verdict concluded that the allegations were not substantiated or credible nor warranting any additional investigations (Overview of Investigation, 2020), there was an overwhelming amount of evidence in the King assassination that had too many odd coincidences. For example, Memphis police department's "sudden and unexplained withdrawal of King's security" detail (Melanson, 1991, 66); the Black police officer Reddit (assigned surveillance of King and the Lorraine) "claim[ing] that he was removed from security duty under the pretext of a false threat against his life" (Melanson, 1991, 68); the retreat of three to four tactical units "patrolling within the five to six block area 'immediately surrounding' the Lorraine…on the morning…of the assassination (Melanson, 1991, 71); the failure of Memphis police dispatch to broadcast an accurate description of the suspect, a code "signal," indicating "certain units were to proceed immediately to prearranged locations blocking all main exits from Memphis" and not issuing an "All-Points Bulletin" to "neighboring states of Arkansas, Mississippi, and Alabama" of the suspect's description (Melanson, 1991, 64); the April 3, 1968 temporary transfer of two Black firefighters "from Fire Station 2, located across the street from the Lorraine Motel…to fire station[s] far removed from the Lorraine Motel" by orders of the Memphis police; the two U.S. Army officers going to the roof of the fire station, saying "they wanted a lookout for the Lorraine Motel." They had cameras and were carrying briefcases. They "had a bird's-eye view of Dr. King's balcony doorway and could also look down on the brushy area adjacent to the fire station." And finally, after a witness reported a puff of white smoke coming from some brush near the scene and after the assassination, the Memphis police ordered the sanitation department to cut the brush away the next morning (Douglass, 2000), all suggesting a law enforcement conspiracy to kill Dr. King.

Opposition to the Vietnam war may have been the driving force behind the assassination of Dr. King. A Central Intelligence Agency's document "had intelligence that Martin Luther King, Jr., constituted a threat to National security — particularly to the Vietnam War effort" (Melanson, 1991, 17). Yet, there was a striking similarity in the killing of a slave preacher in Virginia in 1846 or 1847. "Tom Ashbie's [plantation owner] father went to one of the cabins late at night; the slaves were having a secret prayer meeting. He heard one slave ask God to change the heart of his master and deliver him from slavery so that he may enjoy freedom. Before the next day, the man disappeared . . . When old man Ashbie died, just before he died, he told the white Baptist minister that he had killed Zeek for praying" (Maffly-Kipp, 2005). Likewise, Dr. King prayed and dreamed that White America's heart would change and awaken its morale conscious, as he declared:

> ***When we allow freedom ring, when we let it ring from every village and every hamlet, from every state and every city, we will be able to speed up that day when all of God's children, Black men and white men, Jews, and Gentiles, Protestants, and Catholics, will be able to join hands and sing in the words of the old Negro spiritual: Free at last. Free at last. Thank God almighty, we are free at last - Excerpts from Martin Luther King's***

I Have a Dream speech.

Dr King said, "I want you to say that I tried to love and serve humanity" (King, 1968). Yet, the King of love was shot and killed. Author James Cone said in his book, "While Martin Luther King, Jr., saw America as essentially a dream as yet unfulfilled, Malcolm X viewed America as a realized nightmare (Cone, 2001).

While researching for this book, a Caucasian co-worker asked me, "what are you reading"? After I showed him the book I was reading, he replied, "Dr. King was a good man." He then explained to me that he's not racist, yet one of his neighbors is extremely hateful, and that she refers to Blacks as "jigaboos." He paused and said, "but I don't know about that, Malcolm X." A likely response is that Malcolm X and Martin Luther King, Jr., are often viewed as competing forces in the fight for civil rights and against white supremacy. However, Malcolm X stated, "Dr. King wants the same thing I want — freedom. Now his method of going about getting it is the nonviolent way. We may differ in method, but that does not mean we differ in objective" (Gallen, 1992, 91). However, the modern-day police, indiscriminately armed with weapons of violence and death, believe that they can frighten, maim, or kill Malcolm X and Dr. King with the same recklessness that once drove the slave patrol.

While modern-day police may be subconsciously practicing slave patrol tactics, Malcolm X is unequivocally the modern-day version of Nat Turner and John Brown combined in speech. While most Blacks gave credence to Dr. King's philosophy on nonviolence and passive resistance, Malcolm X was erroneously perceived to be violent. Malcolm X explained, "We're nonviolent with people who are nonviolent with us. But we are not nonviolent with anyone who is violent with us" (Increase My Knowledge, 2011). Malcolm X also declared, "Our religion teaches us to be intelligent. Be peaceful, be courteous, obey the law, respect everyone; but if someone puts his hand on you, send him to the cemetery. That's a good religion" (Breitman, 1965, 12).

Malcolm X's understanding of American slavery precipitated his dialogue that centered on the dichotomy of African Americans on the plantation. In explanation to this, Malcolm X describes the house negro and the field negro:

> ***The house Negro and the field Negro — back during slavery. There were two kinds of slaves. There was the house Negro and the field Negro. The house Negroes – they lived in the house with master, they dressed pretty good, they ate good 'cause they ate his food — what he left. They lived in the attic or the basement, but they still lived near the master; they loved their master more than the master loved himself. They would give their life to save the master's house quicker***

than the master would. The house Negro, if the master said, "We got a good house here," the house Negro would say, "Yeah, we got a good house here." Whenever the master said 'we,' he said 'we. 'That's how you can tell a house Negro.

If the master's house caught on fire, the house Negro would fight harder to put the blaze out than the master would. If the master got sick, the house Negro would say, 'What's the matter, boss, we sick?' We sick! He identified himself with his master more than his master identified with himself. And if you came to the house Negro and said, 'Let's run away, let's escape, let's separate,' the house Negro would look at you and say, 'Man, you crazy. What you mean, separate? Where is there a better house than this? Where can I wear better clothes than this? Where can I eat better food than this?' That was that house Negro. In those days, he was called a 'house nigger.' And that's what we call him today because we've still got some house niggers running around here. This modern house Negro loves his master. He wants to live near him. He'll pay three times as much as the house is worth

just to live near his master and then brag about 'I'm the only Negro out here.' 'I'm the only one on my job.' 'I'm the only one in this school.' You're nothing but a house Negro. And if someone comes to you right now and says, 'Let's separate,' you say the same thing that the house Negro said on the plantation. 'What you mean, separate? From America? This good white man? Where you going to get a better job than you get here?' I mean, this is what you say. 'I ain't left nothing in Africa,' that's what you say. Why you left your mind in Africa?

On that same plantation, there was the field Negro. The field Negro — those were the masses. There were always more Negroes in the field than there was Negroes in the house. The Negro in the field caught hell. He ate leftovers. In the house they ate high up on the hog. The Negro in the field didn't get nothing but what was left of the insides of the hog. They call 'em 'chitt'lings' nowadays. In those days, they called them what they were: guts. That's what you were — a gut-eater. And some of you all still gut-eaters.

The field Negro was beaten from morning to night. He lived in a shack, in a hut; He wore old, castoff clothes. He hated his master. I say he hated his master. He was intelligent. That house Negro loved his master. But that field Negro — remember, they were in the majority, and they hated the master. When the house caught on fire, he didn't try and put it out; that field Negro prayed for a wind, for a breeze. When the master got sick, the field Negro prayed that he'd die. If someone came to the field Negro and said, 'Let's separate, let's run,' he didn't say, 'Where we going?' He'd say, 'Any place is better than here.' You've got field Negroes in America today. I'm a field Negro. The masses are the field Negroes. When they see this man's house on fire, you don't hear these little Negroes talking about 'our government is in trouble.' They say, 'The government is in trouble.' Imagine a Negro: 'Our government'! I even heard one say, 'our astronauts.' They won't even let him near the plant — and 'our astronauts'! 'Our Navy' — that's a Negro that's out of his mind. That's a Negro that's out of his mind. (Breitman, 1965,

10-12)

By presenting the views of Malcolm X, describing himself as a "field negro" I hope it will be readily seen that he will be viewed by modern-day law enforcement and White society as a modern-day Nat Turner. He's rhetorically identifying himself as a Black separatist. Malcolm X was letting America know that we'll get our freedom and do anything to get it.

Malcolm X had the courage to speak about what Black Americans thought but were too afraid to say it. According to Dr. Michael Eric Dyson:

> ***It was Malcolm's unique ability to narrate the prospects of black resistance at the edge of racial apocalypse that made him both exciting and threatening. Malcolm spoke out loud what many blacks secretly felt about racist white people and practices but were afraid to acknowledge publicly. Malcolm boldly specified in lucid rhetoric the hurts, agonies, and frustrations of black people chafing from an enforced racial silence about the considerable cultural costs of white racism. (Dyson, 1995, 10)***

Thus, Malcolm X became as dangerous to the U. S. as a leader of a slave rebellion was to the slave master.

Just as Virginia Governor John Floyd in 1831 responded to Nat Turner's Rebellion that the "most active among ourselves, in stirring up the spirit of revolt, have been the negro preacher" and that the "public good requires the negro preachers to be silence[ed] (Floyd, 1832). Malcolm X's speech would incite the masses of Black Americans, thus causing the F.B.I. Director J. Edgar Hoover, on June 6, 1964 to issue a directive to F. B. I. agents to "do something about Malcolm X" (Popli, 2023). The FBI established a file on him shortly after Malcolm X was released from a Boston prison in March 1953. The F.B.I. maintained a file on Malcolm X until he was assassinated, which totaled thirty-six hundred pages (Carson, 2012). Likewise, similar to Dr. King, the F.B.I. had no evidence of Malcolm X committing a crime.

One of the FBI's most thorough espionage operations ever focused on Malcolm X. A lawsuit under the Freedom of Information Act revealed:

> ***COINTELPRO was set in motion against Black movement. One memo, signed by J. Edgar Hoover and sent to FBI agents across the country, said, 'The purpose of this new counterintelligence endeavor is to expose, disrupt, misdirect, discredit, or otherwise***

> ***neutralize the activities of black nationalists, hate-type organizations and groupings, their leadership, spokesmen, membership, and supporters… (Breitman, Porter & Smith, 1991, 168)***

These secret COINTELPRO documents revealed a national government operation to repress, disrupt, and, more significantly, neutralize Black organizations, particularly the Organization of African American Unity and Malcolm X.

The F.B.I. used the word "neutralize" instead of "kill," "murder" or "eradicate." According to the Oxford Learner Dictionary, to "neutralize somebody/something is to remove the threat of someone or something that might be dangerous, especially by killing them or destroying it" (Oxford Learner's Dictionaries, n.d.). Neutralization involves "a dimension in which persons may be subjected to punishment by the state's agents without any official acknowledgment. Known or suspected offenders may be neutralized by…assassination instead of official execution" (Turk, 1982, 141-142). The United States backed a few assassination plots before there was an official ban on them in the country. A Senate committee that looked into and recorded these activities came to the conclusion that U.S. government officials thought assassination was a legal line of action (Johnson III, 1992). According to Minister Nuri Muhammad of the Nation of Islam, "Malcolm X was not killed by the F. O. I., Malcolm X was killed by the F. B. I." (BreakfastClub, 2019). The F. O. I. (aka the Fruit of Islam) is the paramilitary security and disciplinary wing of the Nation of Islam.

On February 21, 1965, Malcolm X, at the age of 39 years old, was assassinated at the Audubon Ballroom as he was introduced to an audience of 400 people. His pregnant wife, Betty Shabazz, and their four children were present and had to duck for cover. Someone yelled, "Nigger! Get your hand outta my pocket!" Malcolm X said, "Hold it," ten times. A man rushed the stage and shot Malcolm X in the chest with a sawed-off shotgun, and two or three other men charged the stage, shooting him with semi-automatic handguns.

To avoid acknowledgment of governmental neutralization, the assassination of Malcolm X was a prevaricate way to blame the Nation of Islam. The argument is a variety of similarities that Elijah Muhammad ordered the Nation of Islam to kill Malcolm X because he split from the group and started his own movement, exposing the domestic life of Elijah Muhammad, and/or the Nation of Islam has a violent history (Goldman, 1973; Friedley, 1992; Taylor, 2003; Palmer, 2004). However, Elijah Muhammad said at the 1965 Savior's Day convention, a few days after the assassination, with Malcolm X's two brothers, Wilfred and Philbert, standing beside him, "his two brothers know all about it. They stand here like men, like Muslims. They know me. They know their brother. They know I didn't harm their brother. They know I loved their brother" (Muhammad, E., 1965, 18).

More recently, some have blamed Minister Louis Farrakhan because he wrote in Muhammad Speaks newspaper, "The die is set, and Malcolm shall not escape... Such a man as Malcolm is worthy of death." Yet, they ignore Minister Louis Farrakhan's statement that followed, "and would have been met with death if it had not been for Muhammad's confidence in Allah for victory over his enemies" (Louis X, 1964, 15). However, there was no evidence or recordings obtained from the FBI's intense surveillance of the Nation of Islam and Elijah Muhammad. There was no evidence produced to indict Elijah Muhammad, Minister Farrakhan, or any of its top officials for Malcolm X's murder (Muhammad, D., 2004). Such criminal charges would have been detrimental to the continued existence of the Nation of Islam. Malcolm X knew that he would be killed, but near the end of his life, he began to have doubts that the Nation of Islam would be the perpetrators.

Malcolm X told close associates that he was "not all that sure it's the Muslims" (Breitman, Porter, & Smith, 1991, 56) trying to kill him and that he was going to quit saying it was. Things that happened after the February 21, 1965 bombing of his house appeared to be bigger than what the Nation of Islam can do. He said, "I know what they can do. Things have gone beyond that" (Breitman, Porter, & Smith, 1991, 82). Perhaps Malcolm X was referring to how the French government refused to allow him to leave his plane to make a speech in Paris, with it being speculated that the French government "feared they would be embarrassed by having him assassinated on French soil" (Breitman, Porter, & Smith,

1991, 84). He could have thought of how he was poisoned while he was in Cairo, or maybe he recalled how the CIA "truth squad" followed him throughout Africa and the Middle East wherever he went - slandering him and attempting to undo what he was doing (Breitman, Porter, & Smith, 1991, 83).

Malcolm X was aware that the Nation of Islam lacked the means to plan his assassination on a global scale. Certainly, the FBI and CIA desired to prevent Malcolm X from bringing an indictment of racism against the United States government before the United Nations as he had planned (Breitman, Porter, & Smith, 1991, 117). Arguably, on March 13, 1964, "Leon 4X Ameer died of an overdose of sleeping pills. . .. He had just announced plans to produce tapes and documents of Malcolm's proving [that the government was responsible for [the] assassination" (Breitman, Porter, & Smith, 1991, 16).

After a half of century, the scales of Justice were tilted in favor of dissenters and conspiracy theorists regarding who was culpable for the assassination of Malcolm X. In 2021, two of the three men convicted of killing Malcolm X were exonerated, compelling the New York District Attorney to admit that "the FBI and NYPD at the time withheld evidence." The third man, Thomas Hagan (a.k.a. Talmadge Hayer and Mujahid Abdul Halim), confessed to the crime. He said that Norman 3X Butler (a.k.a. Muhammad Abdul Aziz) and Thomas 15X Johnson (a.k.a. Khalil Islam) were innocent, it took the 2020 Netflix documentary series

Who Killed Malcolm X and the Innocence Project to convince Manhattan District Attorney Cyrus Vance Jr. to re-examine the case. Investigative journalist Abdur-Rahman Muhammad uncovered facts and evidence in the documentary to prove that Aziz and Islam were innocent. A judge overturned their convictions, and the city of New York was ordered to pay them $26 million for their erroneous convictions for murder. “The FBI and NYPD did not honor their obligation to disclose exculpatory evidence to prosecutors and the accused, including ‘information that implicated other suspects; that identified witnesses who failed to identify defendant Islam; and that revealed witnesses to be FBI informants.’ The [New York District Attorney’s] office also said at the time that FBI records suggested ‘that information was deliberately withheld.’” The family of Malcolm X is suing the FBI, New York Police Department, and CIA for $100 million (Popli, 2023). While the only admission thus far is that the FBI and the NYPD withheld evidence, upon meticulous scrutiny, there are circumstantial occurrences that suggest that perhaps the FBI and the New York police department were "death squads” to which surreptitious repression may have been carried out.

The most explosive and compelling evidence is the missing second gunman, who was arrested at the scene. The New York Herald Tribune, The New York Times, and another paper all first reported in a headline that "Malcolm X Slain by Gunmen . . . Police Rescue Two Suspects," but all three of the late city editions of the same newspapers on the same day reported that the police rescued only one suspect. Officer Thomas Hoy arrested the second suspect, but his existence never surfaced except in the earlier newspaper accounts (Breitman, Porter, & Smith, 1991, 51-53). The NYPD explained the arrest of the second suspect as a journalistic error (Breitman, Porter, & Smith, 1991, 161). However, the New York Times edition gives details from patrolman Hoy's arrest:

> ***Patrolman Thomas Hoy, 22, said he had been stationed outside the 166th Street entrance when 'I heard the shooting, and the place exploded.' He rushed in, saw Malcolm lying on the stage, and 'grabbed a suspect' who, he said, some people were chasing. 'As I brought him to the front of the ballroom, the crowd began beating me and the suspect,' Patrolman Hoy said. He said he put this man, not otherwise identified later for newsmen, into a police car to be taken to the Wadsworth Avenue station. (Kihss, 1965)***

Contemplate that Hagen "was taken to Bellevue Prison Ward…sealed off by a dozen policemen" (Breitman, Porter, & Smith, 1991, 51) due to his gunshot injury, not the Wadsworth police station.

A police inspector interviewed immediately after the assassination said, "Well, we have two suspects in custody now. [I] wouldn't know that at this time where they were arrested. One of these men was arrested on the street by one of our patrolmen close by" (Noble, 2020). The NYPD police five days later arrested two members of the Nation of Islam (Aziz and Islam).

The police actions at the Audubon Ballroom were extremely suspicious. A top-ranking police official admits that several members of the highly secretive Bureau of Special Services (BOSS) were present in the audience at the time of Malcolm's assassination (Breitman, Porter, & Smith, 1991, 54). A deputy police chief claimed that the NYPD offered Malcolm X protection on many occasions, and he refused, to which his widow Betty Shabazz said, "That's a lie" (Breitman, Porter, & Smith, 1991, 57).

The police are sworn to protect people and are supposed to prevent murder. However, they failed to protect Malcolm X. According to a NYPD spokesman, "the department knew in mid-January that an attempt was to be made on Malcolm's life" (Breitman, Porter, & Smith, 1991, 57). Perhaps they learned that from Gene Roberts, one of Malcolm X's bodyguards, who attempted to give Malcolm mouth-to-mouth resuscitation after the assassination. Roberts was actually an undercover Bureau of Special Services NYPD officer assigned to the Red Squad to infiltrate Malcolm's organization (Breitman, Porter, & Smith, 1991, 13, 72, 86). The actions of police assigned to the Audubon were extremely prejudicial.

The testimony of a black NYPD patrolman, Gilbert Henry,

shed some light on the police inactions, in spite of the fact that they knew Malcolm's life was in danger. Henry and his partner, John Carroll, were assigned to the Audubon Ballroom on the assassination day. Normally, at least six uniformed NYPD officers would be present during Malcolm X's speaking engagements. However, they both were stationed in another ballroom with orders to remain concealed and to call the command post across the street with their walkie-talkie radio if anything were to happen. After Henry heard gunshots, he called for backup on the radio but got no response. He responded to the main auditorium, but no suspects, uniform, or plain-cloths officers were present (Breitman, Porter, & Smith, 1991, 93).

According to Deputy Police Commissioner Walter Arm, a special NYPD detail of two sergeants and eighteen officers was assigned to the Audubon Ballroom on that day (Breitman, Porter, & Smith, 1991, 58). Yet, Hayer was caught after a bodyguard shot him in the leg, a mob beat him, and two officers on scout car patrol, who just happened to hear gunshots, rescued him (Breitman, Porter, & Smith, 1991, 59). Who was the other suspect arrested by police at the scene that disappeared?

The missing second suspect has been identified as a Black NYPD undercover officer named Raymond A Wood. Wood was assigned to the Bureau of Special Services and Investigation (BOSSI) unit. His identity was disclosed in 2011 from handwritten notes from the late Japanese American activist Yuri Kochiyama.

Kochiyama took notes at an OAAU's members meeting on March 6, 1965. Kochiyama, a close friend of Malcolm X, wrote on a piece of paper, "Ray Woods is said to have been seen also running out of Audubon; was one of two picked up by police. Was the second person running out" (Felber, 2015). While the NYPD refused to disclose or release its surveillance files on Malcolm X, Wood made a deathbed confession regarding his role in the assassination.

Exactly 56 years after the assassination of Malcolm X, on February 21, 2021, Reggie Wood, along with attorney Ben Crump and three of Malcolm X's daughters - Qubiliah, Ilyasah, and Gamilah Shabazz held a press conference demanding the Malcolm X assassination be re-investigated. Reggie Wood is the cousin of former NYPD officer Ray Wood, and he released a signed confession letter from Ray Wood, where he admitted that he was responsible for weakening Malcolm X's security on the day of the assassination. When he thought his cancer would claim his life in 2011, according to Reggie Wood, the former officer admitted to his role. In the end, he experienced remission and survived until November 2020. (Confession letter former cop, 2021). The confession letter follows in its entirety instead of a summary for the reader to examine firsthand:

January 25, 2011, TO WHOM IT MAY CONCERN

I, Raymond A. Wood, being of sound mind and body, wish to confess the following:

I was a black New York City undercover police officer from April 1964 through May of 1971. I participated in actions that, in hindsight, were deplorable and detrimental to the advancement of my own black people. My actions on behalf of the New York City Police Department (BOSS) were done under duress and fear that if I did not follow the orders of my handlers, I could face detrimental consequences. Presently, I am aging with failing health; recently, I have learned of the death of Mr. Thomas Johnson and are deeply concerned that with my death, his family will not be able exonerate him after being wrongly convicted in the killing of Malcolm X.

THE FACTS ARE AS FOLLOWS:

April 17, 1964. I was hired by the New York City police department. Without training, I was

immediately assigned to the BOSSI investigation unit.

My job was to infiltrate civil rights organizations throughout New York City to find evidence of criminal activity so the FBI could discredit and arrest its leaders.

After witnessing repeated brutality at the hands of my coworkers (Police), I tried to resign; instead, I was threatened with arrest by pinning marijuana and alcohol trafficking charges on me if I did not follow through with the assignments.

Under the direction of my handlers, I was told to encourage leaders and members of civil rights groups to commit felonious acts.

The Statue of Liberty bombing idea was created by my supervisor handler. Using surveillance, the agency learned that Bowe and Sayyed were key players in Malcolm X's crowd control security

detail. It was my assignment to draw the two men into a felonious federal crime so that they could be arrested by the FBI and kept away from managing Malcolm X's Audubon Ballroom door security on February 21, 1965. On February 16, 1965, the Statue of Liberty plot was carried out, and the men were arrested just days before the assassination of Malcolm. At that time, I was not aware that Malcolm X was the target.

On February 21, 1965 I was ordered to be at the Audubon Ballroom, where I was identified by witnesses while leaving the scene. Thomas Johnson was later arrested and wrongfully convicted to protect my cover and the secrets of the FBI and NYPD.

I have placed my full confession into the care of my cousin Reginald Wood Jr. I have requested that this information be held until after I have passed away.

It is my hope that this information is received

with the understanding that I have carried these secrets with a heavy heart and remorsefully regret my participation in this matter.

Raymond A. Wood. (Wood, 2021, iii)

Kelly Wood, the daughter of former NYPD BOSSI officer Ray Wood, said that the confession letter is fake. She said, "[m]y father is not a coward. He would have never ever asked anybody to speak on his behalf after his passing. If he had something to say, he would have said it when he was alive. I'm certain of that. If he was involved in any way, he would have spoken up earlier." She also said that because the media had already blown her father's cover, "[t]hey were not going to run the risk of having him [at the Audubon]."

However, on February 16, four persons were arrested on suspicion of attempting to blow the Statue of Liberty's head off, and Wood was given credit for infiltrating the organization on the front page of the New York Times. Guards at the Audubon Ballroom were unable to stop the murder of Malcolm X on February 21 (Hawkins, 2021). Secondly, according to witnesses, Woods was leaving the Audubon when he was attacked by a crowd, arrested by Officer Hoy, and later disappeared from police custody (Felber, 2015).

According to Reggie Wood, Ray Wood told him that on the

morning of February 21, 1965, he received a call telling him to leave his apartment and get into a black Buick four-door. Once inside the vehicle, he was met by two FBI agents. They told him to go to the Audubon Ballroom and "check it out." He was told just to observe and report. Wood noticed a lack of usual security for a Malcolm X rally. He went in and sat in the front of the ballroom. He heard a man shout, "Get your hands out my pocket," and heard gunshots. He headed to the closest exit and saw Malcolm X lying on the stage. As he was exiting, he saw a man drop a shotgun, but he did not retrieve it. He heard someone yell, "grab that son of a bitch," and was held by a crowd of people. He was arrested by a uniformed police officer and taken to a police station. Wood spent three hours in a holding cell. He was finally released to the custody of the same two previous FBI agents and driven away in an unmarked vehicle. They asked him a few questions before releasing him and telling him, "Forget you were ever there, forget you even spoke with us. You did your part, now get outta here. And lay low for a while" (Woods, 2021, 59-69).

There are still many questions concerning who committed the assassination of Malcolm X; however, the main suspects are the law enforcement agencies, particularly the NYPD and the FBI. The circumstantial evidence presented falls short of an indictment against them, yet to resolve these suspicions, the NYPD, the FBI, and other surveillance agencies must make their files and records public.

There are numerous incidents between modern-day law enforcement and religious groups. The passage is lengthy because of my passion for the subject. In 2004, I wrote my Master's Essay at Wayne State University titled, Religious Policing: Suppression of Innovative Social and Political Change. I learned from that essay that "the interaction of religious institutions and religious people with law and politics provide some of the most potent cultural conflicts in contemporary American society" (Muhammad, D., 2004, 4). Secondly, two of the most prominent African American leaders, Dr. King and Malcolm X, may have been "neutralized" by law enforcement due to their religious and social influence that challenged America's white supremacy, voting rights, racial violence, and economic injustice. Thus, the slave states had a special interest in controlling slave religious leaders who could influence a revolution or the quest for freedom. For example, after the Nat Turner insurrection, the Virginia legislature passed a law that said, "Blacks were prohibited from holding religious meetings without the supervision of white pastors" (Hillman, 2005, 3). Scholars and historians should conduct more empirical studies on the correlation between Malcolm X and Dr. King's treatment by law enforcement and the similarities of the slave patrol tactics against slave preachers. After the LAPD murdered Nation of Islam secretary Ronald Stokes, Malcolm X openly told Black people they did not have to continue to be abused and that they had the right to protect themselves.

The following section contains violent content which may be too intense for some readers. ***Reader discretion is advised.*** The following analysis is provided for informational purposes only. All the information about the Dallas police massacre is provided in good faith as to research and study. However, I do not condone Micah Johnson's murderous behavior of any kind or anyone killing individuals as acts of retaliation to resolve grievances of any nature.

Imagine if Black people had enough of police killings and physically retaliated. Riots by African Americans often occurred in reaction to police killings where there appears to be no accountability. Since 1960, rioting in the United States was triggered after a police encounter with a Black person, resulting in death or serious brutality and the Black community perceiving no justice. Some of the deadliest riots or insurrections sparked by police were in 1965 Watts, resulting in "34 dead and tens of millions of dollars" in damages; 1967 New Jersey, "26 dead and 1,500 injured"; 1967 Detroit, 43 deaths and 2,000 injuries; 1968 King assassination, 125 cities, "46 dead and 2,600 injured"; 1992 Los Angeles Rodney King acquittals, "59 dead and more than 2,300 injured"; 2014 Ferguson - Michael Brown; 2015 Baltimore - Freddie Gray; and 2016 Charlotte, North Carolina - Keith Lamont Scott, just to name a few (France-Presse, 2020).

In 1968, the National Advisory Commission on Civil Disorders, known as the Kerner Commission, released its report on the cause of civil disorder, which indicated, "Our nation is moving toward two societies, one black, one white- separate and unequal…The police are not merely a spark factor. To some

Negroes police have come to symbolize white power, white racism, and white repression" (National Advisory Commission on Civil Disorders, 2016). Dr. Martin Luther King said the report was a "physician's warning of approaching death, with a prescription for life" (Doss, 2021). Unfortunately, no one in the government or the police implemented reasonable solutions. Thus, this neglect and continued police violence may lead to deranged violent retaliation.

Micah Xavier Johnson assaulted a group of police officers on July 7, 2016, in Dallas, Texas, murdering five of them and wounding nine others with gunfire. Johnson, an Army Reserve veteran of the Afghan War, was enraged by the shootings of black individuals by police. After a demonstration protesting the recent police deaths of Alton Sterling in Baton Rouge, Louisiana, and Philando Castile in Falcon Heights, Minnesota, the shooting took place. After the incident, Johnson hid inside a building on the El Centro College campus. Police followed him, and a standoff resulted. Johnson was slain by police early on July 8 when they detonated a bomb using a remote-control bomb disposal robot. According to initial reports, the attack was the bloodiest for American law enforcement personnel since September 11, 2001. Johnson said that "he was upset about Black Lives Matter…he was upset about the recent police shootings…he was upset at White people…he wanted to kill White people, especially white [police] officers." (Fernandez, Perez-Peña & Bromwich, 2016). There's no justification for killing innocent people or innocent police officers. Unfortunately, the reality is that people are tired of police killing unarmed Black people.

Some White people are getting fed up with unarmed Black people being killed by police also. A recent Monmouth University poll reveals that the majority of White Americans believe the protestors' anger is "fully justified," and early data suggest that during the George Floyd protest in 2020, White protesters will make up the majority of the crowds in various places with a majority-minority population (Chudy, 2020). A White reader of the New York Times responded with a comment regarding the Dallas police massacre:

> ***I'm White, safe in my nice neighborhood, really don't have a dog in this fight, but I completely sympathize with the shooter's anger. Cops shoot handcuffed black man; cops shoot black man reaching for wallet in minor traffic stop; cops choke black man to death for selling cigarettes; cops kill kid looking at pellet gun in store etc., etc., etc. Cops almost never held accountable. This sucks, not acceptable. (Pearson, 2016)***

Even the former President took notice of the increased presence of White citizens protesting against police killing unarmed Blacks. Former President Barack Obama observed "a far more representative cross-section of America out on the streets … that didn't exist back in the 1960s, that kind of broad coalition" (Chudy, 2020). Equivalently, the slaves were tired of not having liberty, and they fought back against slavery and the slave patrol.

The slaves of the American South did not always accept their reality of bondage. The History Channel documentary *Slave Catchers, Slave Resisters* depicts how the slaves fought back in one of the most renowned patrol attacks:

> ***One winter evening in Alexandria, Virginia, the local patrol acts on a tip that slaves are frequenting a certain stretch of road. All the men have passes except two. As they March the two slaves back for punishment, the Patrol doesn't realize that the balance of power has now shifted. They pause to rest, and two of the men stalking them, Alfred [and] Spencer, spring out of the darkness, [beating the patrollers with clubs], free their friends, and disappear into the night. Spencer is later executed, and Alfred sold to a slave trader. Their owner receives fair market compensation for both men. (Buzz Luttrell, 2014)***

The slave was determined to make it clear that you were now

facing a person and not a piece of property, which frequently challenged the slave patrol. This resulted in a cat-and-mouse sort of game. A common slang a lookout uses in the neighborhood is "5-O" to alert others of the presence of police officers—a popular nickname for police after the television show Hawaii Five-O. Likewise, a slave on the lookout would shout "patrol" to alert other slaves of the presence of patrollers (Hadden, 2001, 109). This may alert slaves to the "unwelcome intrusion" from patrollers into the slave quarters. A "quick-thinking slave scooped up ashes from the fireplace, opened the door, threw the ashes into the patrollers' faces, and then everyone inside ran past the blinded [slave patroller] (Hadden, 2001, 107). Former slave Fannie Dorum recalled slaves tied vines across heavily used highways or paths "in order to knock the patrolman off his horse" and would later laugh about it (Hadden, 2001, 132). These agonizing games would get much more serious when "two patrolmen had…their homes burned down, while another had his barn and cattle destroyed" (Hadden, 2001, 132).

Another occasion where the confrontation became violent was when male slaves attacked the slave patrol as they broke up a party:

> ***Led by a newly arrived African slave…hand to hand they fought and struggled with each other amid the terrific explosion of firearms — oaths and curses mingled with prayers of the wounded***

> ***and the groans of the dying! Two patrollers died in the conflict, and another had his arm broken, while six slaves perished, and two of their fellow bondsmen lay wounded as well. (Hadden, 2001, 133)***

Perhaps it was the possibility that emancipation for slaves might be possible that caused frustration that was previously denied by the slave patrol and became unbearable. Slaves resisted slavery by pretending sickness, slow work pace, poor production, hiding or destroying tools and equipment, and up to active, aggressive resistance. The fragile relationship between the police and African Americans arguably hasn't changed since the days of slavery. The mistrust, protest, and active, aggressive resistance still continue.

In addition to this, the two, the modern police and the slave patrol, do share a slight similarity in the description of the weapons they used to maintain their control over society. Renowned sociologist of policing Egon Bittner, in his notable work, The Functions of the Police in Modern Society (1970), contends that police are defined by their capacity to use force. Bittner argues that "police work refers to the fact that policemen are viewed as the fire it takes to fight the fire." He argues that "what separates the police from other institutions is their capacity and license to use force, including deadly force. Who does not realize that the police have guns, sticks, handcuffs, and fast cars and the authority to use them against us?" (Bittner, 1980, 14). As is still reflected in the heavily armed modern police forces, all policing has its roots in the function of men of weapons.

To better safeguard themselves and the public from any threats they may meet, police officers must be outfitted with standard equipment in all police agencies across the United States. These equipment and weapons they may carry include extra ammunition, body camera, bulletproof vests, duty belt, flashlight, handcuffs, radio, baton, knife, pepper spray, pistol or firearm, shotgun or assault rifle, and a TASER gun. Officers may not carry all the listed items simultaneously, but they are available for them.

In comparison, the slave patrol weapons were much more archaic. The slave patrol was often equipped with "guns, whips, and binding ropes…[a] few slaves reported that patrollers carried paddles instead of whips, but this appears to have been unusual" (Hadden, 2001, 123). These instruments were a means of intimidation, but occasionally, lethal force was used against resisting slaves. The rope was often used to bring slaves back to their owners, that is if they were not mauled to death by the slave-hunting dogs.

In Birmingham, Alabama's Kelly Ingram Park, there is a statute of a teenage boy being attacked by the police and a dog. The image appeared on the front page of the New York Times, the Los Angeles Times, the Washington Post, and newspapers in Asia, Europe, Africa, and Latin America. It's a photograph showing

White police officer Dick Middleton attacking 15-year-old African American Walter Gadsden with a police dog in May of 1963. In response to Dr. Martin Luther King Jr.'s call for 3,000 black schoolchildren to demonstrate, aka the “Children's Crusade,” against segregation in the streets, police commissioner Eugene "Bull" Connor let loose police dogs and fire hoses and ordered the children to be arrested in large numbers. “President John F. Kennedy said it made him sick” (Davis, 2023; LeDuff, 2015). Conner told police to let White residents get closer, and he said: “I want ‘em to see the dogs work. Look at those niggers run” (Spruill, 2016, 61).

Malcolm X believed that the only way to stop a police dog from attacking civil rights protesters was to kill the dog:

> ***If a dog is biting a black man, the black man should kill the dog, whether the dog is a police dog, a hound dog, or any kind of dog. If a dog is sicced on a black man when that black man is doing nothing but trying to take advantage of what the government says is supposed to be, then that black man should kill that dog...or any two-legged dog who sics the dog on him.” (Spruill, 2016, 57)***

I reflected on this Birmingham “teenage boy, police, and

dog" image in 2022 when I, as the chief of police at WCCCD, established the first K-9 unit for the college. A colleague police chief advised me that when he started a K-9 unit at his university a few years prior, the Board of Regents asked him if he was trying to remind the students of "Selma." I advised my command team to procure a K-9 exclusively for bomb searching. Attacks by police dogs on Black people often brought up unsettling memories of the time of slavery, when slave catchers and the slave patrol used bloodhounds to hunt down runaway slaves.

While slaves often sought their God-given right of freedom and ran away, they were pursued and often captured by the most feared and ferocious "negro dogs." The bloodhound was perhaps the fugitive slave's worst nightmare. The narrative of former slave Henry Waldon described the terror of being hunted by these bloodthirsty beasts:

> ***Them hounds would worry you and bite you and have you bloody as beef ... They would tell you to stand still and put your hands over your privates ... They would set them on you to see them bite you. Five or six or seven hounds bitin' you on every side, and a man settin' on a horse holding a doubled shotgun on you." (Spruill, 2016, 53)***

There is no exaggeration in saying that these "negro dogs" were a savage breed capable of mauling a slave to death. Perhaps it is true that the common practice of using dogs for tracking is based on the desire to prevent slaves, mostly Black Africans, from fleeing. According to slave narratives, they never forgot what the slave patrol, slave catchers, and hounds were going to do:

> ***In every district dey had about twelve men dey call patterrollers. Dey ride up and down and round looking for niggers without passes... When slaves run away, dey always put de bloodhounds on de tracks... Dey had de dogs trained to keep dey teeth out you till dey told' em to bring you down. Den de dogs would go at your throat, and dey'd tear you to pieces, too. After a slave was caught, he was brung home and put in chains. (Spruill, 2016, 53)***

During American slavery, the slave catcher and the slave patrol used the "negro dogs" or bloodhounds to hunt, attack and intimidate African American slaves. A police officer charging his K-9 dog to attack defenseless Black males was once a slave patroller savagely unleashing his bloodhounds to pursue slaves. Bull Conner and White racist police unleashed their German Shepard police dogs on Civil Rights protestors, exercising their 1st Amendment rights. In situations where they do not treat White people identically, the police nonetheless utilize vicious K-9 dogs against Black people throughout the United States (Stewart, 2020). After the Civil War and the 13th Amendment abolished slavery, the use of attack dogs against African Americans continued. The German shepherd is currently the most common breed of police canine. During World War II, the breed was employed against prisoners in German concentration camps. “Hitler often referred to the German shepherd as the canine equivalent to the Aryan race” (Dowd, 2022).

Today, a dog is a White man’s best friend if the dog is a modern-day police K-9 and a Blackman’s worst enemy. The Marshall Project reported that police dog bites send more people to the hospital than any other kind of use of police force, and the bite victims are predominantly Black. A 1991 lawsuit filed by the American Civil Liberties Union and the NAACP against the LAPD, alleging that the LAPD was committing excessive force using dogs, indicated that “900 Los Angelenos [were] bitten by dogs between 1990 and 1993, [and] 90 percent of whom were Black and Hispanic” (Dowd, 2022). A 2015 US Department of Justice report on the Ferguson police department determined that the “Ferguson Police Department engages in a pattern of deploying canines to bite individuals when the articulated facts do not justify this significant use of force... leaving serious puncture wounds to nonviolent offenders, some of them children” (Spruill, 2016, 45). The report also concluded that the Ferguson police department “appears to use canines not to counter a physical threat but to inflict punishment" (Stewart, 2020, 192). A 2015 Center for Policing Equity study found that "the rate at which officers used force by canine against Black people was more than double that for White people" (Stewart, 2020, 193).

Fatal police K9 dog attacks are uncommon, and the Courts ruled that a death caused in the apprehension of a felon doesn't "outweigh the dogs' proven benefits for effective law enforcement" (Robinette v. Barnes, 1988). However, there are a few cases where a police dog killed someone that requires serious scrutiny:

> ***1984.*** ***A man suspected of being in the course of a commercial burglary, hiding inside a darkened building, was apprehended by a police dog who bit him on the neck. The suspect died shortly thereafter.***
>
> ***1990.*** ***A homeless woman, Laurene MacLeod, was sleeping in an abandoned house when she was attacked by a police K-9 in West Palm Beach, Florida. The dog involved in the incident was a 108 lb. German Shepherd. The K-9 bit the victim extensively throughout her body, even after being handcuffed and while she was lying face down on the ground. MacLeod died 15***

> ***hours later in the hospital.***
>
> ***2012:*** ***An elderly man sleeping under a bush in a residential area was attacked by a police K-9 deployed to search for a burglary suspect. The victim died about a month later in [a] hospital from complications of the attack.***
>
> ***2018:*** ***The victim, Joseph Pettaway, was in a private residence making house repairs in Montgomery, Alabama. He was mistaken for a burglar. The police were called used their K-9 to search the house. The victim died from a ruptured artery in his leg (Polsky, n.d.).***

Attack-trained police dogs are extremely aggressive, and they have the potential to inflict lethal force.

It's apparent that people and the Courts value police dogs over the lives of African Americans. The peril is that some modern-day police often use the K-9 dogs against African Americans, similar to how the slave patrol used the bloodhounds against slaves. For example, a 14-year-old boy suspected of trespassing, waiting for his friend inside an abandoned house, was attacked by a police K-9, causing puncture wounds to his arm. The boy said that the police officers afterward laughed about the attack (Stewart, 2020, 192). While the slave patrol used horses as a means of transportation, the modern-day police-mounted horse units do not appear to affect African Americans disproportionately negatively.

In 2014 and 2015, I had the opportunity to attend Police Week with WCCCD's Honor Guard in Washington, D.C. In 1962, President Kennedy proclaimed May 15 as National Peace Officers Memorial Day and the calendar week in which May 15 falls as National Police Week. Established by a joint resolution of Congress, National Police Week pays special recognition to those law enforcement officers who have lost their lives in the line of duty for the safety and protection of others. I was deeply impressed with the various police department's attractive mounted horse units on display. There had to be at least 100 mounted units from different agencies across the country lined up near the police memorial. Police officers in various uniforms sat on their horses, side by side with their brothers and sisters in blue, as part of the police week activities. Many of them participated in the North American Police Equitation Council (NAPEC) competition. Police-mounted units are an excellent form of public relations engagement. A mounted unit was added to the Wayne State University Police Department's outstanding collection of law enforcement equipment in 2017 (Hunter, 2020). A police officer could stand on a corner all day and go unnoticed, but if the officer were riding a horse, they would stick out, and people would stop to talk to them, especially children, who would want to touch the horses. It's often said that a police officer on a horse is equal to ten officers on foot. The police-mounted unit is excellent for crowd control. Occasionally, the police on horseback are deployed during protests, civil disturbances, or riots. There is a risk of people being trampled during these protests, which may result in injury or death.

Coincidentally, the most frequent mode of transportation accessible in the eighteenth and nineteenth centuries was utilized by slave patrols in rural areas: they rode horses. The slave patrol on horses had a huge advantage over the runaway slaves who were on foot. "Patrollers also relied upon horses for purposes of intimidation. A mounted man presents an awesome figure, and the power and majesty of a group of men on horseback at night could terrify slaves into submission. And since patrollers carried no distinguishing equipment, in the dark, any cluster of mounted men might be mistaken by a slave for patrollers" (Hadden, 2001, 121).

Typically, slave patrols traveled on horseback in packs of four or five White men, very similar to today's modern police-mounted unit. In many American cities nowadays, it's common to see police officers riding horses. Police still use this antiquated yet effective mode of transportation and patrol. An online media outlet erroneously portrayed the Lake County Sheriff's Department as dressing their police horses like the KKK when their intent was to dress up their police horses as ghosts for Halloween (Mann, 2022).

The American public does not get a clear picture from the media when it comes to police corruption. A critical thinker should be able to see that sensationalism is a strategy employed to try to capture an audience's attention. Only 0.02% of American police officers are involved in corruption, according to the Bureau of Justice. The police "breaking news" headlines that open the five o'clock news are not necessarily genuine despite the fact that the media generates money by selling stories (Morey, n.d.).

However, police corruption has been around for a long time. Some of the worst cases involved in 1895 NYPD captain Alexander Williams "collect[ing] money from criminals, including the madams of several brothels, and make a fortune as a result"; in the 1980s, Miami police played a part in large amounts of cocaine being smuggled into South Florida from Latin America; 1960, the Chicago police having eight officers charged with running a large-scale burglary ring; the Philadelphia police department in the 1990s conducted a series of unreported raids on crack houses where officers would steal from suspects; and 2012 towing scandal by the Baltimore police department involving 50 officers and generating hundreds to thousands of dollars just to mention a few (7 of the most corrupt police, n.d.). My analysis of police corruption follows a critical evaluation of the modern police correlation with southern slave patrols.

On one occasion, a slave wrote a letter to his slave master complaining that the slave patrol "told a good many miserable lies on me which has given me a great deal of trouble" in hopes of being spared a beating (Hadden, 2001, 118). In comparison, in 2018, a Black teenager, Christopher Parham, was arrested by plainclothes NYPD for driving his scooter recklessly and without a helmet. The police officers accused Parham of violently resisting, and they did not use force to arrest him. A surveillance video was released that proved the NYPD officers lied. Parham did not resist, and the officers tackled and tased him repeatedly. The district attorney dropped the charges (Stern, 2020). A list of 74 Wayne County police officers who have been found to be unreliable witnesses and or liars in court cases was published by Wayne County Prosecutor Kym Worthy under the Brady-Giglio list in 2022, including a former police officer from WCCCD named DaJuan Dickerson mentioned previously (Neavling, 2022). A man was exonerated after serving 19 years in prison after the "Innocence Project" uncovered that police officers lied under oath to cover up shooting him.

Termaine Joseph Hicks, a 26-year-old Popeyes manager, was shot by a police officer in 2001. The officer later testified in court that Hicks reached for a revolver after he was caught raping a lady in an alleyway in Philadelphia. After a jury found Hicks guilty of rape, the judge handed down a sentence of up to 25 years in jail. Hicks, however, has always given a different tale, claiming that he rushed into the alley to aid the woman after hearing her scream. He reached for his phone to call 911, but the cops arrived out of nowhere, shot him in the back, and then wrongfully arrested him.

However, the conviction was based on shaky evidence and fabricated police testimony, presumably in an effort to cover up a botched police shooting. "Mr. Hicks' case is yet another example of the pervasive problem of police perjury in the criminal legal system.

The cover-up of shooting an innocent man required the false testimony of three officers and the acquiescence of a dozen more." The Innocence Project, in collaboration with the Philadelphia Conviction Integrity Unit (CIU), took on Mr. Hicks' case and, with exculpatory post-conviction evidence, compelled District Attorney Larry Krasner to concede and moved to vacate Mr. Hicks' conviction (Innocence staff, 2020). Another slave patrol malfeasance was bribery.

At times, some members of the slave patrol could be bribed "if slaves had the right goods and patrolmen had weak principles. Enslaved blacks who provided food, liquor, or other goods (stolen or not) could receive safe passage from a patroller, despite not having a valid ticket" (Hadden, 2001, 118). The modern police today are identical to receiving exactions as the slave patrol that birthed them. For example, in 2018, Detroit Deputy Police Chief Celia Washington was sentenced to a year in prison for accepting nearly $4,000 in cash bribes, accepted a $5,000 Ford Fusion, allowed the owner of a tow company to pay her nearly $800 birthday party bar tab in 2016, accepted free oil changes, $2,400 in repair work to her vehicle and a $2,700 loan from another towing company.

Deputy Chief Washington was in charge of the police department's municipal towing permits and was accused of rigging the towing rotation in favor of the tow company owner who bribed her (Burns, 2018). It's not uncommon for food establishments to offer free or discounted meals and drinks to police officers on duty, which many do not consider to be bribery, even though the payback is for the store or restaurant to have more police presence. I even recalled a bar that occasionally offered off-duty officers free alcoholic drinks.

Alcoholism is a bad habit that attached itself to modern-day police as it evolved from the slave patrol. Modern-day law enforcement personnel typically have more alcohol-related issues than a cross-section of the rest of the general population in a given community. Police officers tend to get arrested more often than other drivers for driving while intoxicated (Parker, 2012), and driving drunk could be so much more dangerous to the community. For example, on August 4, 2001, NYPD off-duty officer Joseph Gray killed four pedestrians, including a pregnant mother and her unborn child, when he was driving drunk in Brooklyn. It was later discovered that other officers were drinking with Gray in the NYPD parking lot and at a topless bar. His blood alcohol level was at least twice over the legal limit. Gray was sentenced to 5-15 years in prison for second-degree manslaughter (Donnelly, 2011). Alcoholism was also a problem for the slave patrol officers during slavery.

Hadden describes the slave patrol's "shameful neglect" in patrolling while being drunk on duty:

> ***Masking the serious nature of their work, patrol groups could become quite rowdy and boisterous***

> ***in carrying out their duties. Slaves like Charity Bowery, born in 1782, remembered that the slave patrol near her North Carolina plantation was 'frequently intoxicated.' South Carolina patrol groups were particularly well known for excessive drinking, according to slave testimonies and references in colonial law. In the wake of the 1739 Stono rebellion, the South Carolina legislature noted that since 'many irregularities have been committed by former patrols, arising chiefly from their drinking too much liquor before or during the time of their riding on duty . . . any person whatsoever who shall be drunk during the time of his service on the patrol, shall be subject to the penalty of forty shillings. (Hadden, 2001, 85-86)***

It is inevitable that the slave patrol and police officers would turn towards alcohol consumption. "Socializing and drinking with other patrollers helped pass the time during tedious nights of patrol duty" (Hadden, 2001, 86). I assume that the slave patroller drank alcohol to relieve the guilt associated with oppressing and beating slaves in light of the Declaration of Independence. Yet the very nature of police work increased the likelihood that officers would get drunk. "They respond to domestic disturbances, bar fights…fatality accidents and suicides in which alcohol was a factor" (Parker, 2012).

In conclusion, the tasks and obligations of the slave patrol and contemporary law enforcement are comparable. Both of them were involved in beating Black people who fled or ran away, stopping and searching people, seizing firearms, patrolling an area or attacking Black people, and using discretion while carrying out their tasks and stakeouts. Secondly, we addressed the requirements of the appointments to the slave patrol as well as a police officer. In particular, they both took an oath of office and wore badges, and their activities were subject to judicial interpretation of the laws and statutes. Next, with a significant discussion of the role religion played in the fears of slave rebellions, the slave patrol waged a war on religious leaders.

Religion is potent with power; what else will convince a person to strap a bomb to themselves and kill and die "in the name of God." The Black preacher's allegiance is to the Gospel of Christ. Minister Louis Farrakhan stated, *"I love the preachers because these are the men and women; if they do their job right, Black people would be free overnight; that is the truth"* (Farrakhan, 1983). Nat Turner and John Brown saw themselves as religious freedom fighters. It's this fear of the threat of religious leaders that may have resulted in the assassination of Dr. Martin Luther King Jr. as well as Malcolm X at the hands of modern-day law enforcement. Organized policing was one of the many types of social controls imposed on enslaved African Americans in the South as well as Blacks in modern-day America.

To accomplish this task, they both carried weapons to inflict punishment, including guns, whips, chains, clubs, and so forth. Lastly, we contrasted a familiar problem, which was caused by the very nature of their jobs: abuse of alcohol.

Dr. Larry H. Spruill, Professor of History, contends that "[S]lavery is not dead yet. It is pretending to be dead, only that it may be let alone and rise again to do mischief" (Spruill, 2016, 59). Consider that on August 27, 2019, a White Aurora, Colorado police officer, Levi Huffine, hogtied in the back of a patrol car a Black female named Shataean Kelly. She complained that she couldn't breathe after falling face-first inside onto the car floor. Kelly's narrative sounded like a scene of a punished slave in the movie Roots. She pleaded, "I don't want to die like this, officer…I'm a good person…This is some slavery shit. I'm sorry. I'm so sorry, God ... It hurts so bad ... Please don't let me die back here…Master, I'll be good" (Cohen, 2020). "Slave patrols were, as are modern police forces, the face of white despotic power – enforcers of white domination" (Spruill, 2016, 60). "Slaves' unapproved absence changed their status to "fugitives" resulting in dreadful consequences and punishment" (Spruill, 2016).

Modern day police refer to suspects wanted for an outstanding warrant as a fugitive. I recall several arrests that I made for a suspect wanted for warrants where the title of the report was "one arrest – fugitive." If modern-day police stop and search like a slave patrol, have dogs like a slave patrol, and shoot and kill like a slave patrol, then they probably are the modern version of the slave patrol.

Chapter 6: The Solution to Reforming the Police

"No one is more hated than he who speaks the truth." – Plato

"You're either part of the solution or you're part of the problem." - Eldridge Cleaver

"Sometimes the best solution is the most painful option" — Dr. Jacinta Mpalyenkana, Ph.D., MBA

Throughout this writing, my main focus has been on the slave patrol and how it has evolved into modern-day police. I do not loathe law enforcement; I actually love law enforcement— it motivates me to criticize and seek a solution. I've been in the security police profession for at least 40 years. Because the focus of this section is on reasonable solutions to police abuse against African Americans, an issue that is important in the context of police reform, it may be worthwhile to explore why telling the truth matters. I'm sure I will lose some friends, and enemies will reveal themselves for sharing my perspective on law enforcement. If my analogy is wrong, then present historical evidence and/or facts to refute my arguments. However, please don't get mad at me for pointing out wrong. As *Minister Farrakhan* said at the 1985 Million Man March:

> ***I come in the tradition of the doctor who has to point out, with truth, what's wrong. And the pain is that power has made America arrogant. Power and wealth have made America spiritually blind, and the power and the arrogance of America make you refuse to hear a child of your slaves pointing out the wrong in your society…we must not shrink from the responsibility of pointing out wrong."(Farrakhan, 2020)***

You can't slap the medical doctor if they say you have cancer. You simply take medicine that will help your body heal itself. It's not enough just to point out what's wrong with policing; we must offer solutions.

> ***The truth is very important, no matter how negative it is. It is imperative that you learn the truth. Not necessarily the facts, I mean that that***

> ***can come. But the facts can stand in front of the truth and almost obscure the truth. It is imperative that students learn the truth of our history; however sad, however mordant, however terrible, we must know it. The only way out of something is all the way through it. You must see it, read it, study it, and then you can pass through it. You see it is imperative that young white men and women study Black American history. It's imperative that blacks and whites [know what happened]. (Angelou, 2024)***

Maya Angelou powerfully emphasizes the importance of seeking and learning the truth about our shared history; however unpleasant parts of it may be. We can only move forward in understanding and bringing people together as equals by facing hard truths. Students of all backgrounds would benefit from her wisdom here.

Dr. Martin Luther King said, *"We can never be satisfied as long as the Negro is the victim of the unspeakable horrors of police brutality"* (Waxman, 2020). It's evident today that African Americans haven't experienced a society free of police brutality.

In our previous discussion, *"I Can't Breathe," "Police Brutality and Race,"* and *"Similarities between Police and the Slave Patrol,"* I criticized that law enforcement today is an evolution of a

White supremacy system that utilizes police to keep controls and oppress the Black community. My arguments are not desolate. Retired Philadelphia police captain Ray Lewis, who is Caucasian, is scolding U.S. policing and shows up at various protests wearing his police uniform. Lewis proclaimed, "[p]olice really are oppressing not only the black community but also the whites" (Wood, 2014).

Many scholars today, including Harvard professor of history, race, and public policy Khalil Gibran Muhammad, "traces the history of policing in America to 'slave patrols' in the antebellum South, in which white citizens were expected to help supervise the movements of enslaved Black people" (Walsh, 2021).

It is worth mentioning, however, that most police officers are not consciously racist, trained to act as judge, jury, and executioner in their interactions with the Black community. The regrettable truth is that the decent officers - the ones who take seriously their oath of office to respect the Constitution, serve and protect their fellow citizens, and keep the peace - are increasingly being overshadowed by the few "bad apple" police officers. These "good" officers tend not to get much, if any, attention from the press. Loyola University criminology professor Dr. Ronal Serpas, former head of three large police agencies, said:

> ***The bad apples are not unique to policing. Every profession on earth has some group of people***

> ***who are bad apples in their profession – lawyers, doctors, dentists, nurses. Police exercise a power that those people don't. You can pick your lawyer or your doctor. You don't get to pick your cop. So, police officers have to be held to a higher standard than other professions." (Wagner, 2020)***

There are some good police officers; it's getting more difficult for the public to tell the difference. We similarly need to ask, *where are the good officers*?

We seldom hear about police like Officer Alexis Callaway of the Senoia, Georgia, Police Department. She responded to a citizen's residence and saved a choking baby using life-saving first aid. She said afterward, *"I think he was one month old, now gets the rest of his life."* Obscured from America's living rooms during the evening news was Jamestown, New York Police Officer Mark Conklin. He ran towards danger, risked his own life, entered a house engulfed in flames, and rescued an entire family from a certain death.

What about Florida Highway Patrol Trooper Toni Schuck? She crashed her patrol vehicle into a car driven by a drunken driver who was headed toward a bridge where thousands of walkers and runners were participating in a 10K race for charity. There are officers ready, willing, and able to neutralize the threat of an active shooter all across the United States, like the officers of the Nashville police department. On March 27, 2023, these courageous officers stopped an active shooter at a school, saving many lives (Heroic Stories, 2021). These are just a few of the good officers who truly protect and serve every single day. Such are like retired Detroit police and retired WCCCD police officer Eric Eaves, who often told me, "Chief, I love what I do, and I thank you every day for giving me the opportunity to serve." Being a police officer is really a noble profession.

Being a police officer is analogous to being a mighty warrior for God. The police are to serve and protect people and humanity from the evils of the world and community. The Holy Bible (Matthew 5:9) reads, "Blessed are the peacemakers, for they will be called children of God." This does not mean for someone to be passive and meek. A "peacemaker" is someone who reconciles people in their conflicts and disagreements with one another. A police officer brings about peace by taking the initiative to intervene in disputes with the aim of mending fences between the disputing parties. No wonder that police officers are sometimes referred to as peace officers. Yet, somehow, in the Black community, the role of the police officer has gone off track. Unfortunately, it's the unwarranted aggressive, hostile, brutal, and fatal actions of the police that have ignited the phrase, *"no justice, no peace."*

In his non-fiction book, An American Crime Fighter, Lee Richardson Jr. describes the daily task of a lawman:

> ***You must be a social worker, a psychiatrist, a big brother or sister, a marriage counselor, deliver babies, give first aid, give legal advice, appear in court whenever summoned, be prepared for any violent contingency, and take control of any emergency situation, hazmat (handling hazardous materials), hazardous storms, flood emergencies, barricaded gunman, attempted suicides, hostage situations, bomb threats, explosions, assist firefighters and fire victims, save lives whenever and wherever possible and, most of all, be prepared for ambush to protect your partner and yourself. This will enable you to live to fight crime and save lives another day. To be able to return to duty day after day is an absolute must. (Richardson, 2017, 12)***

Maintaining peace, combating crime, addressing safety and security issues, and upholding the law are the objectives of policing.

Just as the LAPD intended when they created the motto, “Serve and Protect,” this should be the aim and purpose of the profession. Serving crime victims, the community, their superiors, one another, the organization, and the profession is the primary responsibility of police officers. Service must be the primary focus of the police to the community, including the Black community. How do we arrive at the belief that the institution of policing is perfectible, and how can society restore legitimacy to the police in the United States?

Before it is too late and extreme measures such as defunding or abolishing police become a reality, we must reform and change the behavior of the American police. The problem is not entirely the police itself nor the Black community, but the history of American slavery, which we don't like to talk about. A systemic overhaul is required before a police reform can be implemented. The African American community wants to feel protected by the police, but the police struggle to successfully communicate with the Black residents in the neighborhoods they serve because they lack knowledge of how slavery contributed to their racial superiority complex. Police reform should start by giving proper training on how modern police evolved from the slave patrol to new recruits and veterans, enhancing community policing and police accountability. The police must change how they do things in their interactions with Black people.

In 2017, I attended the International Chief of Police conference in Philadelphia. At the opening ceremony, Philadelphia police commissioner Richard Ross Jr., in his opening remarks, said something that struck a nerve and stuck with me throughout the years. Commissioner Ross said:

I remember my dad tells me a story. It was a day he was sitting around and he was watching my mom cook; I guess football wasn't on. He didn't have anything better to do, so he was harassing her about how she was cooking. She happened to be making a roast that day. [He said], I saw her cut the ends of the roast off before she put it in the roasting pan. My dad, being curious, says babe, why did you do that? She says, I really don't know. I just learned it from watching my mom, and that's how you make a good roast. That's just how I do it. But if you want to know, call my mom up and ask her. And he did that. He said, mom because, he called grandma mom, he says, why does your daughter cut the ends of the roast off before she put it in the roasting pan? And she says that's the way you make a good roast. Why are you asking me that? That's how I learned it; that's the way it's done. That's the way my mother taught me, and that's the way it should be done. You shouldn't ask questions like that. So, fortunately, my mom's grandmother was still living. So, my mom-in-law said, why don't you call her and ask her? It's really simple. So,

> ***he called the 90-year-old grandmother and said, Grandma, can you just explain why? You know your daughter and granddaughter are cutting the ends of the roast off before they put it in the roasting pan. And she said, baby they're still doing that? My pan simply wasn't big enough. That's why I did it. So, I say that not to be funny, but to say that sometimes we are guilty of that in policing. How many times have you heard that's just the way we do it? So, it is those things that can hold us back. Those mentalities, but I submit to you that as police professionals, as long as we're willing to step beyond that and go beyond that, I know that we can continue to advance this profession. And I know that [policing] will be much better for it. (Ross, 2017)***

The future of policing in the United States can't afford to say or act as if, "That's the way we have always enforced the law."

The murder of George Floyd at the hands of former police officer Derek Chauvin and the Minneapolis police department was a wake-up call to White America that change was imperative. I witnessed hundreds or maybe thousands of people marching in the streets of Downtown Detroit as we increased patrols near the Curtis L. Ivery Central Educational Complex during the pandemic in 2020.

Most of the protesters, to my surprise, were young Caucasian men and women. They made demands for police reform, defunding, and/or abolishment, and they want America to seriously consider the issue of racial inequality. A White Republican journalist wrote:

> ***Seeing it unfold before my eyes — or maybe seeing this act unfold after seeing so many other similar acts unfold in a similar fashion over the last few years — has had a profound effect on me. George Floyd's death was a tipping point, not just for the Black Lives Matter movement or the movement to reform policing, but even for many white Republicans like me who once chose to believe — perhaps were taught to believe — that the fight to end institutionalized racism had already been won. Something inside me had been reluctant to believe the system was still being perpetuated today. No more…I've accepted that something in my white heart still needs to change. I am pushing myself to come to terms with my own heritage, my white privilege and my flawed beliefs, as well as to develop a better understanding of the experiences that people of color have living in America today. (Austin, 2020)***

It appears that some White Americans became aware of the institutional and individual racism and prejudice that affects African Americans and the need to eradicate it. The growth of the Black Lives Matter hashtag is a sign that people want an end to police violence against African Americans.

The Black Lives Matter hashtag was born after the July 13, 2013 acquittal of George Zimmerman of the murder of Trayvon Martin by Twitter users. A year later, in 2014, after Darren Wilson was not indicted for the murder of Michael Brown, the hashtag became predominant in an expression of anger and grief. After the George Floyd murder and the police assault in Lafayette Square a week later, when former President Trump did a photo op with the Bible, the #BlackLivesMatter hashtag skyrocketed. The hashtag "generated approximately 3.4 million original posts with 69 billion engagements—or roughly 13% of all posts and 15.5% of all engagements on Twitter in that period. #BlackLivesMatter content peaked on June 8, with some 1.2 million original posts mentioning the hashtag". It had been used in more than 25 million original Twitter posts as of April 30, 2021, and each of those posts had received around 444 billion likes, retweets, comments, or quotes, or roughly 17,000 engagements each. Today, the Black Lives Matter hashtag internet discussion continues to draw consistent attention (Wirtschafter, 2021). It's becoming evident that if policing does not change, internal grappling maybe its demise.

Police departments are becoming divided along racial lines, and officers are working in a toxic environment. After the George Floyd murder and protest in December 2020, a group of anonymous Black LAPD officers sent a letter to police chief Michael Moore complaining that White officers were expressing racist viewpoints in private group chats, on social media, and in the workplace. It was alleged that White officers posted bigoted and offensive comments such as, "Breonna Taylor is a fat slob and deserved what she got,"; "George Floyd had a criminal history, so he got what he deserved,"; and "these negro people kill their own and blame others for it." Chief Moore had to update the LAPD social media policy and issued disciplinary action to seven officers. In addition, two LAPD detectives retired in lieu of disciplinary action (Scott, 2022). The death of a retired Memphis police sergeant, who was considered a whistleblower in the Tyre Nichols murder, ignited many conspiracy theories.

On July 9, 2023, a retired Memphis homicide sergeant named Mark Lesure was found dead, lying face down in his driveway. Lesure was outspoken in criticizing the Memphis police department after the Tyre Nichols beating death by five of its officers. In an interview with the New York Times, Lesure said:

> ***Rookies were getting put on specialized units where they had no business being…Human beings' man, that's what happened. They let***

> ***their emotions get the best of them, and there was no veteran officer there to stop them. Usually, when vets are there, things go differently because we have that experience to say, 'I understand you're mad, but you got to stop. You can't do this; it isn't right. (Wright, 2023)***

Social media posts on Twitter claimed that LeSure was "found shot and dead in his driveway" and that he was a "good cop who got silenced by dirty cops" (Wright, 2023). However, these claims were not substantiated by law enforcement. Before police lose all credibility and legitimacy, change must be implemented.

To eliminate racial bias in policing, the solution must not involve "defunding the police" or "abolishing the police." First, let's examine the concept of defunding the police and what does it mean. The phrase "defund the police" refers to the idea of reallocating funds from police departments and redistributing them to community resources, including social services, youth programs, housing, education, and healthcare that don't involve policing. When using this phrase, activists may have different goals in mind; some advocate for small cuts, while others push for complete divestment as a first step toward ending modern police services. According to activists, defunding police agencies would better serve the purpose of preventing crime in communities by investing in community initiatives that deal with social concerns, including homelessness, poverty, and mental illnesses (Levin, 2020). Another peril to public safety would be abolishing the police.

The police abolition movement is a political movement that is mostly active in the United States and supports alternate public safety measures in place of policing. Police abolitionists disagree with the philosophy of police reformists and hold that policing is an intrinsically defective system that cannot be improved (Mertz, 2020). The War on Drugs has been the main factor in "the systematic mass incarceration of people of color in the United States," according to abolitionist scholars who claim that Americans are being over-policed, disproportionately African Americans and low-income people of color (Chilton, 2023). Neither “defund the police” nor “abolish the police” is practical.

While the idea of moving funding away from police departments and into community resources such as mental health appears plausible, a critical analysis reveals otherwise. First, the mental health crisis in America was created by the government taking away funding from mental hospitals. John Engler, a former governor of Michigan, closed more than a dozen psychiatric hospitals in 1997 to return treatment to the community in his opinion. The burden has shifted to encounters with law enforcement (Gutierrez, 2022). The solution would be for the State of Michigan to allocate and restore funding for mental health hospitals in Michigan. Decreasing funds for the police would likely reduce officers' salaries, which are already underpaid compared to professional athletes, despite the critical role they play in helping and protecting society from danger. Thus, lowering the salaries of police would likely increase corruption. Corruption within the Mexican police force is primarily caused by extremely low wages (Quinones, 1994). "Defund the police" would ultimately result in police taking bribes to ignore crimes and actively participate in criminal activity such as extortion and drug trafficking.

As for "abolishing the police," it is ludicrous to suggest society is able to function without police. What alternate public safety measure would respond to neutralize an active or mass shooter? According to the FBI, the annual numbers of active shooter incidents in the United States were: 2022 = 50; 2021 = 61; 2020 = 40; 2019 = 30; and 2018 = 30 (Active shooter, 2022). Much more alarming is the annual numbers of mass shootings in the United States, which were: 2022 = 647; 2021 = 690; 2020 = 610; 2019 = 417; and 2018 = 336 (Mass shootings, 2023). When I was chief of police at WCCCD, I made it mandatory that all armed officers had to attend quarterly active shooter response training. This by no means was a guarantee that an active shooter incident would not occur, but only that the WCCCD police authority department would rapidly respond. As proficient as police are in rapid deployment to an active shooter, the inaction of the 376 law enforcement personnel response to the Uvalde School shooting provokes the question: who else could do this? Even the school police chief, Pete Arredondo, was criticized for waiting more than an hour in the hallway of Robb

Elementary School (Despart, 2022). If there's no police, what entity would engage the shooter in the number one priority of stopping the killing?

Since we need police, our solution is reform. One area of reform would be education and training. As Malcolm X has stated, "Of all our studies, history is best qualified to reward our research." We can't be like Ron DeSantis, who depicts Jonathon Harris's painting, Critical Race Theory, as he'd prefer to ban discussions of American slavery. Modern-day police must be taught the true history of the American police. Slavery existed in colonial America during much of the history of police. The first unofficial police force in America was slave patrols, which were tasked with catching runaway slaves and returning them to their owners in the South, where slavery was essential to the economy (Hadden, 2001). This history should be part of the curriculum in the police academy and should be included in annual maintenance training for all police in the United States. Police annual maintenance training typically includes firearms re-qualification, legal updates, defensive tactics, and/or CPR/first aid. While these all are important, neither of them and the lack of them may lead to police extinction as racial violence and murder will. Perhaps, if police are made aware of how the slave patrol tactics contribute to how they treat African Americans, they may become more sensitive to police brutality toward Black citizens. Will teaching police about the tactics of the slave patrol modify their behavior?

Danny Glover said, “We have to begin to say, to tell ourselves the truth. James Baldwin, the great writer, once said, ‘If we cannot tell ourselves the truth of our past, we become trapped in it.’ And that's what we are; we're trapped in it. This country is trapped in not telling the truth” (@myskincolorisnotacrime, 2023). So, let’s tell the truth about the police evolving from the slave patrol. Police are trained to look at evidence and make conclusions based on facts. Perhaps such authentic conclusions were made by The National Law Enforcement Officers Memorial Fund, as they wrote in an article on their website:

> ***After the Civil War, Southern police departments often carried over aspects of the [slave] patrols. These included systematic surveillance, the enforcement of curfews, and even notions of who could become a police officer. Though a small number of African Americans joined the police force in the South during Reconstruction, they met active resistance. Though law enforcement looks very different today, the profession developed from practices implemented in the colonies. (Slave Patrols NLEOMF, n.d.)***

The National Law Enforcement Officers Memorial Fund

was established with the intention of remembering the sacrifices and bravery made by law enforcement, educating the public, and making the community a safer place for those who serve (NLEOMF Our purpose, n.d.). While some have criticized them for this publication, their efforts to educate the public are remarkable. Some other police chiefs have decided to tell the truth about the evolution of American policing.

In an open letter to fellow members of law enforcement, retired Detroit police chief and former Detroit Public Schools chief of police Ralph L. Godbee, Jr passionately argues:

> ***[Police] are surreptitiously the instrumentation that enforces the structural and, at times, exacerbates the social inequities of systemic racism that starts with the first organized police forces in America; slave patrols from Bull Connor to the War on Drugs; the Omnibus Crime bill to the seminal moment in our history where America witnessed a tipping point moment when George Floyd was murdered by four Minneapolis police officers right in front of what had been for 401 years our proverbial lying eyes. (Godbee, 2020)***

Chief Godbee opined that due to practices inherited from the slave patrol and the disproportionate criminalization of Black people, American policing requires comprehensive reform. Chief Godbee is joined by a White colleague in the narrative of the slave patrol's influence on policing.

Former Seattle police chief Norm Stamper, who authored two books, *To Protect and Serve: How to Fix America's Police (2016)* and *Breaking Rank: A Top Cop's Exposé of the Dark Side of American Policing (2005)*, acknowledges that the history of America policing includes the slave patrol:

> ***Is what we're doing [in policing] today working? No. The relationship between white cops and people of color, particularly Black people, is abysmal. The institution of American policing dates back to the formation of the slave patrols, where local police were actually assisting the slave patrols, if not replacing them. White people might say that was a long time ago, that trainings, policies and psychological screenings have improved. I would ask, how's that working for us? How's it working in the relationship between young people, poor people, and black people particularly? (Radke, 2020)***

Stamper believes that the slave patrol was responsible for the dysfunction of modern policing. The evidence is crystal clear. People came to the conclusion that something was toxic and seriously wrong with the policing system after witnessing George Floyd being slain by cops.

A recruit in a police academy asked a bewildered question to the biased policing instructor, “If Lady Justice is blindfolded, why are we studying differences in people” (Cultural Diversity, n.d.)? We all own prejudices that have an impact on all facets of our lives as well as the lives of others we interact with. Although everyone has both implicit and explicit biases, the latter are more worrisome because they are the ones we are least aware of. This includes police officers; they have their biases as well. Whether making an arrest based on probable cause, a detention based on reasonable suspicion, or a consensual interaction with a member of the neighborhood, the police officer treats everyone equally. That is what we as a society need to get to concerning law enforcement. The history of slave patrol tactics serves as a training objective to equip police officers with cultural competencies. Yet, there are two types of individuals who harbor prejudices.

Prejudice is particularly the act of assuming the worst about a person or a group of people without sufficient reason; it is a feeling, whether positive or negative, that is held before or unrelated to actual experience. According to Coffey, Eldefonso & Hartinger, the two types of prejudice are cultural condition and character condition prejudice:

> ***Culture-Conditioned Prejudice is a learned social phenomenon. As its name might imply, culture-conditioned prejudice is primarily learned or acquired in the normal process of social interaction. Thus, most people raised in an environment verbalizing antipathy toward blacks assume prejudicial behavior, for they have been taught deliberately and by subtle examples that the black is both different and inferior; they have known no other explanation from childhood on…Culture-conditioned prejudice can be 'unlearned'… [by bring[ing] them into contact with minority groups.***
>
> ***Character-Conditioned Prejudice is pure hatred or bias. This type of prejudice is quite firmly imbedded in the personality makeup, and attempts to rid people of it must be, needless to say, far more formidable than the just-cited techniques of eradicating culture-conditioned prejudice…[A] character-conditioned prejudice [person] almost has to hate, and if one of their***

> ***scapegoats or objects of venom is somehow eliminated from focus, they will inevitably seek out some other victim. "[A] character-conditioned prejudice [person] is more dangerous than the sociologically or culture-conditioned prejudiced person in a twofold sense. He or she is (1) present in all areas of the population among the educated, wealthy, and influential as well as the poor and ill-educated and is (2) more likely to be actively prejudiced and in a position to translate hatred into effective political or social action." (Coffey, A., Eldefonso, E., & Hartinger, W., 1982, 10-12)***

Thus, the culturally conditioned prejudiced person may be cured by confronting one another's unfavorable viewpoints. In other words, social exposure to other cultures and experiences helps to overcome prejudices. Some people might be unable to let go of their preconceptions, but that does not mean they have to act on them. Unfortunately, the character-conditioned person may already be educated about other cultures, yet they still harbor hate. Hate becomes an essential part of their personality. Therefore, culturally conditioned police officers should be exposed to the history of slave patrol tactics from southern societies. The character-conditioned police officer, on the other hand, must be "weeded out" by the use of psychological testing and expelled from law enforcement. Perhaps Derek Chauvin was a character-conditioned prejudiced police officer, and he was least concerned about how the public viewed his demonic behavior.

As we have already explained, Peel's police were not only the first modern police model, but they were, in every respect, the first form of community policing. From a historical perspective, there is uncertainty regarding who created community policing. Sir Robert Peel is frequently credited with developing the community policing concepts that served as the foundation for professional policing in London in the early 19th century. Peel's guiding principles emphasized proactive policing that relies on good ties with community people to reduce crime and increase police effectiveness. Peel's principles for "community policing" state that:

- ***The power the police hold depends upon public approval.***
- ***In order to maintain public respect, police must secure willing public cooperation as well as obey laws themselves.***
- ***The cooperation of the public diminishes proportionately with police use of public force.***
- ***Police must demonstrate impartial service to the***

law in order to maintain the favor of the public.

- ***The ultimate goal recognizes police are the public and public are police. (DeMeester, LaMagdeleine, Norton, Austin, Johnston & Nadeau, n.d.)***

Any police officer can implement community policing by adhering to Peel's "community policing" standards, even the police that captured slaves.

Of far greater interest is the story of the slave patrol of Virginia participating in community policing with captured bondsmen. There is no foundation for this story; it is simply apocryphal, intended to indoctrinate by example. On one occasion, slave patrollers heard hymns and religious music sung by slaves. They followed the music to a slave gathering in the woods and swamps. Instead of breaking up the religious meeting, the slave patrol allowed it to continue and joined in singing hymns with the slaves. This would've been a good example of community slave patrolling; however, it did not occur. Likewise, modern-day police rarely practice community policing with controversial or Black religious groups.

Instead of community policing, police in New York arrested the Reverend Al Sharpton on May 8, 2008, along with hundreds of demonstrators as they protested the acquittal of three detectives in the 50-bullet shooting of an unarmed black man on his wedding day (Gardner, 2008). On the contrary, in 1961, the Monroe Police Chief and 30 armed officers broke into the local Nation of Islam temple's prayer service, beating Minister Troy X Cade, as well as men, pregnant women, and children. Cade's necktie was used in an unsuccessful attempt by the police to hang him from the temple's rafters. Despite being given a six-year term in Angola, a White racist mob was permitted to free him from his prison cell. He was taken back to North Louisiana, where the gang assaulted him and abandoned him there, believing he had been drowned. He miraculously survived by pretending to be drowned. His sentence was overturned after the Monroe incident, but Nation of Islam members countrywide began wearing bow ties instead of neckties to prevent the ties from being used as hanging cords. Troy Cade, now known as Minister Abdul Bey Muhammad, was 93 years old and still alive and well in 2023 (Minister Abdul Bey Muhammad, 2022).

Enhancing community policing is essential to the survival of modern-day American policing. President Barack Obama issued an executive order on December 18, 2014, establishing the President's Task Force on 21st Century Policing. President Obama started it in response to the turmoil that erupted in Ferguson, Missouri, after Michael Brown was shot by a police officer there (Kaste, 2015). One of the essential recommendations was for police to embrace community policing:

> ***It must also be stressed that the absence of crime is not the final goal of law enforcement. Rather, it is the promotion and protection of public safety while respecting the dignity and rights of all. And public safety and well-being cannot be attained without the community's belief that their well-being is at the heart of all law enforcement activities. It is critical to help community members see police as allies rather than as an occupying force and to work in concert with other community stakeholders to create more economically and socially stable neighborhoods…Community policing is not just about the relationship between individual officers and individual neighborhood residents. It is also about the relationship between law enforcement leaders and leaders of key institutions in a community, such as churches, businesses, and schools, supporting the community's own process to define prevention and reach goals. (President's Task Force on 21st Century Policing, 2015, 42-43)***

The task force emphasized that the development of constructive relationships with community people is a necessary component of community policing.

Although the police can and frequently do use force to coerce compliance, they can also win the cooperation of those they deal with by using collaboration and consent, earning buy-in from the community. People respond primarily based on their perceptions of the fairness of the processes they go through and a corresponding assessment of whether they trust the intentions of the authority they are interacting with. The public's assistance is crucial to the police. They rely on voluntarily respecting police judgment, routinely abiding by the law, and actively working with police to reduce crime. When the public is less supportive of the police, these forms of collaboration decline. “Studies suggest that people value having the police talk to citizens and cooperate with citizens to solve community problems. They support more bike and pedestrian patrols because they like to perceive the police as friends and helpers, and they would support endeavors to improve the work of the police force much in the sense of what community and problem-oriented policing propose" (Tyler, 2003, 348). Community policing involves focusing on what fair policing means to people in the community. There were some in law enforcement who recognized the value of community collaboration early on.

Former NYPD officer, former Kansas City police chief, and former San Jose police chief Joseph D. McNamara was considered by some police professionals as the “father” of community policing. Chief McNamara taught San Jose police officers how to build connections with local businesses, citizens, and community leaders in high-crime areas, elevating those who did and demoting those who did not. He added African Americans and minorities to the predominantly white police force in the city and removed officers who had been accused of using excessive force repeatedly. In response to the 1991 Rodney King beating, he was the lone police chief who called for the resignation of the LAPD chief, Daryl Gates. Chief McNamara said, “that [Rodney King] tape has cast a cloud over the credibility of all police.” He criticized the militarization of police and the war on drugs extensively (Vitello, 2014).

Police agencies today must acquire this concept and be more responsive to the community's needs. I recognized this as the chief of police at WCCCD. Our department participated every October in the nationwide community initiative called *Coffee with a Cop.* The idea was to bring the college police officers and community members together over a cup of coffee, donuts, and sometimes sandwiches to discuss issues and learn more about each other. I saw it as successful when a student told us where to set up a speed trap on campus to get drivers to slow down. We even hired a dispatcher from the student body when she asked, “How can I get a job with you guys?” WCCCD police additionally participated in an annual hat, scarf, and glove drive to support and donate to homeless shelters as a means of community engagement. Unlike former Detroit police Chief James Craig, his predecessor, Chief James White, appeared to understand the importance of community support.

Former Detroit police Chief Craig appeared to have alienated some metropolitan residents. In September of 2021, James Craig traveled to Belle Isle to formally announce his intention to run for governor of Michigan. However, demonstrators from the community yelled over him at the microphone and forced him to leave after only uttering a few words. The protestors surrounded the podium, blasting blow horns, carrying anti-Craig signs, and chanting, "James Craig has got to go" (Hutchinson, 2021). Contrastingly, Chief White, in 2022, launched a city-wide community outreach program called "Walk a Mile Wednesday with Chief James E. White." Chief White explains:

> ***We do walk a mile to get out and engage the community and to have a feel-good day with the community. We let them tell me how good I'm doing or how bad I'm doing, and we talk about what I can do better. I believe that DPD's success stems from the relationships we have with the residents we serve. For decades, our selfless officers have built strong bonds and bridges, and we will do our best to not only sustain them but to build many more. (Barmore, 2022)***

The only people who have the authority to judge whether the

police have succeeded or failed in the communities they serve are the residents of the community themselves. Instead, too often, the police and the community are isolated from each other in the “we vs them” mindset.

Through officer selection, training, and job experience, an "us versus them" mentality is established and perpetuated. This mentality shows in cynical views toward the public and implicit acceptance of misconduct, also referred to as "the blue wall of silence” (Nhan, 2014). When you work in law enforcement, you have the potential to either save or take another person's life. Officers think we are a unique set of individuals since we were chosen from hundreds or perhaps thousands of other applicants. We gradually start to distance ourselves from the rest of society due to this elitist feeling, which reinforces the belief that we are superior to the majority of people.

One of the main causes of the us vs. them syndrome is this feeling of elitism, together with the development of cynicism and the general lack of public awareness of the challenges faced by police officers throughout their careers. The typical police officer will experience more human tragedy in their first three years than most people do in their lifetimes. After their shift, police officers gather to swap "war stories" over a few cold ones. Earlier in their careers, these similar stories were more frequently shared with friends and family, who, being outside the profession, never truly understood. This kind of conduct sets off a risky cycle of social isolation. Police lose their optimism. It is inevitable that cops eventually develop dark, aloof souls and lose much of their trust in society, thus creating the "us versus them" police officer (Gugliotti, 2016).

Minister Louis Farrakhan analyzed the problematic heavy-handed policing tactics that may have resulted from the "we versus them" syndrome:

> ***The community is suffering. The people need a better relationship with the police, not with an oppressive force or an occupying army, but with a force that is present to serve and protect the people. Most policemen do not understand the common people of urban cities and the nature of problems that exist in the community. Their tactics are often heavy-handed. Some of the communities' own officers try to show their brother of blue officers how hard and vicious they can be in their handling of their own people. On the other hand, there are good law officers who sincerely wish to work to make the community safe for all who live and work there. People like to be policed by their own. The police who have grown up in the communities and live and understand the community would be the best***

ones to serve and protect as well as police their own community.

The police need to be sensitized, properly educated, and trained better. Each person who desires to become a police officer must be analyzed psychologically to determine their motives and a psychological profile should be done on each officer, particularly when they are serving a community where there are great cultural differences. A system of selection with a psychological analysis has to accompany the hiring.

It appears that many police are sick individuals who only want a license to maim, beat, and kill those who might fall victim to the law or who might fall into their hands for one reason or another. The community must be involved at the academy level and help in the sensitizing and education of the police so that the people feel that the police in their community are an extension of their community and not an occupying army in foreign territory. (Farrakhan, 1992, 20)

Minister Farrakhan's comments should be taken seriously as feedback on how the community perceives the police. Responding to public input regarding the community's needs and the best methods the police may assist in meeting those needs is a requirement for effective community policing. It considers the public's assessment of its own issues seriously.

I believe there are ways to offset the "us vs. them" syndrome and the negative attitudes developed over time. The key is for police chiefs, command staff, and supervisors to consistently emphasize community policing, especially in African American neighborhoods. Talks among police leaders must be about the direction of community policing and prompting city administrations to invest more substantially in encouraging police innovation and community engagement. The police must adopt the title of the *people's police.*

Police in the People's Republic of China are known as the "People's Police." The name signifies the importance placed on the concept of service. Local police stations put considerable effort into community relations and administer excellent crime prevention programs. A police officer's duties include knowing the general whereabouts of all residents in his district, educating the people concerning the country's laws and the government's philosophy, investigating crimes, and providing needed services to the public. These services include mediating disputes, transporting sick people to the hospital, helping lost persons find their way home, and identifying potential neighborhood safety hazards (Patterson, 1988).

It may appear that police in China do not spend as much time enforcing the law as officers in the United States. However, the major difference is that the Chinese perform what we consider non-law enforcement social services to build a rapport with the people. This effort to build respect is enhanced by a regulation requiring officers to salute pedestrians and drivers before correcting their mistakes. Executions are performed in public places and carried out by a single shot to the head. Following the philosophy that everyone in society is responsible for crime prevention, especially one's family. The family of a person being executed must buy the bullet, attend the execution, and dispose of the body (Patterson, 1988).

Thus, community policing is an essential ingredient to police reform, just as it was during the Peel period. The police and the community should function as two sides of the same coin, where the people are the police and vice versa. Too often in the Black community, the police have neglected to engage with religious groups and have frequently resorted to heavy-handed tactics. The modern-era police chief will need to be creative in devising innovative ways to engage the community.

The police will adopt community policing to become the people's police of the future. A straightforward process involves changing the ideas, perceptions, and attitudes of the community and the police through engagement, which will generate behavioral changes. This, in turn, will help control crime and foster positive relationships within the urban communities. However, it is inevitable that a small percentage of police officers—perhaps five percent—will neglect community policing and engage in acts of brutality. These police officers must be held to a higher standard and held accountable for their actions.

There is a dichotomy within the police departments: those who endorse community policing and equal treatment for all, including African Americans, and those who are racist and brutal. As early as 2006, the FBI warned that White supremacists were infiltrating law enforcement throughout the United States (Kanu, 2022). There is not only a need to enact department policies and legislature to prohibit police from being affiliated with white supremacist groups, but there needs to be strict accountability for excessive force and abusive actions of officers, particularly against African Americans. Civil Rights attorney Ben Crump applauded the quick arrest of the five Memphis police officers who beat and killed Tyre Nichols.

Crump declared, "We look at how swiftly the district attorney brought charges against them in less than twenty days. We want to proclaim that this is the blueprint going forward for any time any officers, whether they be Black or white, will be held accountable. No longer can you tell us we've got to wait six months to a year" (Hauck, 2023). However, a critical inquiry leads to the conclusion that those officers were quickly arrested because they were Black. Enhanced police accountability is essential in the

United States.

One of the impediments to police accountability is the “blue wall of silence.” The police in the United States have a rule of silence known as the "blue wall of silence" that forbids officers from disclosing the mistakes, wrongdoings, or crimes of their comrades, particularly when those mistakes or crimes involve police brutality. The officer being questioned would commit perjury or lie if asked about a case of alleged misconduct involving another officer by pretending not to know about the violation (Skolnick, 2002). I recall when I was a sergeant at Fairlane Town Center Security Police, a White male lieutenant and I witnessed three white officers stomping and kicking a handcuffed Black male as he lay on the pavement. I said to the lieutenant, “Do you believe this”? He replied, “Let’s put a stop to it.” I reported the incident with a recommendation for disciplinary action, but the security police director told me that my complaint could not be substantiated because there were no witnesses, and the lieutenant denied that the brutality occurred. Another Black female officer who had initially complained to me about the incident seemed to have had a case of amnesia. However, the “blue wall of silence” gets much worse than a mere “mall cop” episode.

A more intricate and striking illustration of the "blue wall of silence" occurred on October 20, 2014, when Laquan McDonald, an African American teenager, was shot and killed by Chicago Police. White police officer Jason Van Dyke and four other officers claimed "that McDonald had been slashing tires with a knife, ignored police requests to drop the knife, and approached or "lunged" at officers putting them in fear for their life... [Officer Van Dyke] shot McDonald in the chest and he was pronounced dead at the hospital" (Huq & McAdams, 2016, 216). However, it was later discovered from police dash cam video and a civilian witness that McDonald did not lunge towards officers and was walking away with the knife on his side. Van Dyke shot McDonald once, causing him to fall to the ground, then proceeded to empty his magazine, shooting his body 16 times (Huq & McAdams, 2016, 217).

As for officers who violate the "blue wall of silence," they risk their law enforcement careers, putting their lives and safety in peril. In 2012, after Baltimore detective Joe Crystal reported two officers for beating a drug suspect, "he became a target for taunts and harassment while on the job. His peer officers repeatedly failed to respond to his calls for backup; he received threats of perjury prosecution in the criminal matter that his whistle-blowing prompted; and a dead rat was left on his vehicle's windshield." Crystal resigned two years later (Huq & McAdams, 2016, 214).

The 1992 Mollen Commission, which investigated police corruption in the NYPD, concluded that "adherence to a 'code of silence' that keeps even honest cops silent about the misdeeds of their colleagues" was one of the reasons why officers didn't cross the line (Baer & Armao, 1995, 79). The general population believes that police abuse of authority is on the rise. Public disclosure regulations are seen as a check against this abuse of police power by various interest groups, most notably the press. A handful of towns have started using civilian review boards to handle accusations of police misconduct. The usage of these external boards developed from police departments' inability to adequately handle citizen complaints, much as the press' push for lax disclosure rules. The "Blue Wall of Silence" may be the most complex challenge in a police internal affairs inquiry to overcome (Powers, 2000), referred to as a "virtually impenetrable obstruction" (Skolnick, 2002).

Finding the facts is extremely difficult due to the police's "Blue Wall of Silence. The walls of silence in police stations can be even more challenging to break down than the world of organized crime. This is because you are dealing with individuals who are familiar with the system and know how to work around it. An oppositional criminal subculture that defends the rights of police who break the law thrives on a sense of loyalty and blue brotherhood. One straightforward guideline governs how many officers behave regarding the code of silence: an officer is not allowed to speak ill of or tell on a fellow cop. For example, the fact that so many cops witnessed the beating of Rodney King suggests that those involved thought they could rely on their coworkers to lie in the event of an investigation (Skolnick, 2002). As was foreseeable, the world was shocked by the killing of George Floyd on May 25, 2020, because Darnella Frazier witnessed the murder and posted a video of the incident on Facebook and Instagram. The footage contradicted the Minneapolis Police Department's official reports of Floyd's death (Bump, 2021).

While publicly exposing the “blue wall of silence” was once considered a remedy to encourage police officers to disclose wrongdoing by their peers, I propose an alternative method to minimize its effects: offering a monetary reward or a whistleblower reward. Nobody wants to unleash a snitching and counter-snitching campaign within the police department. Instead of simply punishing police officers who commit excessive force or brutality, states should offer monetary rewards to police officers who, when they are witnesses to such, turn in the officer who commits these acts. It is common knowledge that underpaid public servants and law enforcement officials are more likely to accept a reward to supplement their poor salaries (Becker & Stigler, 1974). Police officers are always looking for new law enforcement jobs where they may make more money and receive other benefits they don’t receive at their current agency. In an effort to solve crimes, law enforcement organizations have long offered rewards. Since 1950, the FBI has maintained a list of its "Ten Most Wanted" suspects, and since then, it has offered a reward of up to $100,000 for information that results in the immediate arrest of any person on the list. Crime Stoppers employed rewards to encourage anonymous information that led to the arrest of offenders (Corley, 2019). Offering monetary rewards to police officers to report bad cops has the potential to create its own set of problems.

As one could imagine, there’s the potential for retaliation, as well as the risk of officers lying for monetary gain or simply because another officer is not part of their clique. First, a police officer who reports a bad officer risks their personal safety. Officers may refuse to provide back up or may inflict serious bodily injury or death. However, whistleblower officers may be provided witness protection, reassigned to desk duty, or placed on temporary administrative leave with pay, depending on the potential threat level. Second, a whistleblower reward program within a police department may encourage willfully making any false, fictitious, or fraudulent statements. To combat the potential for making false statements, enact legislation imposing severe penalties including jail time, and revoke the law enforcement officer's license for committing such offense. Finally, it would be a serious mistake to consider only the risk of this proposal without considering its benefits. The primary benefit, of course, is the reduction of police brutality against African Americans and the elimination of slave patrol policing tactics simply because good officers would have an incentive to report bad cops. The 1970s Knapp Commission, which also investigated corruption within the NYPD, was told by Detective Frank Serpico, "We must create an atmosphere in which the dishonest officer fears the honest one, and not the other way around (Baer & Armao, 1995, 85). Three years after the George Floyd murder, police reform has proven to be a difficult objective.

Democrats in the US Congress drafted the George Floyd Justice in Policing Act of 2020 as a policing reform measure. The bill was introduced in the US House of Representatives (George

Floyd Justice in Policing Act, 2020). The bill seeks to ban several police tactics, such as carotid artery and choke holds, which have the potential to be lethal. It also aims to fund community activities that will enhance policing, advance new laws, and enhance police training. Other clauses in the bill include:

- ***Ban no-knock warrants in federal drug cases and, as with chokeholds, encourage local and state agencies to comply by tying bans to federal funding. A no-knock warrant led to the fatal shooting of 26-year-old Breonna Taylor by police in Louisville, Kentucky.***

- ***End "qualified immunity," which protects law enforcement officers from most civil lawsuits.***

- ***Make it easier to prosecute police officers accused of misconduct by lowering the legal standard from willfulness to recklessness.***

- ***Prohibit racial, religious, and discriminatory profiling by law enforcement agencies at the local, state, and federal levels and mandate training against such discriminatory profiling.***

- ***Local and state police agencies are required to use existing federal funds to ensure the use of*** *body cameras, all federal uniformed officers are required to wear body cameras, and all marked federal police vehicles are required to use dashboard cameras.*

- *Create a national police misconduct registry to prevent police officers who are fired or pushed out for bad performance from being hired by other agencies.*

- *Use federal grants to help communities establish commissions and task forces to study police reforms.*

- *Address police militarization by limiting how much military-grade equipment is awarded to state and local law enforcement agencies.*

- *Enhance "pattern and practice" investigations of police departments by granting the Justice Department subpoena power and establishing grant programs for state attorneys general to conduct their own probes. (Gomez, 2021)*

Just as Congress failed to act on preventing active shooters, mass killings, and gun control, they failed to pass the George Floyd Justice in Policing Act.

The George Floyd Justice in Policing Act twice passed the House of Representatives in June 2020 and March 2021. However, Republican opposition to the bill caused it to stall in the Senate. Democrats Karen Bass of California and Senator Cory Booker of New Jersey negotiated with Republican Senator Tim Scott in a failed attempt at bipartisan passage of the legislation. The breakdown in negotiations appears to center around "qualified immunity, a legal principle that shields police officers from civil liability for misconduct" (Greve, 2023). As Jay-Z says in his rhyme, "This pain, this pain again. Politics as usual" (Jay-Z, 1996). Reverend Al Sharpton said, "[t]his nation needs a clear, standard policy for police accountability, which is why it's so important Congress finally pass the George Floyd Justice in Policing Act" (Three years since George Floyd, 2023). Tyree Nichols's mother, RowVaughn Wells, urged Congress to pass the George Floyd Justice in Policing Act, stating that "[w]e need to get that bill passed. Because if we don't, the next child that dies – that blood is going to be on their hands" (Greve, 2023). The George Floyd Justice in Policing Act is opposed by police unions, taking issue with the elimination of qualified immunity (Edmondson, 2020). The question arises as to whether qualified immunity is illogical, unjust, and a doctrine that should be considered unlawful.

Qualified immunity is "[a] legal doctrine that shields [police officers] from liability if their conduct did not violate clearly established civil rights that a reasonable person would have known about" (Siegel, L. & Worrall, J. 2014, 541). I am suspended in judgment regarding whether qualified immunity for police officers should be eliminated. I concur that police officers, on some occasions, may need qualified immunity to do their jobs. Police officers, in particular, carry out crucial duties that can call for split-second decisions under pressure. If qualified immunity were removed, police could hesitate to act when it was most needed (Fawbush, 2023).

We cannot elaborate an argument on qualified immunity because it would be beyond our scope. However, the U. S. Supreme Court introduced the qualified immunity doctrine to protect Jackson, Mississippi, police officers in 1961 for arresting a group of 15, including three black priests, violating their civil rights who were participating in a so-called prayer pilgrimage. The priests appeared to have been attempting to desegregate a coffee/lunch counter at a bus terminal (Pierson v. Ray, 1967), and the police actions simply shocked the conscience. Speculation comes into play regarding whether the Supreme Court was paid off in deciding a qualified immunity case in Mullenix v. Luna. In Mullenix v. Luna, the U. S. Supreme Court ruled that a police trooper, Chadrin Mullenix, who shot and killed a suspect (Israel Leija Jr.) by shooting at his car during a high-speed pursuit was entitled to qualified immunity (Mullenix v. Luna, 2015). Assistant Professor of Clinical Legal Education & Director of the Criminal Defense Clinic at the University of Alabama School of Law John P. Gross argued that the Supreme Court in Mullenix v. Luna "transform[ed] what is reckless into something which is reasonable" (Gross, 2017, 91). According to a 2023 ProPublica article, billionaire Harlan Crow gave Supreme Court Justice Clarence Thomas opulent gifts during a twenty-year span, including extravagant vacations, yacht cruises, private jet flights, the home of Thomas's mother, and the nephew of Thomas's grandchild's tuition (Kaplan, 2023). Unfortunately, the Black community does not feel connected to Judge Thomas, but they need to feel that way for the police.

As I have already explained, and I can't overemphasize enough, that community policing is key to the success of modern-day law enforcement. A critical element of community policing has not been accomplished between African Americans and the police — trust. NYPD Commissioner Bill Bratton made a profound observation. He said he was "troubled by the realization that, although crime had been reduced to record lows, the public, particularly in communities of color, was angry at the police. Why,' he asked, 'had the public safety successes not translated into public confidence?' 'His goal,' he said, 'was to restore that public trust in the police'" (Travis, 2015). After I and Deputy Chief Bahrija Livadic, in June or July 2016, represented the WCCCD police department at the White House 21st Century Policing Briefing in Washington, D. C., I was sure that President Barack Obama desired to strengthen the trust between the community and the police. I was so excited to attend the briefing, and knowing that the President of the United States was passionate about "community policing," we gave him a plaque on behalf of the department. Of course, we had to leave it with White House staffers, and I don't even know if he received it. I wholeheartedly supported President Obama's choice to establish the Task Force on 21st Century Policing and that their recommendations should be adopted.

The Task Force on 21st Century Policing was established by an executive order signed by President Barack Obama on December 18, 2014, after civil disorder erupted in Ferguson, Missouri, after the killing of unarmed Black youth Michael Brown by White police officer Darren Wilson. The task force was given by the President the assignment of finding best practices and making suggestions regarding how policing strategies might support efficient crime reduction while fostering public trust.

The Task Force members were Charles H. Ramsey (co-chair) Commissioner, Philadelphia Police Department; Laurie Robinson (co-chair) Professor, George Mason University; Cedric L. Alexander Deputy Chief Operating Officer for Public Safety, DeKalb County, Georgia; Jose Lopez Lead Organizer, Make the Road New York; Tracey L. Meares Walton Hale Hamilton Professor of Law, Yale Law School; Brittany N. Packnett Executive Director, Teach for America, St. Louis, Missouri; Susan Lee Rahr Executive Director, Washington State Criminal Justice Training Commission; Constance Rice Co-Director, Advancement Project; Sean Michael Smoot Director and Chief Counsel, Police Benevolent & Protective Association of Illinois; Bryan Stevenson Founder and Executive Director, Equal Justice Initiative; Roberto Villaseñor Chief of Police, Tucson (Arizona) Police Department; and Ron Davis,

Director of the COPS Office, serves as Executive Director of the Task Force. On May 18, 2015, the Task Force released its final report (President's Task Force on 21st Century Policing, 2015).

The Task Force on 21st Century Policing generated 59 recommendations with 92 action items. The Task Force recommendations are organized around six main topic areas or "pillars": *Building Trust and Legitimacy, Policy and Oversight, Technology and social media, Community Policing and Crime Reduction, Officer Training and Education,* and *Officer Safety and Wellness* (President's Task Force on 21st Century Policing, 2015). I strongly suggest that anyone interested in police reform read the Task Force's final report, as it is a must-read. President Obama said:

> ***When any part of the American family does not feel like it is being treated fairly, that's a problem for all of us. It's not just a problem for some. It's not just a problem for a particular community or a particular demographic. It means that we are not as strong as a country as we can be. And when applied to the criminal justice system, it means we're not as effective in fighting crime as we could be. (President's Task Force on 21st Century Policing, 2015, 5)***

President Obama’s comments laid down the foundation for the Task Force to increase trust between residents and their peace officers so that all community members are committed to ensuring public safety in an environment of mutual respect and are treating one another fairly and justly.

Unfortunately, U.S. law enforcement may have neglected to reform itself by not fully achieving the goals of President Obama’s Task Force on 21st Century Policing. President Obama expressed his frustration, indicating, “Change has been too slow, and we have to have a greater sense of urgency about this.” Task force member Brittany Packnett acknowledged an obstacle towards change; she commented, “We are dealing with issues that are deeply rooted in systemic racism and oppression, and those roots go all the way back to the founding of this country. It’s unrealistic to think that in a year’s time, we’re going to uproot systemic oppression and racism.” Only nine states and localities in the US had enacted the task force's recommendations despite having at least 18,000 police agencies nationwide (Rhodan, 2016).

Nearly four years later, in 2020, former President Obama stated that he shares the "anguish" that many feel about the police murder of George Floyd. After referencing a viral video of a song by 12-year-old Keedron Bryant titled, “I just want to live, God protect me,” the former President said, “This shouldn't be ‘normal’ in 2020s America. It can't be ‘normal.’ If we want our children to grow up in a nation that lives up to its highest ideals, we can and must be better" (Farrington, 2020). Perhaps President Obama and the Task Force should've addressed how the slave patrol evolved into modern-day law enforcement and how to eradicate it. It's not that police don't know about community policing—they do it well in White communities. But now that America is seriously discussing police reform, Norman Stamper is one of the voices we should be paying heed to.

In his monumental book "How to Fix America's Police," Norm Stamper argues that American policing was "doomed from the start." Stamper wrote:

> ***[C]orruption and misconduct have been an integral part of the structure and culture of American policing from the very beginning. Although some agencies have shown halting progress, the institution itself has failed to make necessary, lasting changes. And the American people, particularly young people, poor people, and people of color, those most in need of fair, equitable, and caring police work- are making their discontent known. (Stamper, 2016, 29-30)***

Stamper believes the modern police mindset is so far removed from Sir Robert Peel's "vision of virtuous, accountable police work, and steadily moving further and further away from it" (Stamper, 2016, 28).

Stamper places the blame of police in crises on police aggression, misconduct, racism, the rise in police militarism, and the failed war on drugs. He believes trust in policing never existed. He contends:

> ***The 'few bad apples' theory is not enough to explain police misconduct. The kind of behavior widely questioned and condemned today is, in reality, part of a deeply ingrained, historically dysfunctional structure, that is, a moldering orchard or, if you prefer, a rotten barrel. A fresh, healthy apple will quickly turn in such an environment (Stamper, 2016, xvi).***

While Stamper's perspective on police reform may appear fatalistic and hopeless, he does believe that the solution is in a "community-driven system of policing." The stakes are too great to risk anything else (Stamper, 2016, xx).

I concur with Stamper's perspective that the federal government, working with local communities, must undertake a comprehensive project to reform the police in the U.S. He said:

> ***[It is] imperative that the federal government set and enforce standards for policing in America—much as it has done for air traffic control through the Federal Aviation Administration, agricultural products through the U.S. Department of Agriculture, and pharmaceuticals through the U.S. Food and Drug Administration (Stamper, 2016, 272).***

I don't believe that it's appropriate to point out a policing problem and the root cause of it without offering proposed solutions. Even if police reform includes some proposed solutions, such as Stamper's, which calls for a sweeping overhaul of policing in America, his proposal would definitely ignite an argument against federalism and the need for local control. However, policing in America is a failing institution, and the need to do something is overwhelming. Thus, I include Stamper's recommendations as an alternative for the reader.

Norm Stamper's manifesto for police reform in America:

> 1. ***The campaign will persuade Congress to pass legislation transforming the Department of Justice's traditional,***

largely reactionary police accountability role to one that sets and enforces binding national standards for police conduct. Such standards will govern police hiring and training, use of force policies and procedures, stop-and-frisk and arrest standards and procedures, investigations into use of force, ethical conduct, leadership and supervision, citizen complaint policies and practices, and citizen oversight.

2. *DOJ will establish a program of standards-based certification for both law enforcement agencies and individual officers and will exercise concomitant authority over decertification, based on established cause, of both agencies and individual officers.*

3. *Special, federally trained, and certified teams of regional (not federal, not local) investigators will investigate all homicides at the hands of police, including in-custody deaths, regardless of circumstances. Independent prosecutors will replace grand juries in all such cases.*

Criminal proceedings, if justified by the facts, will be heard by local courts and in accordance with existing rules of evidence. Moreover, all local, state, and federal law enforcement agencies will report every officer-involved shooting and in-custody death and injury to the Department of Justice, which, in addition to serving as a clearinghouse for statistical data, will order investigations as appropriate.

4. *Every police officer in the country will undergo intensive, ongoing classroom and "experiential" training in shoot/no-shoot scenarios; body-camera policies and procedures; use of less-lethal weapons and other defensive tactics, nondiscriminatory police practices; crisis intervention; de-escalation techniques; response to civil disorders; ethical behavior; and policing in a democratic society. Citizens will be invited and encouraged to attend training sessions, and local jurisdictions will be obligated to welcome and accommodate them.*

5. ***Citizens will be involved in all aspects of police operations: policymaking, program development, police oversight, use of lethal-force review panels, police officer recruitment, candidate screening and hiring; academy and in-service training, co-planning, co-preparation, and co-policing of all scheduled and spontaneous events that carry the potential for neighborhood and citizen-police conflict.***

6. ***The Department of Justice will, in conjunction with community activists, community-based organizations, representatives of local police departments, academics, and subject-matter experts, develop and host a national, ongoing community-police leadership academy for America's promising beat cops and detectives.***

7. ***Congress, with the grassroots support of the people, will end the War on Drugs and replace prohibition with a rigorously enforced regulatory system, thereby dramatically reducing mass incarceration, particularly of young***

people, poor people, and people of color.

8. *The tens of billions of dollars saved by ending the drug war will be used in three ways: to finance a drug-use regulatory system and provide resources for local drug education, abuse prevention, and treatment, to underwrite the costs of a comprehensive realignment of Department of justice functions and resources; and to develop and enforce constitutional standards of police performance and conduct in every political jurisdiction throughout the country. (Stamper, 2016, 273-274)*

While Stamper's police reform proposal will most likely be controversial, only a simpleton would disagree with the need to eradicate the war on drugs.

People who are addicted to drugs and are nonviolent lawbreakers need intense narcotics therapy and definitely not prison. I recall many years ago, a security police sergeant at Fairlane Town Center shopping center arrested a shoplifter and transported him to the Dearborn police station. Upon arrival, he started to walk with a limp. Being aware that some experienced shoplifters pretended to be sick or injured to avoid going to jail and instead be transported to a hospital, where they would be issued an appearance citation. I told the desk sergeant that nothing was wrong with my suspect. After the desk sergeant had a brief conversation with my shoplifting suspect, he pulled me to the side, and what he told me shocked my conscience.

The desk sergeant told me that my shoplifting suspect was a heroin addict and had no good veins left in his arm, so he was injecting himself with heroin into his penis, which was causing him to walk with a limp. Any man who resorts to such behavior has to be insane. We should regard adult drug use as a public health concern, becoming a criminal justice issue only if an individual decides to drive impaired, furnish to a minor, or commit any other violation while under the influence, as with alcohol. By addressing drug misuse, especially addiction, as the medical issue that it is— just as with the incarceration of the mentally ill— the jailing of drug-addicted people is both widespread and heinous (Stamper, 2016). President Nixon's War on Drugs in the 1970s contributed to an increase in drug overdoses and promoted and maintained the formation of powerful drug gangs. Almost half of the 186,000 individuals jailed in federal prisons in the United States are there for drug-related crimes (Coyne & Hall, 2017).

As a final offer of solution, I hope and pray for the nation's redemption. Slavery was and is a sin against God's law. In Exodus 21:16, we quote, "Whoever steals a man and sells him, and anyone found in possession of him, shall be put to death" (Holy Bible, NIV, 1983, Exodus 21:16). I assume that Nat Turner read this scripture in the Bible to justify his killings of his White slave masters. African Americans carried to the New World of North America were unquestionably stolen people. Owning a stolen person was always a mortal sin. It's of no wonder that "Thomas Jefferson said he trembled for this country when he reflected that God was just and that His justice could not sleep forever" (Farrakhan, 2020).

God's promise to Abraham elucidates this even further. In Genesis 13-14, we quote, "And he said unto Abram, know of a surety that thy seed shall be a stranger in a land that is not theirs, and shall serve them; and they shall afflict them four hundred years; And also that nation, whom they shall serve, will I judge: and afterward shall they come out with great substance" (Holy Bible, KJV, n.d., Genesis 15:13-14). According to Minister Farrakhan, "While the Jewish people have claimed the Biblical prophecy of Abraham's children being lost and afflicted in a strange land, and many misguided Christians have repeated that claim, there is no historical record of Jews in bondage in Egypt for four centuries. The prophecy fits the Black people of America, who have been strangers in the United States and deprived of freedom, justice, and equality for over 400 years" (Muhammad & Muhammad, 2010). If you disagree with Minister Farrakhan's interpretation of the Bible, perhaps a White pastor may convince us.

Reverend John A. Kilpatrick of Church of His Presence in

Daphne, Alabama, who in 2019 predicted that President Trump wouldn't serve a second term, said that Black people are the chosen people of God due to their suffering during slavery and would be rewarded. Reverend Kilpatrick said in a video clip that went viral:

> ***Now, let me say something right quick. I think back on African American people in America. I think how they were taken against their wills, put in the belly of ships brought over here, beat, cussed. Many of them died in the guts of those ships, thrown overboard. They were pulled from families over there. You ain't never heard a gut-wrenching song 'til you hear a black person sing one of those black negro spirituals. (Nobody knows the trouble I've seen).***
>
> ***When you experience hell, it comes out of your voice. If you're one of those people that you've got problems with black people or whatever, you better shut your mouth, 'cause they're God's people, you better hear what I'm saying to you. Shut your mouth, you better shut your white mouth.***
>
> ***I know some of you [were] raised in the deep South, raised by prejudiced people, bigoted***

> ***people, you better get that out of your system, get it out of your system. It'll cause you to suffer right along with those masters. It'll cause you to suffer right along with them. These are God's people.***
>
> ***I know that there's wicked in the white race and wicked in [the] black race, I'm not justifying none of that stuff. I'm just saying God knows what happened to the black race. He knows how they wound up over here, and God is going to reimburse the black people for all their trouble and all their labor. You watch what I tell you. (Blair, 2021)***

Reverend Kilpatrick was saying that everyone should be cautious in their treatment of African Americans because they have been through a lot in the U.S. This is a Pastor who is in charge of his flock and is concerned about their misdeeds. Many white preachers will never bring up the subject in their churches, and millions of their congregations will go to damnation because of their hatred for another race. People need the word that will lead them to heaven, not the one that will make them feel good.

Based on scripture, God was always opposed to slavery and oppression and raised individuals to fight against it. This is illustrated in the story of Moses. According to the Holy Bible scriptures, Moses was born at a time when Pharaoh feared the multiplication of the Israelites. Pharaoh enacted a law to kill the newborn male child and spare the female as a means of population control. So, Moses' mother placed him in a basket and sailed him down the river, and Moses ended up in Pharaoh's kingdom. One day, an adult, Moses, went among his people in slavery and saw them hard at laboring. Moses saw an Egyptian beating an enslaved Hebrew person so badly that he lost his temper and killed the Egyptian. Moses fled across the Red Sea to Midian, where God spoke to him from a burning bush, asking him to save his people who were enslaved in Egypt and lead them to the Promised Land. Moses returned to Egypt and told Pharaoh, "To let my people go." The Pharaoh was not pleased with this request and did not want to lose all the people he had enslaved, so he declined. God became enraged as a result, and he brought ten plagues to Egypt. After the 10th plague, which killed all firstborn sons (including the Pharaoh's), Pharoah was eventually forced to liberate the captive people. This enraged the Pharaoh, who dispatched an army to pursue them. As the Israelites met the Red Sea, they realized they were trapped. God told Moses to lift his staff, and when he did, the Red Sea parted to let them through. The sea closed on and killed the Egyptian army and Pharaoh.

Some scholars assert that the story of Moses is mendacious. According to William G. Dever, "the overwhelming scholarly consensus today is that Moses is a mythical figure" and that archeology can't confirm his previous existence (Dever, 1993). To respond to the skeptical scholars regarding God's Prophet Moses, we turn to a YouTube video titled, "Pharaoh's (Ramesses II) Mummy: Sea-salt traces prove the miracle of the Holy Quran":

> ***We all know that…Pharaoh is a very significant character in Islam, especially when Allah [God] is talking about the Prophethood of one of His messengers [Moses]. In this particular context, the Quran refers to Pharaoh Ramesses II. Ramesses II is believed to be one of the most powerful Pharaohs of the Egyptian dynasty, whose mummy was discovered in 1881. His mummy is considered to be one of the most well-preserved mummies ever found. However, after nearly 100 years of its discovery, in 1976, the mummified body of Ramesses II was suddenly required to be transported to France. The mummy was getting affected by some external fungus, which needed immediate treatment to avoid complete decay. Very interestingly, due to the French passport law, Ramesses II was even issued a passport by the Egyptian government as a prerequisite for visiting France.***

The French surgeon Maurice Bucaille was the scientist in charge of the study on the mummy of Ramesses II. It was he who discovered the traces of sea salt in the body of Ramesses II.

It is very commonly known that salt was a major ingredient in the process of mummification, but that was Natron salt, which is completely different from sea salt. Therefore, it was a very clear indication that Ramesses II died by drowning in the sea, and his body was soon recovered and mummified after his demise.

The question that came to Dr Bucaille's mind was, 'How could the body of Ramesses II remain so undamaged compared to the other mummies, although his body was recovered from the sea?'

Now, let's find out what the Quran has said about the death of the Pharaoh:

And We let the children of Israel cross the sea. So, Pharaoh and his troops chased them in transgression and hostility until when he was about to drown, he said, 'I believe that there is no god but the One in whom the children of Israel believe, and I am among those who submit to Allah.'

(Allah said,) 'Is it now (that you have come to believe) while you were rebellious all along, and you were among the mischief-makers? So, today, We shall save your body so that you may become a sign for those after you. And many of the people are heedless of Our signs.' Surah Yunus: 90-92

[A]lthough this incident of Pharaoh's death was mentioned in the Bible and the Torah; however, they did not mention that the Pharaoh's body was recovered and preserved…the discovery of the mummies in Egypt started taking place roughly at the beginning of the 19th Century…the first mummy in Egypt was discovered in the year 1817.

Then, 1400 years ago, how could the Quran make such a surprisingly appropriate statement about the Pharaoh and the preservation of his body? (TAQWA995, 2020)

The narrative of Moses teaches us how so many people were

saved, how one man, Moses, could stand up to a tyrant like Pharaoh, and how God delivered them from tyranny and injustice.

The story of Moses is significant to the struggles for freedom throughout the world. Harriet Tubman, an Underground Railroad conductor and American Civil War warrior, was nicknamed "Moses" for her varied missions in freeing and ferrying fugitive enslaved people to freedom in the United States (Clinton, 2004). Prophet **Moses is mentioned more than any other person in The Holy Quran, and his life is chronicled and told more than any other prophet's (**Mediapro, 2019). There's a synchronicity between the fight against slavery and oppression and the religion of Islam.

There is an Ayat (verse) in the Holy Quran, which is the Muslim Holy Book, that relates to fighting to be delivered from the persecution of an oppressor. In *Sura* (Chapter) *An-Nisa* 4:75, it states:

> ***And what reason have you not to fight in the way of Allah, and of the weak among the men and the women and the children, who say: Our Lord, take us out of this town, whose people are oppressors, and grant us from Thee, a friend, and grant us from Thee, a helper." (The Holy Quran, 2011)***

This clearly establishes that the fight against oppression and tyranny is a direct command of God to all Muslims. While the Holy Quran doesn't outright abolish slavery, Prophet Mohammed (PBUH - May the peace and blessings of God be upon him) set a good example of freeing a slave with his companion, Bilal.

While there is disagreement among scholars on whether or not some Muslims engage in slavery, Prophet Mohammed (PBUH) set free all of his 39 male and female slaves, regardless of whether they had been seized during the war (Kannoun 1966). Former African slaves, most notably Bilal, were among Prophet Mohammed's (PBUH) closest and most notable companions. A notable figure in Islamic history, Bilal was a Black Ethiopian slave. Bilal renounced the polytheistic religion of his wealthy Quraish master, Umayyah Ibn Khalaf, and embraced Islam instead, which emphasized that a man is only a slave to God and not to other men. Bilal was starved and chained by Umayyah out of rage, yet he insisted on saying "Ahad, Ahad" (one God). Umayyah ultimately decided to kill Bilal by dumping him in the scorching desert and placing a boulder on his chest. To purchase Bilal from Umayyah for five pounds of gold, Prophet Mohammed (PBUH) dispatched Abu Bakr. After being purchased, Bilal was granted his release. Every morning, Bilal, the Prophet Mohammed's (PBUH) first muezzin (Minister), would call the Muslims to prayer (Muhammad, D. 2007). The story of Bilal is significant in my argument that God does not condone slavery by way of his Prophet Mohammed (PBUH), which is exemplified through the ministry of Jesus Christ.

Jesus was never in favor of slavery. Except for the fact that he discusses slaves in his stories and that it is frequently noted as a feature of the civilization he lives in, he doesn't really acknowledge it. However, ignoring it does not constitute an endorsement (Thiessen, 2016). Jesus does not express opposition to slavery anywhere in the New Testament. Jesus, however, stood in the synagogue to read the following scripture of Luke 4:18 as he launched his public ministry:

> ***The Spirit of the Lord is upon me because he has anointed me to proclaim good news to the poor. He has sent me to proclaim liberty to the captives and recovering of sight to the blind, to set at liberty those who are oppressed. (Morrow, 2013)***

Thus, Jesus articulated that part of his mission was to free those who were captive. Malcolm X claimed that if Jesus were alive today, he would go to give freedom to African Americans who were being held in bondage in America.

According to the Holy Bible, Jesus was not White; he had blond hair and blue eyes, as depicted in pictures throughout American Literature. He is described in the King James Version,

Revelation 1:14-15 as, “His head and his hairs were white like wool, as white as snow; and his eyes were as a flame of fire; and his feet like unto fine brass, as if they burned in a furnace; and his voice as the sound of many waters.” Malcolm X said that this thick hair, dark-complexioned man would’ve come to the oppressed African Americans:

> ***They said [Jesus] was discriminating because he told his disciples not to go the way of the Gentiles but rather go to the lost sheep. He discriminated. Don't go near the Gentiles; go to the lost sheep. Go to the oppressed. Go to the downtrodden. Go to the exploited. Go to the people who don't know who they are. Who are lost from the knowledge of themselves and who are strangers in a land that is not theirs. Go to those people. Go to the slaves. Go to the second-class citizens. Go to the ones who are suffering the brunt of Caesar's brutality. And if Jesus were here in America today, he wouldn't be going to the white man. The white man is the oppressor. He would be going to the oppressed. He would be going to the humble. He would be going to the lowly. He would be going to the rejected, the despised. He would be going to the so-called American negro.***

(Ishi Utube, 2022)

Malcolm X was interpreting Jesus' life, teachings, and mission as a metaphor to rescue the former Black slaves of America, held in bondage to a cruel tyrant slave master. Upon Jesus's arrival, African Americans were freed and became slaves of God, now obedient to a good master.

One may wonder what this religious discussion has to do with policing. The main purpose of this religious dialogue is to show sinful people such as slave masters, slave catchers, slave traders, the slave patrol, and modern police, the few who continue to practice their tactics…that they're guilty before a Holy God. They must repent and break away from their oppressive policing before the chastisement of God reaches them. Pharaoh was drowned and killed because he refused to let the children of Israel go to freedom.

While the 13th Amendment abolished slavery, there was a loophole in the law that kept slavery alive, "except as a punishment for crime." The police are on the frontline making arrests, and the prosecutors and the courts work in conjunction to sustain a disproportionate prison rate for incarcerated African Americans. According to the Declaration of Independence, we have not only the right but also the obligation to change or overthrow any government that does not uphold our fundamental liberties, such as the right to life, liberty, and the pursuit of happiness. The 2020 killing of George Floyd by a Minneapolis police officer nearly put American policing on life support as calls for defunding and abolishing the police grew louder. It's the slave patrol tactics of modern-day police that are causing its downfall.

Following a lengthy police pursuit, a police K-9 dog mauled a Black man named Jadarrius Rose in Ohio during a 2023 July Fourth traffic stop after he surrendered with his hands raised in the air. A Circleville police officer named Ryan Speakman released and ordered the K-9 dog to attack Rose as an Ohio State trooper repeatedly shouted, "Do not release the dog with his hands up." Another trooper yelled, "Get the dog off of him! Get the dog off of him!" "Was I not loud enough?" the trooper who cried, "Do not release the dog," was heard asking of his fellow officers. Another officer answered, "You said it three, four times" (Gill, 2023).

It was as if a ghost from the slave patrol was speaking to former officer Speakman, urging him louder to release the dog, regardless of the fact that Rose was surrendering. As we discussed previously, it was the echo of the "slave" or "negro" dogs used to hunt runaway slaves by the slave patrol and often mauled them mercilessly after they were captured (Wills, 2023). Thus, some modern-day police are still practicing slave patrol tactics and keeping America bound by the chains of slavery. God's judgment may be upon America today!

America must inquire how do we repent for slavery and police brutality before it is too late. Malcolm X said in a speech:

The Honorable Elijah Muhammad teaches us that as it was the evil sin of slavery that caused the downfall and destruction of ancient Egypt and Babylon, and of ancient Greece, as well as ancient Rome, so it was the evil sin of colonialism (slavery, nineteenth-century European style) that caused the collapse of the white nations in present-day Europe as world powers…we…are also witnessing how the enslavement of millions of black people in this country is now bringing America to her hour of judgment, to her downfall as a respected nation. The Honorable Elijah Muhammad teaches us that as it was divine will in the case of the destruction of the slave empires of the ancient and modern past, America's judgment and destruction will also be brought about by divine will and divine power. Just as ancient nations paid for their sins against humanity, America must now pay for her sins against twenty-two million 'Negroes'…America should be asking herself: 'What does God want for these twenty-two million ex-slaves.' (Malcolm X, 1963)

Malcolm X is saying that the God of the universe wants a

world of international brotherhood founded on the values of justice, equality, righteousness, truth, and peace; otherwise, suffer His divine wrath. God wants the same attributes for modern-day police.

Police reform should transform law enforcement into an institution that interacts with Black Americans in the same way they do with White Americans. The police should be a servant of God. Retired Inkster and Highland Park police Chief Hilton Napoleon describes it like this:

> ***As a peacemaker, it is a great honor to be called a child of God. Whether you are Baptist, Methodist, Catholic, Protestant, or any other denomination of the Judeo-Christian tradition, this honor comes with tremendous responsibility in serving our citizens. Law enforcement officers must be fully aware of the tremendous ethical responsibilities of their position and must strive to consistently fulfill these responsibilities to the highest professional standards.***
>
> ***Police officers are the official representatives of the government, and they also represent God. No government can exist in a safe, secure environment without police officers responsibly enforcing the laws of the land. Police officers are***

required to work within the law, and they are entrusted to ensure the rights of all to liberty, equality, and justice…

Being considered a child of God, police officers should take on the nature of God. God represents love, peace, patience, empathy, humility, fairness, courtesy, confidence, righteousness, service, sacrifice, and equality. It is imperative that police departments across the nation make every attempt to recruit candidates who exhibit these attributes.

People who desire to be police officers should love all the people they have sworn to protect and serve. In fact, all of us who serve the public must keep love in the forefront of our minds and hearts. Love is the strongest voice in the world. As police officers, we must utilize the voice of love to unify and strengthen our communities for the greater good. We must utilize love to improve and strengthen our police departments nationwide. Our humanity comes to its fullest bloom when we display a loving disposition. We become a more beautiful society when we give love. As police officers and public servants, this love must not be selective or discriminatory. It

must be genuine and true to the public we serve. Can't nothing be love, but love. (Napoleon, 2022, 1-2)

If police officers were to reform into servants of God, there would be no more police brutality, no more George Floyd incidents, and no more malicious police dog attacks. Unfortunately, when I discussed my conclusions from this book with a co-worker, she said, "They've had 400 years to change; I don't think they ever will."

Will the efforts to reform the American police system be successful? Can the police be accountable, consistently adhere to the rule of law and operate through procedural justice for African Americans? There are arguments in favour of either outcome, although there are more reasons for pessimism than optimism, particularly after the 2024 election of President Donald Trump. President Trump will emboldened White police officers to peel off their mask of civility and then you will see murder coming out of their hearts and their eyes. George Floyd, Ahmed Arberry and Breonna Taylor all occurred under Trumps previous presidency. Minister Farrakhan warned that Mr. Trump would put America "on a rocket ship to hell" (Muhammad, A., 2016). At a 2024 rally in Erie, Pennsylvania, to end crime immediately, President Donald Trump called for one real rough, nasty, and violent day of police retaliation (Wren, 2024). How much worse could it become? My unfortunate prediction is that President Trump will encourage police brutality and absolve them of responsibility, resulting in another "George Floyd" incident within four years.

If American policing has obtained a hardened heart and is too arrogant to acknowledge its mistakes and refuse to reform, only Heaven will help us. God help this world; God help this nation. God bless America, or as Reverend Wright said:

> ***Not God bless America, God damn America. That's in the Bible, for killing innocent people. God damn America for treating her citizens as less than human. God damn America for as long as she acts like she is God and she is supreme. The United States government has failed the vast majority of her citizens of African descent. Think about this, think about this. (Wright, 2001)***

So, I say, "God damn America," if there is no appropriate police reform, and some law enforcement continues to kill innocent unarmed Black people, and some modern-day police continue to practice slave patrol tactics.

References

Abbey-Lambertz, K. 2014. Mall security guards who killed unarmed Black Man won't be charged. The Huffington Post. September 20, 2014. Available at: https://www.huffingtonpost.com.au/entry/mckenzie-cochran-northland-mall-died_n_5849348 (Accessed: October 12, 2020).

ABC 24 Staff. 2023. In eulogy, Rev. Al Sharpton likens Tyre Nichols to Joseph, recalls Dr. King's death in Memphis. ABC 24 News. February 1, 2023. Available at: https://www.localmemphis.com/article/news/local/rev-al-sharpton-full-remarks-tyre-nichols-funeral/522-3f07e50a-7265-4241-8f32-f0c73efc622b (Accessed: March 24, 2023).

Active shooter. 2022. Active shooter incidents in the United States in 2022. FBI. Available at: https://www.fbi.gov/file-repository/active-shooter-incidents-in-the-us-2022-042623.pdf (Accessed: July 13, 2023).

Abdollah, T. 2013. Review: Firing of ex-LAPD officer Dorner justified. Associated Press. June 4, 2013. Available at: https://apnews.com/article/1a08b14ea06342e7bf034cc1faeee0d3 (Accessed: January 1, 2021).

Abel, R. 2006. The Black shields. Bloomington: Author House.

Adler, J. 2010. Review of Holmes and Smith, Race and police brutality: roots of an urban dilemma. H-Law, H-Net Reviews. March, 2010. Available at: http://www.h-net.org/reviews/showrev.php?id=29274 (Accessed: December 4, 2020).

Ahmaud Arbery: What do we know 2020. Ahmaud Arbery: What do we know about the case? BBC News. June 5, 2020. Available at: https://www.bbc.com/news/world-us-canada-52623151 (Accessed: June 25, 2020).

Akinyela, M. 2003. Battling the serpent: Nat Turner, Africanized Christianity and a Black ethos. Journals of Black Studies. 33 (3), 255-280.

Al Jazeera and News agencies. 2021. Nightmares for a long time: police joked of beating Black man. AlJazeera. March 12, 2021. Available at: https://www.aljazeera.com/news/2021/3/12/nightmares-for-a-long-time-cops-joked-of-beating-black-man (Accessed: January 4, 2024).

Almaguer, M., Seward, B. & Ortiz, E. 2017. Dashcam Video Shows Death of Georgia Teen Nicholas Dyksma in Fatal Police Stop. NBC News. March 3, 2017. Available at: https://www.nbcnews.com/news/us-news/dashcam-video-shows-death-georgia-teen-nicholas-dyksma-fatal-police-n728906 (Accessed: November 5, 2020).

Alpert, G., Kenny, D. J., & Dunham, R. 1997. Police pursuits and the use of force: recognizing and managing "the pucker factor". Justice Quarterly. 14 (2), 371-385.

Alston, Jasmina. 2018. Woman: Restaurant called police because of my service dog. WGCL-TV. March 7, 2018. Available at: https://www.cbs46.com/news/woman-restaurant-called-police-because-of-my-service-dog/article_9df2beb7-23cf-5358-9b18-fc958c9e5037.html

(Accessed: October 28, 2020).

Anderson, C. 1994. Black labor, White wealth: the search for economic justice. Maryland: Duncan & Duncan.

Angelou, M. [@250wpm]. (2024, January 21). The truth is very important, no matter how negative it is. [Post]. Instagram. Available at: https://www.instagram.com/reel/C2XXizBt04c/?igsh=eDQ5d3ZwOW00eDVq (Accessed: February 18, 2024).

Annals of Congress. 1875. 2nd Congress, 2nd Session, pp. 1413 & 1414 of 1456, American Memory, Library of Congress, accessed January 17, 2022.

Annual Report. 2022. WCCCD 2022 Annual Security Report. WCCCD. Available at: https://www.wcccd.edu/dept/pdf/CS/2022_Clery_Security_Report.pdf (Accessed: August 20, 2023).

Assad, S., Hacker, C. & Savini, D. 2020. Left in the dark. CBS 2 Chicago. November 15, 2020. Available at:

https://storymaps.arcgis.com/stories/3603ef8cc492488c847cffbe03ad0f1d

(Accessed: November 29, 2020).

Associated Press, 1989. Man pushed through glass alleges police racism. New York Times. January 17, 1989. Available at: https://www.nytimes.com/1989/01/17/us/man-pushed-through-glass-alleges-police-racism.html(Accessed: December 27, 2020).

Associated Press, 1992. Undercover cop is shot after being mistaken for a robber. Associate Press News. November 19, 1992. Available at: https://apnews.com/article/d61db4ddcfd188ea90929941319c1d43 (Accessed: December 23, 2020).

Austin, D. 2020. George Floyd's death has to be a tipping point. White people like me must fight racism. THINK Opinion, Analysis, Essays. June 14, 2020. Available at: https://www.nbcnews.com/think/opinion/george-floyd-s-death-has-be-tipping-point-white-people-ncna1229181 (Accessed: July 9, 2023).

Baer, H. & Armao, J. 1995. The Mollen commission report: an overview. New York Law School Lae Review, 40 (1), 73-85. Available at: https://digitalcommons.nyls.edu/cgi/viewcontent.cgi?article=2017&context=nyls_law_review (Accessed: July 26, 2023).

Baldas, T. 2020. Michigan attorney general agrees to review 2014 'I can't breathe' case at Northland mall. Detroit Free Press. June 16, 2020. Available at: https://www.freep.com/story/news/local/michigan/oakland/2020/06/16/mckenzie-cochran-i-cant-breathe-dana-nessel/3201811001/ (Accessed: October 11, 2020).

Barlow, D. & Barlow, M. 2002. Racial profiling: A survey of African American police officers. Police Quarterly 5 (3) 334-358. Available at: http://citeseerx.ist.psu.edu/viewdoc/download?doi=10.1.1.833.994&rep=rep1&type=pdf(Accessed: November 22, 2020).

Barmore, J. 2022. Detroit Police Chief James White takes regular walks through city — with dozens of others. Detroit Free Press. July 30, 2022. Available at: https://www.freep.com/story/news/local/detroit-is/2022/07/30/detroit-police-chief-james-white-walk-mile/10173430002/ (Accessed: July 21, 2023).

BBS Trending. 2015. 'Blue Lives Matter' trends after officers shot. BBC News. March 12, 2015. Available at: https://www.bbc.com/news/blogs-trending-31853299 (Accessed: November 22, 2020).

Becker, G. & Stigler, G. 1974. Law enforcement, malfeasance, and compensation of enforcers. Journal of Legal Studies, 1 (6), 1-18.

Bittner, E. 1980. The function of Police in modern society. Policing Perspective. Los Angeles: Roxbury.

[blackmuslimculture]. (2023, December 21). For most of us, when we complete any post assignment (Minister, Captain, Imam, Secretary, etc.) given to us. [Post]. Instagram. Available at: https://www.instagram.com/p/C1I72QGNcqJ/?igsh=c21jNTBlMTkzbzBx (Accessed: February 18, 2024).

Blair, L. 2021. Pastor who predicted end to Trump's presidency says God's going to 'reimburse' black Americans. The Christian Post. April 15, 2021. Available at:

https://www.christianpost.com/news/pastor-kilpatrick-says-god-will-reimburse-black-americans-for-their-troubles.html (Accessed: August 4, 2023).

Board of police commissioners, n.d. City of Detroit. Available at: https://detroitmi.gov/government/boards/board-police-commissioners#Board-Police-Commissioners-Policy-Directives (Accessed: May 31, 2023).

Bobic, I. 2014. Obama reacts to Eric Garner decision: This is an American problem. The Huffington Post. December 3, 2014. Available at: https://www.huffpost.com/entry/obama-eric-garner-decision_n_6264762 (Accessed: October 15, 2020).

Bonita Carey-Powers and Alexis Holmes vs WCCCD and Darrick Muhammad. 22-008022-CD. Wayne County Circuit Court. July 5, 2022.

Bonner v. WCCCD, et al. Transcript of the Testimony of Regina Bonner. Tri-County Court Reporters. March 10, 2021.

Bonner v. WCCCD, et al. Transcript of the Testimony of Derrick Bonner. Tri-County Court Reporters. February 1, 2022.

Bork, H. 2023. No need for speed: the inherent unreasonable of high-speed police chases and a new approach to excessive litigation. Brooklyn Law Review. 88 (2), 649-685. Available at: https://brooklynworks.brooklaw.edu/cgi/viewcontent.cgi?article=2339&=&context=blr&=&sei-redir=1&referer=https%253A%252F%252Fscholar.google.com%252Fscholar%253Fhl%253Den%2526as_sdt%253D0%25252C23%2526q%253Dpolice%252Bchase%252Bexcessive%252Bforce%2526btnG%253D#search=%22police%20chase%20excessive%20force%22 (Accessed May 8, 2023).

Bragg, S. 2007. Ossian Sweet 1895-1960. Black Past. Available at: https://www.blackpast.org/african-american-history/sweet-ossian-1895-1960/ (Accessed: December 19, 2023).

Brand, J. 2020. Police brutality as an extension of white supremacy: social control of African Americans in contemporary America. Master thesis, University of North Carolina at Greensboro. Available at: https://libres.uncg.edu/ir/uncg/f/Brand_uncg_0154M_12982.pdf (Accessed: May 26, 2023).

BreakfastClub. (2019, December 18). Brother Nuri Muhammad speaks on Malcolm X, valuable relationships, economic empowerment [Video]. Available at: https://youtu.be/BNsy44O7fmQ (Accessed: June 19, 2023).

Breitman, G. 1965. Malcolm X speaks: selected speeches and statements. New York: Grove Press.

Breitman, G., Porter, H. & Smith, B. The assassination of Malcolm X. New York: Pathfinder Press.

Browne-Marshall, G. 2013. Stop and frisk: from slave-catchers to NYPD, a legal commentary. Trotter Review, 21 (1), 98-119. Available at: https://scholarworks.umb.edu/cgi/viewcontent.cgi?article=1345&context=trotter_review (Accessed: May 22, 2023).

Brucato, B. 2020. Policing race and racing police: the origin of US police in slave patrols. Social Justice. 47 (3/4), 115-136. Available at: https://www.jstor.org/stable/27094596 (Accessed: July 2, 2023).

Bruinius, H. 2016. Why police are pushing back on body cameras. The Christian Science Monitor. August 30, 2016. Available at: https://www.csmonitor.com/USA/Justice/2016/0830/Why-police-are-pushing-back-on-body-cameras (Accessed: November 29, 2020).

Bruno, T. 2016. Nat Turner after 9/11: Kyle Baker's Nat Turner. Journal of American Studies, 50 (4), 923-951.

Bump, P. 2021. How the first statement from Minneapolis police made George Floyd's murder seem like George Floyd's fault. The Washington Post. April 20, 2021. Available at: https://www.washingtonpost.com/politics/2021/04/20/how-first-statement-minneapolis-police-made-george-floyds-murder-seem-like-george-floyds-fault/ (Accessed: July 26, 2023).

Burns, G. 2018. Ex-Detroit deputy police chief sentenced to prison for corruption. MLive. April 19, 2018. Available at: https://www.mlive.com/news/detroit/2018/04/ex-detroit_deputy_police_chief.html (Accessed: July 3, 2023).

Bush, G. 1992. Public papers of the Presidents of the United States: George H. W. Bush, Book I. U. S. Government Publishing Office.

Buzz Luttrell. 2014, July 16. Slave catchers slave resisters [Video]. YouTube. Available at: https://youtu.be/j3iLCyxjfEw (Accessed: June 25, 2023).

Cannon, L. 1999. Official Negligence. Boulder: Westview Press.

Capelouto, S. 2014. Eric Garner: The haunting last words of a dying man. CNN. December 9, 2014. Available at: https://edition.cnn.com/2014/12/04/us/garner-last-words (Accessed: October 15, 2020).

Carlson, J. 2011. A state of violence? A historical look at civilization, criminalization and the politics of legitimate and illegitimate force in Michigan. Vandeplas Press.

Carr, B. 2024. Detroit Public School police officer convicted of fabricating carjacking incident. Click on Detroit. March 27, 2024. Available at: https://www.clickondetroit.com/news/local/2024/03/28/detroit-public-school-police-officer-convicted-of-fabricating-carjacking-incident/ (Accessed: May 3, 2024).

Carroll, N. 2021. USA Today investigation finds widespread retaliation against police whistleblowers. USA Today. November 12, 2021.

Carson, C. 2012. Malcolm X: the FBI file. New York: Skyhorse Publishing.

Carson, S. & Jones, M. 2020. Kenosha businesses damaged and vehicles burned after police officer shoots Jacob Blake in the back. Milwaukee Journal Sentinel. August 24, 2020. Available at: https://www.jsonline.com/story/news/2020/08/24/kenosha-protests-escalate-after-police-shoot-black-man-jacob-blake/3427941001/ (Accessed: October 1, 2020).

Carter, C. 2017 Police Brutality, the Law & Today's Social Justice Movement: How Police Brutality, the Law & Today's Social Justice Movement: How the Lack of Police Accountability has Fueled #Hash tag Activism. The City of New York University Law Review. Fall 2017. Available at: https://academicworks.cuny.edu/cgi/viewcontent.cgi?article=1440&context=clr (Accessed: June 24, 2020).

Carter, S. 2015. Policing and oppression have a long history. Bloomberg. October 29, 2015. Available at: https://www.bloomberg.com/opinion/articles/2015-10-29/policing-and-oppression-have-a-long-history#xj4y7vzkg (Accessed: May 31, 2023).

Chan, J. 2016. What is 'All Lives Matter'? A short explainer. The Wrap. July 13, 2016. Available at: https://www.thewrap.com/what-is-all-lives-matter-a-short-explainer/ (Accessed: November 22, 2020).

Chilton, J. 2023. What do "defund the police" and "police abolition" mean? And what do they not mean? Close Up Washington DC. February 22, 2023. Available at: https://www.closeup.org/what-do-defund-the-police-and-police-abolition-mean-and-what-do-they-not-mean/ (Accessed: July 13, 2023).

Chudy, J. 2020. Many whites are protesting with Black Lives Matter. How far will their support go? Washington Post. June 15, 2020. Available at: https://www.washingtonpost.com/politics/2020/06/15/many-whites-are-protesting-with-black-lives-matter-how-far-will-their-support-go/ (Accessed: June 25, 2023).

Chughtai, A. n. d. Know their names: Black people killed by the police in the US. Al Jazeera. No date. Available at: https://interactive.aljazeera.com/aje/2020/know-their-names/index.html (Accessed: November 22, 2020).

City News Service. 2023. Man sues LA County over alleged beating after getting caught in the middle of wild SoCal chase. ABC7 Los Angeles Eyewitness News. FEBRUARY 2, 2023. Available at: https://abc7.com/police-chase-crash-driver-detained-lawsuit-alleged-beating/12762140/ (Accessed: May 8, 2023).

Civil War Casualties. n.d. Civil War Casualties: The cost of War: Killed, Wounded, Captured, and Missing. American Battlefield Trust. Available at: https://www.battlefields.org/learn/articles/civil-war-casualties (Accessed: April 29, 2921).

Clinton, C. 2004. Harriet Tubman: the road to freedom. New York: Little Brown and Company.

CNN wire. 2023. Police officer clings to roof of suspect's car in new video of Iowa car chase. ABC North Carolina. May 18, 2023. Available at: https://abc11.com/new-video-carroll-iowa-police-traffic-stop-suspect-speeds-away/13264409/ (Accessed: December 27, 2023).

Coffey, A., Eldefonso, E. & Hartinger, W. 1982. Human relations: law enforcement in a changing community. Englewood Cliffs: Printice-Hall.

Cohen, L. 2020. Former Aurora cop admits to ignoring Black woman's cries for help after she fell head-first on the floor while hogtied in a patrol car. CBS News. October 1, 2020. Available at: https://www.cbsnews.com/news/aurora-police-officer-ignored-black-woman-back-of-patrol-car/ (Accessed: January 4, 2024).

Cohen, W. 1969. Thomas Jefferson and the problem of slavery. The Journal of American History, 56 (3), 503-526. Available at: 200.144.254.127:8080/iea/english/journal/38/cohenjefferson.pdf (Accessed: December 15, 2010).

Cone, J. 2001. Martin and Malcolm on nonviolence and violence. Phylon. 49 (3/4) 173-183.

Confession letter former cop. 2021. Confession letter from former cop claims link between NYPD, FBI and Malcolm X. 4 WNBC New York. February 21, 2021. Available at: https://www.nbcnewyork.com/news/local/confession-letter-from-former-cop-claims-link-between-nypd-fbi-and-malcolm-x-killing/2901005/ (Accessed: June 30, 2023).

Conrad, A. & Meyer, J. 1958. The economics of slavery in the ante bellum south. Journal of Political Economy, 66 (2) 95-130.

Cook, D. n.d. Anti-Black punitive traditions in early American policing. The Metropole. Available at: https://themetropole.blog/2021/06/08/anti-black-punitive-traditions-in-early-american-policing/#_ftn7 (Accessed: May 31, 2023).

Copehart, J. 2019. The story of Bloody Sunday and today's pilgrimage to Selma: 'Voices of the Movement' Episode 4. The Washington Post. April 25, 2019. Available at: https://www.washingtonpost.com/opinions/2019/04/25/story-bloody-sunday-todays-pilgrimage-selma-voices-movement-episode/ (Accessed: August 26, 2020).

Corley, C. 2019. Do cash rewards for crime tips work? NPR News. September 17, 2019. Available at: https://www.npr.org/2019/09/17/761183202/do-cash-rewards-for-crime-tips-work (Accessed: July 26, 2023).

Costello, D. 2020. Louisville police is firing officer Brett Hankison involved in Breonna Taylor shooting. USA Today. June 19, 2020. Available at: https://www.usatoday.com/story/news/nation/2020/06/19/breonna-taylor-shooting-louisville-police-fire-officer-brett-hankison/3222169001/ (Accessed: August 25, 2020).

Court clears Ali (1971) Court clears Ali of charges. Associated Press. June 28, 1971. Available at: https://news.google.com/newspapers?id=gO5VAAAAIBAJ&sjid=PuEDAAAAIBAJ&pg=5441%2C6461911 (Accessed: July 6, 2020.

Coyne, C. & Hall, A. 2017. Four decades and counting: the continued failure of the war on drugs. CATO Institute. April 12, 2017.

Crepeau, M., Gutowski, C., Meisner, J. & St. Clair, S. 2019. How the day unfolded: Inside the courtroom for former Chicago police Officer Jason Van Dyke's sentencing. Chicago Tribune. January 18, 2019. Available at: https://www.chicagotribune.com/news/breaking/ct-met-laquan-mcdonald-jason-van-dyke-sentencing-20190118-story.html (Accessed: November 28, 2020).

D'Angelo, B. 2023. Ohio officer placed on leave after police dog attacks surrendering truck driver? KIRO 7. July 24, 2023. Available at: https://www.kiro7.com/news/trending/ohio-officer-placed-leave-after-police-dog-attacks-surrendering-truck-driver/SI4CJG4YUJBPHI7Z6JTPJH5HBI/ (Accessed: January 2, 2024).

DaJuan Dickerson v. Wayne County Community College District, and Darrick Muhammad, 22-010540. Wayne County Circuit Court. September 6, 2022.

DaJuan Dickerson v. WCCCD and Darrick Muhammad. Transcript of the Testimony of DaJuan Dickerson. Carroll Reporting & Video. June 19, 2023.

Davies, D. 2021. Historian uncovers the racist roots of the 2nd Amendment. NPR News. June 2, 2021. Available at: https://www.npr.org/2021/06/02/1002107670/historian-uncovers-the-racist-roots-of-the-2nd-amendment (Accessed: May 25, 2023).

Davis, A. & Graham, B. 1995. The Supreme Court, race, and civil rights. Thousand Oaks: Sage.

Davis, D. & Hankins, B. 2002. New religious movements and religious liberty in America. Waco: Baylor University Press.

Davis, J. 2023. Birmingham's use of police dogs on civil rights protesters shocked liberal onlookers. But the backstory was all-American. Slate. May 16, 2023. Available at: https://slate.com/news-and-politics/2023/05/birmingham-civil-rights-march-history-dog-photo.html (Accessed: June 26, 2023).

Decaro, L. 2022. Why white evangelicals should claim John Brown. Christianity Today. June 17, 2022. Available at: https://www.christianitytoday.com/ct/2022/june-web-only/john-brown-bible-quote-evangelical-faith.html (Accessed: June 15, 2023).

Deep, S. n.d. Dearborn Officer puts 7s episode behind him. The Detroit News.

Dees, T. 2010. Surveillance technology: an end to stakeouts? Police Magazine. December 13, 2010. Available at: https://www.policemag.com/technology/article/15348312/surveillance-technology-an-end-to-stakeouts (Accessed: May 25, 2023).

DeGruy, J. 2005. Post traumatic slave syndrome: America's legacy of enduring injury and healing. Milwaukie, Oregon: Uptone Press.

DeGue, S., Fowler, K. & Calkins, C. 2018. Deaths due to use of lethal force by law enforcement. American Journal of Preventive Medicine, 51(5 Suppl 3), S173–S187.

Demby, G. & Escobar, N. 2020. From Negro militias to Black armament. NPR News. December 22, 2020. Available at: https://www.npr.org/sections/codeswitch/2020/12/22/949169826/from-negro-militias-to-black-armament (Accessed: May 23, 2023).

DeMeester, D., LaMagdeleine, D., Norton, C., Austin, L., Johnston , E. & and Nadeau, S. n.d. The rebirth of community policing: a case study of success. [Essay, University of St Thomas]. Available at: https://cms5.revize.com/revize/columbiaheights/document_center/Police/The%20rebirth%20of%20community%20policing_2015100713161793 75.pdf (Accessed: July 17, 2023).

Dennis told City Council. 1998. Detroit's Black Slate Digest. May 1998.

Derrick Bonner and Regina Pickett vs WCCCD et al. 20-001062-CZ. Wayne County Circuit Court. January 23, 2020.

Derrick Muhammad v. Taub-Co Management, Inc., the Taubman Company and Fairlane Mall. 1996. Plaintiff's brief in response to defendant's motion for partial summary judgment. U. S. District Court Eastern District Court. March 8, 1996.

Despart, Z. 2022. Systemic failures in Uvalde shooting went far beyond local police, Texas House report details. The Texas Tribune. July 17, 2022. Available at: https://www.texastribune.org/2022/07/17/law-enforcement-failure-uvalde-shooting-investigation/ (Accessed: July 13, 2023).

Dever, W. 1993. What remains of the House that Albright built? The Biblical Archaeologist. University of Chicago Press, 56 (1), 25-35.

Diamond, J. 2020. Jewface and the Nazi gaze: why Amazon's hunters fails. Heyalma. March 3, 2020. Available at: https://www.heyalma.com/jewface-and-the-nazi-gaze-why-amazons-hunters-fails/ (Accessed: May 23, 2023).

DaJuan Dickerson v. WCCCD and Darrick Muhammad. Transcript of the Testimony of DaJuan Dickerson. Carroll Reporting & Video. June 19, 2023.

Diouf, S. 2021. Muslims in America: a forgotten history. Al Jazeera. February 10, 2021. Available at: https://www.aljazeera.com/features/2021/2/10/muslims-in-america-always-there. (Accessed: June 10, 2023).

District Police Authority. 2023. WCCCD Frequently Asked Questions. Available at: https://www.wcccd.edu/dept/safety_faq.htm (Accessed: August 20, 2023).

Donnelly, F. 2011. Parole denied again for Staten Island DWI cop Joseph Gray, who killed 4 people in crash. SILive.com. February 22, 2011. Available at: https://www.silive.com/northshore/2011/02/parole_denied_again_for_staten.html (Accessed: July 5, 2023).

Doss, J. 2021. MLK, the Kerner report, and the fourth estate. New Pittsburgh Courier. January 25, 2021. Available at: https://newpittsburghcourier.com/2021/01/25/mlk-the-kerner-report-and-the-fourth-estate/ (Accessed: June 24, 2023).

Douglas. F. 1852. What to the Slave Is the Fourth of July? Jacobin. July 4, 2019. Available at:

https://www.jacobinmag.com/2019/07/fourth-of-july-frederick-douglass-address (Accessed: December 14, 2020).

Douglass, J. 2000. The King assassination: after three decades, another verdict. The Christian Century. March 15, 2000. Available at: https://www.religion-online.org/article/the-king-assassination-after-three-decades-another-verdict/ (Accessed: June 16, 2023).

Dowd, T. 2022. The violent, racist history of K-9 units. Vice News. September 7, 2022. Available at: https://www.vice.com/en/article/g5vjjb/k9-unit-history (Accessed: June 29, 2023).

Dr. Amos Wilson. [@theblackdetour]. 2018, July 25. Dr. Amos Wilson. [Video]. [Tweet].

Dred Scott v. Sandford, 60 U.S. 393 (1856).

Dukes, W. 2014. Police ethnicity and anomie: exploring organizational adaptation strategies among African American police officers in relation to a socially constructed double consciousness. 87. Doctoral Dissertation. North Carolina A&T

State University. Available at: https://digital.library.ncat.edu/cgi/viewcontent.cgi?article=1086&context=dissertations (Accessed: April 2, 2023).

Dulaney, W. 1984. Black shields: A historical and comparative survey of Blacks in American police forces. (Ph.D. dissertation). Ohio State University, Columbus, Ohio. Available at: https://www.ncjrs.gov/pdffiles1/Photocopy/96354NCJRS.pdf(Accessed: July 6, 2020).

Duvall, T. 2020. Louisville police release the Breonna Taylor incident report. It's virtually blank. Louisville Courier Journal. Available at: https://www.courier-journal.com/story/news/crime/2020/06/10/breonna-taylor-shooting-louisville-police-release-incident-report/5332915002/ (Accessed: August 25, 2020).

Dyson, M. 1995. Making Malcolm: the myth and meaning of Malcolm X. New York: Oxford University Press.

Edmondson, C. 2020. House passes sweeping policing bill targeting racial bias and use of force. New York Times. June 25, 2020.

Edwards, M. & Andone, D. 2017. Ex-South Carolina cop Michael Slager gets 20 years for Walter Scott killing. CNN. December 7, 2017. Available at: https://www.cnn.com/2017/12/07/us/michael-slager-sentencing/index.html (Accessed: November 19, 2020).

11Alive. (2024, February 15). Part 1 Fani Willis takes stand in hearing on motions to disqualify her from Trump case. [Video]. YouTube. Available at: https://youtu.be/FJ0oXkgoKh4?si=PajcLCJw2BkakxGP (Accessed: February 18, 2024).

Eligon, J. 2019. A White officer shoots a Black colleague, deepening a racial divide. New York Times. November 24, 2019. Available at: https://www.nytimes.com/2019/11/24/us/st-louis-race-police.html (Accessed: December 30, 2020).

English, T. 2012. The savage city: race, murder, and a generation on the edge. New York: Harper Collins.

Evanzz, K. 2001. The Messenger: the rise and fall of Elijah Muhammad. New York: Vintage Books.

Eversley, M. 2015. Man who shot S.C. cell phone video speaks out. USA Today. April 8, 2015. Available at: https://www.usatoday.com/story/news/2015/04/08/walter-scott-feidin-santana-cell-phone-video/25497593/ (Accessed: November 19, 2020).

Farrakhan, L. 1983. A savior is born for the Blackman and woman of America. Saviour's Day, Gary, Indiana. Available at: https://youtu.be/TiVCyBifh2I (Accessed: July 6, 2023).

Farrakhan, L. 1992. Are the police present in the community to serve and protect. The Final Call. August 24, 1992.

Farrakhan, L. 1992. The worst is yet to come. Final Call. June 5, 1992.

Farrakhan, L. 2011. The People of The Prophecy, The People of God's Promise. The Final Call. April 21, 2011. Available at: http://www.finalcall.com/artman/publish/Minister_Louis_Farrakhan_9/article_7961.shtml (Accessed: January 30, 2022).

Farrakhan, L. 2020. The historic Million Man March address toward a perfect union. The Final Call. October 13, 2020. Available at: https://new.finalcall.com/2020/10/13/the-historic-million-man-march-address-toward-a-perfect-union/ (Accessed: July 24, 2023).

Farrington, D. 2020. Obama on George Floyd's death and the ‘maddening’ normalcy of racism. NPR News. May 29, 2020. Available at: https://www.npr.org/2020/05/29/865295468/obama-on-george-floyds-death-and-the-maddening-normalcy-of-racism (Accessed: August 3, 2023).

Felber, G. 2015. Malcolm X assassination: 50 years on, mystery still clouds details of the case. The Guardian. February 21, 2015. Available at: https://www.theguardian.com/us-news/2015/feb/21/malcolm-x-assassination-records-nypd-investigation (Accessed: June 23, 2023).

Fawbush, J. 2023. Qualified immunity: both sides of the debate. FindLaw. March 24, 2023. Available at: https://supreme.findlaw.com/supreme-court-insights/pros-vs-cons-of-qualified-immunity--both-sides-of-debate.html#:~:text=Officers%20and%20public%20officials%20n eed,when%20it%20is%20most%20needed. (Accessed: July 31, 2023).

Fenkelman, P. 1995. His soul goes marching on: responses to John Brown and Harpers Ferry raid. Charlottesville: University Press of Virginia.

Fernandez, M., Perez-Peña, R. & Bromwich, J. 2016. Five Dallas officers were killed as payback, police chief says. New York Times. July 8, 2016.

Final Call News. 2012. Rodney King's haunting question lives on: can we all just get along? Final Call. June 21, 2012. Available at: http://www.finalcall.com/artman/publish/Perspectives_1/article_8959.shtml(Accessed: November 13, 2020).

Fisher, L. 2004. Guilt by expression association: political profiling, surveillance and the privacy of groups. Arizona Law Review. 46, 621-675. Available at: https://arizonalawreview.org/pdf/46-4/46arizlrev621.pdf (Accessed: June 11, 2023).

First Black police chief. 1997. City known for civil rights struggles names first black police chief. Associated Press. November 19, 1997. Available at: https://apnews.com/article/355e75c0172f181a99ec45ab56fd0a68 (Accessed: February 26, 2021).

Fisk, C. & Richardson, L. 2017. Police unions. George Washington Law Review, 85(3), 712 – 799. Available at: https://escholarship.org/content/qt0mc2w2kw/qt0mc2w2kw.pdf (Accessed: December 14, 2020).

Fleming, J. 2005 The Death of Jimmie Lee Jackson. The Anniston Star. Available at: https://www.annistonstar.com/article_1290419c-ab42-50c6-ac62-c24c9bdda9f2.html (Accessed: August 26, 2020).

Floyd, C. 2000. Officers killed by friendly fire. Trooper, Fall 2000, 78-79.

Floyd, J. 1832. Excerpts from Governor John Floyd's message to the general assemble. Niles Weekly Register. 41 (1,059), 350-351. Available at: https://encyclopediavirginia.org/entries/excerpts-from-governor-john-floyds-message-to-the-general-assembly-december-6-1831/ (Accessed: June 18, 2023).

48 hours, 2020. 48 hours 1992 - 10 best quotes. YouTube, uploaded by God Loves Movies Too, February 17, 2020. Available at: https://youtu.be/nv1WQUTmqB0. (Accessed: May 29, 2023.

France-Presse, A. 2020. A timeline of US race riots since 1965. VOA News. May 30, 2020. Available at: https://www.voanews.com/a/usa_timeline-us-race-riots-1965/6190204.html (Accessed: June 24, 2023).

Freiman, J. & Carissimo, J. 2020. Police in Wisconsin shoot Black man in back multiple times, sparking protests. CBS News. August 25, 2020. Available at: https://www.cbsnews.com/news/jacob-blake-kenosha-shooting-wisconsin-police-black-man-protesters-gather/ (Accessed: September 25, 2020).

Freivogel, W. 2014. Grand Jury Wrangled with Confusing Instructions. St. Louis Public radio KWMU. November 26, 2014. Available at: https://news.stlpublicradio.org/government-politics-issues/2014-11-26/grand-jury-wrangled-with-confusing-instructions (Accessed: November 16, 2020).

Friedley, M. 1992. Malcolm X: the assassination. New York: Ballantine Books.

Friedman, M. 2022. Don't let these 10 legal myths stop your doing business in the U. S. European American Chamber of Commerce. Available at: https://eaccny.com/news/member-news/dont-let-these-10-legal-myths-stop-your-doing-business-in-the-u-s-myths-6-and-7-the-u-s-is-very-litigious-and-that-is-too-threatening-to-a-small-company-like-ours-as-a-result-the-risk/ (Accessed: December 26, 2023).

Fritsch, J. 2000. The Diallo verdict: the overview; 4 officers in Diallo shooting are acquitted of all charges. New York Times. February 26, 2000. Available at: https://www.nytimes.com/2000/02/26/nyregion/diallo-verdict-overview-4-officers-diallo-shooting-are-acquitted-all-charges.html (Accessed: November 17, 2020).

Gallen, D. 1992. Malcolm X A to X: the man and his ideas. New York: Carroll & Graf Publishers.

Gardner, G. 2008. Al Sharpton arrested at NYC protest. NPR News. May 8, 2008. Available at: https://www.npr.org/sections/newsandviews/2008/05/al_sharpton_arrested_at_nyc_pr.html (Accessed: July 21, 2023).

Garfield, D. 2020. Life's a journey: the voices. The North Star Monthly. June 30, 2020. Available at:http://www.northstarmonthly.com/columns/the-voices/article_475fa250-baf1-11ea-95e7-67f501d60e5a.html (Accessed: November 6, 2020).

Genovese, E. 1979. From rebellion to revolution: Afro-American slave revolts in the making of the modern world. Baton Rouge: Louisiana State University Press.

George Floyd died of asphyxia. 2020. George Floyd died of asphyxia to neck: family medical examiner's report. New York Times Post. June 9, 2020. Available at: https://nytimespost.com/george-floyd-died-of-asphyxia-to-neck-family-medical-examiners-report/ (Accessed: June 9, 2020).

George Floyd Justice in Policing Act of 2020, H.R. R 7120, 116th Congress. 2020. Available at:

https://www.congress.gov/bill/116th-congress/house-bill/7120/all-actions (Accessed: July 30, 2023).

Gibbs, K. 2020. Retired Metro officer recalls police brutality. WTVF 5 Nashville. June 2, 2020. Available at: https://newsystuff.com/news/retired-metro-officer-recalls-police-brutality-33760 (Accessed: December 26, 2020).

Gibson, T. [@tyrese]. (2025, February 4). A surprising amount of Americans don't realize the United States practically stole all the land of Mexico. [Reel]. Instagram. Available at: https://www.instagram.com/reel/DFrmMgeOFP7/?igsh=MTc1NHdoZnVqbmJmZA== (Accessed: February 6, 2025).

Gill, P. 2023. Ohio police dog mauled Black man as he surrendered to officers, video shows. USA Today. July 24, 2023. Available at: https://www.usatoday.com/story/news/nation/2023/07/23/ohio-police-dog-unarmed-jadarrius-rose-case/70453818007/ (Accessed: August 11, 2023).

Gladwell, M. 2005. Blink: the power of thinking without thinking. New York: Time Warner.

Godbee, R. 2020. Open letter to fellow members of law enforcement from Ralph L. Godbee Jr. Atlanta Tribune. June 13, 2020. Available at: https://atlantatribune.com/2020/06/13/open-letter-to-fellow-members-of-law-enforcement-from-ralph-l-godbee-jr/?amp=1 (Accessed: July 14, 2023).

Goldberg, J. 2020. The problem with claiming that police evolved from slave patrols. The Dispatch. June 19, 2020. Available at: https://www.aei.org/op-eds/the-problem-with-claiming-that-policing-evolved-from-slave-patrols/ (Accessed: May 5, 2023).

Goldman, P. 1973. The death and life of Malcolm X. New York: Harper& Row.

Goldman, R. 2013. Christopher Dorner let some live while killing others. ABC News. February 14, 2013. Available at: https://abcnews.go.com/US/christopher-dorner-live-killing/story?id=18504028 (Accessed: January 1, 2021).

Goldstein, J. & Santora, M. 2014. Staten Island man died from chokehold during arrest, autopsy finds. New York Times. August

1, 2014. Available at: https://www.nytimes.com/2014/08/02/nyregion/staten-island-man-died-from-officers-chokehold-autopsy-finds.html (Accessed: October 15, 2020).

Gomez, H. 2021. Here's what the George Floyd Justice in Policing Act would do. NBC News. April 21, 2021. Available at: https://www.nbcnews.com/politics/congress/here-s-what-george-floyd-justice-policing-act-would-do-n1264825 (Accessed: July 30, 2023).

Gottlieb, J. & Maske, M. 2017. Roger Goodell responds to Trump's call to 'fire' NFL players protesting during national anthem. The Washington Post. September 23, 2017. Available at: https://www.washingtonpost.com/news/early-lead/wp/2017/09/22/donald-trump-profanely-implores-nfl-owners-to-fire-players-protesting-national-anthem/ (Accessed: June 10, 2020).

Gottschalk, P., Dean, G. & Glomseth, R. 2011. Police misconduct and crime: bad apples or systems failure? Journal of Money Laundering Control, 15 (1), 6-24. Available at: https://biopen.bi.no/bixmlui/bitstream/handle/11250/93420/Gottsc

halk%20Dean%20Glomseth%20_JMLC_2012_authorversion.pdf?sequence=1&isAllowed=y (Accessed: December 9, 2020).

Grabiner, G. 2016. Who Polices the Police? Social Justice, 43(2 (144)), 58–79. Available at: http://www.jstor.org/stable/26380303 (Accessed: January 30, 2022).

Graves, C. 2020. The killing of George Floyd: What we know. MPR News. June 1, 2020. Available at: https://www.mprnews.org/story/2020/06/01/the-killing-of-george-floyd-what-we-know (Accessed: June 10, 2020).

Gray, R. 2013. Campus safety announces director of the year finalists. Campus Safety Magazine, 21 (1), 54-59. Available at: Spotlight on 2012 Director of the Year Finalist Darrick Muhammad - Campus Safety Magazine (Accessed: October 24, 2024).

Gray, T., Turner, N. & Royster, R. 1831. The confession of Nat Turner. Electronic Texts in American Studies. Available at: https://digitalcommons.unl.edu/cgi/viewcontent.cgi?article=1014&=&context=etas&=&sei-redir=1&referer=https%253A%252F%252Fscholar.google.com%2

52Fscholar%253Fhl%253Den%2526as_sdt%253D0%25252C23%2526q%253DNat%252BTurner%252Bconfession%2526oq%253D#search=%22Nat%20Turner%20confession%22 (Accessed: June 2, 2023).

Greenwald, D. 2017. My view: the problem with the bad apple theory of policing. Vanguard. September 30, 2017. Available at: https://www.davisvanguard.org/2017/09/view-problem-bad-apple-theory-policing/ (Accessed: December 6, 2020).

Gregory, S. 2020. Why Jacob Blake's Shooting Sparked an Unprecedented Sports Boycott. Time. August 27, 2020. Available at: https://time.com/5883892/boycott-nba-mlb-wnba-jacob-blake/ (Accessed: October 1, 2020).

Greve, J. 2023. What is the George Floyd Justice in Policing Act and is it likely to pass? The Guardian. February 6, 2023. Available at: https://www.theguardian.com/us-news/2023/feb/06/george-floyd-justice-in-policing-act-explainer-tyre-nichols (Accessed: July 30, 2023).

Griffing, S., Ragin, D. F., Sage, R. E., Madry, L., Bingham, L. E., & Primm, B. J. 2002. Domestic violence survivors' self-identified reasons for returning to abusive relationships. Journal of Interpersonal Violence, 17 (3), 306-319.

Gross, J. 2017. Qualified immunity and the use of force: making the reckless into the reasonable. Alabama Civil Rights & Civil Liberties Law Review, 8, (1), 67-92. Available at: https://www.law.ua.edu/acrcl/files/2017/04/Qualified_Immunity_and_the_Use_of_Force.pdf (Accessed: July 31, 2023).

Gugliotti, M. 2016. The us vs. them syndrome. Medium. November 4, 2016. Available at: https://medium.com/@michaelgugliotti/the-us-vs-them-syndrome-6a7c663aad9c (Accessed: July 22, 2023).

Gustafson, J. 2013. Diversity in municipal police agencies: A national examination of minority hiring and promotion. Policing: An International Journal of Police Strategies and Management, 36 (4), 719-736.

Gutierrez, A. 2022. State of mental health care in Michigan. CBS Detroit. October 10, 2022. Available at: https://www.cbsnews.com/detroit/news/state-of-mental-health-care-in-michigan/ (Accessed: July 13, 2023).

Hadden, S. 2001. Slave patrol: law and violence in Virginia and the Carolinas. Cambridge: Harvard University Press.

Haney, C., Banks, C., & Zimbardo, P. 1973. Interpersonal dynamics in a simulated prison. International Journal of Criminology and Penology, 1, 69–87.

Hacker, A. 1992. Two Nations: Black and White, separate, hostile, unequal. New York: Ballantine Books.

Hadden, S. 2001. Slave Patrols: law and violence in Virginia and the Carolinas. Cambridge: Harvard University Press.

Haley, A. 1964. The autobiography of Malcolm X. New York: Ballantine Books.

Harris, D. 1999. Driving while black: racial profiling on our Nation's highways. American Civil Liberties Union. University of Toledo College of Law. June 1999. Available at: https://www.aclu.org/report/driving-while-black-racial-profiling-our-nations-highways (Accessed: December 21, 2020).

Hass, J. 2010. The assassination of Fred Hampton. Chicago: Lawrence Hill Books.

Hassett-Walker, C. 2021. How you start is how you finish? The slave patrol and Jim Crow origins of policing. Human Rights Magazine. 46 (2). Available at: https://www.americanbar.org/groups/crsj/publications/human_rights_magazine_home/civil-rights-reimagining-policing/how-you-start-is-how-you-finish/ (Accessed: May 16, 2022).

Hatch, M. 1993. Slave rebellion in Brazil: The Muslim uprising of 1835 in Bahia by Joao Jose Reis. University of Texas at Austin. Available at: https://repositories.lib.utexas.edu/bitstream/handle/2152/82258/Slave%20Rebellion%20in%20Brazil_%20The%20Muslim%20Uprising%20of%201835%20in%20Bahia%20by%20João%20José%20Reis%20%281993%29%20-%20Not%20Even%20P.pdf?sequence=2 (Accessed: June 10, 2023).

Hauck, G. 2023. Ben Crump applauded 'swift justice' in Tyre Nichols killing. Experts say the speed was 'unusual.' USA Today.

January 28, 2023. Available at: https://www.usatoday.com/story/news/nation/2023/01/28/memphis-police-quickly-charged-tyre-nichols-death/11134428002/ (Accessed: July 23, 2023).

Hawkins, D. 2021. An NYPD cop allegedly confessed to aiding in Malcolm X's assassination. His daughter says his letters is fake. The Washington Post. February 27, 2021. Available at: https://www.washingtonpost.com/history/2021/02/27/malcom-x-letter-fake/ (Accessed: June 30, 2023).

Hayes, M. 2012. Malcolm X at the Mosque. Our Weekly Los Angeles. May 16, 2012. Available at: https://www.ourweekly.com/2012/05/17/malcolm-x-at-the-mosque/ (Accessed: June 9, 2023).

Heal, A. 2019. Nowhere to turn: Women say domestic abuse by police officers goes unpunished. The Bureau of Investigative Journalism. Available at: https://www.thebureauinvestigates.com/stories/2019-05-01/police-perpetrators-domestic-violence (Accessed: January 25, 2023).

Hehman, E., Flake, J. & Calanchini, J. 2017. Disproportionate use of lethal force in policing is associated with regional racial biases of residents. Social Psychological and Personality Science. July 27, 2017. Available at: https://journals.sagepub.com/doi/full/10.1177/1948550617711229(Accessed: September 9, 2020).

Henry, H. 1914. The police control of the slave in South Carolina. Nashville: Vanderbilt University.

Hermes, G. 2020. Detroit police release body camera footage of fatal officer-involved shooting. Click on Detroit. July 10, 2020. Available at: https://www.clickondetroit.com/news/local/2020/07/10/protest-in-detroit-over-officer-involved-shooting-escalates-as-crowds-grow/ (Accessed: October 23, 2020).

History.com Editors 2009. Fugitive Slave Acts. History. A & E Television Networks. Available at: https://www.history.com/topics/black-history/fugitive-slave-acts (Accessed: January 17, 2022).

Heroic stories. 2021. Law enforcement heroes. Citizens Behind the Badge. Available at: https://www.behindbadge.org/heroes (Accessed: July 8, 2023).

Hillman, N. 2005. Between Black and White: the religious aftermath of Nat Turner's rebellion. Master Thesis. The College of William and Mary in Virginia. Available at: https://scholarworks.wm.edu/cgi/viewcontent.cgi?article=6498&context=etd (Accessed: June 23, 2023).

Hodder, F. H. 1936. The Authorship of the Compromise of 1850. The Mississippi Valley Historical Review, 22(4), 525–536. Available at: https://doi.org/10.2307/1897319 (Accessed: January 17, 2022).

Holmes, M. & Smith, B. 2008. Race and police brutality: Roots of an urban dilemma. Albany: State University of New York.

Holy Bible, King James Version, n.d., Genesis 15:13-14.

Holy Bible, New International Version, 1983, Exodus 21:16.

Hopfe, L. 1994. Religions of the world. New York: Macmillan.

Hudson, R. 2014. Being a cop showed me just how racist and violent the police are. There's only one fix. The Washington Post. December 6, 2014. Available at: https://www.washingtonpost.com/posteverything/wp/2014/12/06/i-was-a-st-louis-cop-my-peers-were-racist-and-violent-and-theres-only-one-fix/(Accessed: July 6, 2020).

Hunter, G. 2020. Detroit police mounted section trots with 2 new horses. The Detroit News. January 2, 2020. Available at: https://www.detroitnews.com/story/news/local/detroit-city/2020/01/03/detroit-police-mounted-section-new-horses/2783343001/ (Accessed: June 30, 2023).

Huq, A. & McAdams, R. 2016. Litigating the blue wall of silence: how to challenge the police privilege to delay investigation. University of Chicago Legal Forum: 2016 (6), 213-253. Available at: https://chicagounbound.uchicago.edu/cgi/viewcontent.cgi?article=1568&=&context=uclf&=&sei-redir=1&referer=https%253A%252F%252Fscholar.google.com%252Fscholar%253Fhl%253Den%2526as_sdt%253D0%25252C23%2526q%253Dblue%252Bwall%252Bof%252Bsilence%2526oq%253Dblue%252Bwall#search=%22blue%20wall%20silence%22 (Accessed: July 24, 2023).

Hutchinson, B. 2019. Bracing for a shot in my back: Ohio Sheriff's Deputy Alan Gaston speaks out after IRS office security guard pulls gun on him. ABC News. July 16, 2019. Available at: https://abcnews.go.com/US/security-guard-pleads-guilty-pulling-gun-ohio-sheriffs/story?id=64346648 (Accessed: January 10, 2025).

Hutchinson, D. 2021. James Craig shouted down by protesters on Belle Isle while announcing run for governor. Click on Detroit WDIV 4. September 14, 2021. Available at: https://www.clickondetroit.com/news/local/2021/09/14/james-craig-shouted-down-by-protesters-on-belle-isle-while-announcing-run-for-governor/ (Accessed: July 21, 2023).

IACP. 1957. Law enforcement code of ethics. IACP. Available at: https://www.theiacp.org/resources/law-enforcement-code-of-ethics (Accessed: October 3. 2024).

Increase My Knowledge. 2011, March 16. Malcolm X - 08 - We're non-violent with people who are non-violent with us [Video]. YouTube. Available at: https://youtu.be/kXo0lgcOHhg (Accessed: June 23, 2023).

Innocence staff. 2020. Termaine Hicks, shot in the back by Philadelphia police, is exonerated after 19-year cover up. The Innocence Project. December 17, 2020. Available at: https://innocenceproject.org/news/termaine-hicks-shot-in-the-back-by-philadelphia-police-is-exonerated-after-19-year-cover-up/ (Accessed: July 28, 2023).

[Ishi Utube]. 2022, September 26. Malcolm X lost sheep [Video]. YouTube. Available at: https://youtu.be/GjslxEjrmn8 (Accessed: August 11, 2023).

Ivery, C. 2010. Campus safety. WCCCD Chancellor's Weekend Memo. No. 722. March 5, 2010. Available at: https://www.wcccd.edu/about/pdfs/weekendmemo/WEM722.pdf (Accessed: August 20, 2023).

Ivery, C. 2017. District Police Authority: Police Advisory Board. WCCCD Chancellor's Weekend Memo. No. 1088. May 20-26, 2017. Available at: https://www.wcccd.edu/about/pdfs/weekendmemo/WEM1088.pdf (Accessed: August 31, 2023).

Ivery, C. 2021. WCCCD recognizes our director of District Police Authority. WCCCD Chancellor's Weekend Memo. No. 1321. December 4-10, 2021. Available at: https://www.wcccd.edu/about/pdfs/WeekendMemo/WEM1321.pdf (Accessed: August 31, 2023).

Jackson, D. n.d. Who is Don Jackson A.K.A Diop Kamau. Police Abuse. Available at: https://policeabuse.com/index.php?option=com_content&view=article&id=34 (Accessed: December 27, 2020).

Jackson, D. 2020. Long Beach racial profiling. [Video]. Police Abuse. Available at: https://www.policeabuse.com/index.php/component/customvideos/detailvideo?id=2052 (Accessed: December 27, 2020).

Jackson, H. 2013. Who's who in black Detroit: celebrating African American achievement. Real Times Media, 106.

Jacob, D.& O'Brien, R. 1998. The determinants of deadly force: A structural analysis of police violence. American Journal of Sociology, 103 (4) 837-862. Available at:

https://www.journals.uchicago.edu/doi/pdf/10.1086/231291 (Accessed: November 6, 2020).

Jay-Z. 1996. Politics as Usual [Song]? On Reasonable Doubt album. Roc-A-Fella Records.

Johnson III, B. 1992. Executive Order 12,333: the permissibility of an American Assassination of a foreign leader. Cornell International Law Journal. 25 (2), 400-435. Available at: https://scholarship.law.cornell.edu/cgi/viewcontent.cgi?article=1289&context=cilj (Accessed: June 19, 2023).

Johnson, M. 2020. Colin Kaepernick tried to tell white America. The Undefeated. May 30, 2020. Available at: https://theundefeated.com/features/colin-kaepernick-tried-to-tell-white-america/ (Accessed: June 10, 2020).

Johnson, R. 2005. Whistleblowing and the police. Rutgers University Journal of Law and Urban Policy. 1 vol. 3. Available at: https://www.bmartin.cc/dissent/documents/Johnson.pdf (Accessed: July 10, 2020).

Johnson, T. 2006. Being Black, or being a cop: the problem of race in American law enforcement. Forum on Public Policy: A Journal of the Oxford Roundtable, Fall 2006, 1-17.

Jolley, D., Douglas, K, & Sutton, R. 2018. Blaming a few bad apples to save a threatened barrel: The system-justifying function of conspiracy theories. Political Psychology, 39 (2), 465-478. Available at: http://nrl.northumbria.ac.uk/id/eprint/40857/1/Jolley%20Douglas%20Sutton%202017.pdf

(Accessed: December 6, 2020.)

Jury backs King. 1999. Jury backs King conspiracy theory. BBC News. December 8, 1999. Available at: http://news.bbc.co.uk/2/hi/americas/556289.stm (Accessed: June 16, 2023).

Kaepernick, C. [@Kaepernick7]. 2017, June 16. A system that perpetually condones the killing of people, without consequence, doesn't need to be revised, it needs to be dismantled! [Tweet]. Twitter. Available at: https://twitter.com/Kaepernick7/status/875832378501074944 (Accessed: May 31, 2023).

Kaffer, N. 2005. A new breed of panther. Detroit Metro Times. May 4, 2005. Available at: https://www.metrotimes.com/news/a-new-breed-of-panther-2181373 (Accessed: August 15, 2023).

Kagan, J. 1999. The Role of Parents in Children's Psychological Development. Pediatrics. July 1, 1999. Available at: https://pediatrics.aappublications.org/content/pediatrics/104/Supplement_1/164.full.pdf

(Accessed: July 9, 2020).

Kannoun, J. 1966. Islam is the first anti-slavery religious system of the world. The Islamic Review. July-August 1966.

Kanu, H. 2022. Prevalence of white supremacists in law enforcement demands drastic change. Reuters. May 12, 2022. Available at: https://www.reuters.com/legal/government/prevalence-white-supremacists-law-enforcement-demands-drastic-change-2022-05-12/ (Accessed: July 23, 2023).

Kapilango, D. 2019. Uprooting Legacy of racism In Dearborn. Riverwise. Summer/Fall 2019. Available at: https://riverwisedetroit.org/article/uprooting-legacy-of-racism-in-dearborn/ (Accessed: July 8, 2020).

Kaplan, J. 2023. Clarence Thomas and the billionaire. ProPublica. April 6, 2023.

Karimi, F. 2020. Kenosha shooting suspect called a friend to say he 'killed somebody,' police say, and then shot two others. CNN. August 28, 2020. Available at: https://www.cnn.com/2020/08/28/us/kyle-rittenhouse-kenosha-shooting/index.html (Accessed: October 5, 2020).

Kaste, M. 2015. Obama's policing task force begins with public hearing. NPR News. January 13, 2015. Available at: https://www.npr.org/2015/01/13/377024708/obamas-policing-task-force-begins-with-public-hearing (Accessed: July 21, 2023).

Kelly, J. 2013. Christopher Dorner: What made a police officer kill? BBC News. February 16, 2013. Available at: https://www.bbc.com/news/magazine-21476904 (Accessed: January 1, 2021).

Keneally, M. 2017. Trump to police: Please don't be too nice to suspects. ABC News. July 28, 2017. Available at: https://abcnews.go.com/Politics/trump-police-nice-suspects/story?id=48914504 (Accessed: December 9, 2020.

Key, K.L., Rich, C., DeCristofaro, & C., Collins, S. (2010). Use of Propofol and emergence agitation in children: A literature review. AANA Journal, 78(6). Available at: https://writingcenter.ashford.edu/sites/default/files/inlinefiles/Sample%20Literature%20Review_0.pdf (Accessed: December 10, 2020).

Kihss, P. 1965. Malcolm X shot to death at rally here. New York Times. February 22, 1965. Available at: https://archive.nytimes.com/www.nytimes.com/library/national/race/022265race-ra.html (Accessed: June 22, 2023).

King, M. 1968. Drum major instinct - a speech by Dr. Martin Luther King, Jr.

Knight, F. 1994. Justifiable homicide, police brutality, or governmental repression? The 1962 Los Angeles police shooting of seven members of the Nation of Islam. The Journal of Negro History. 79 (2) 137-152.

Kolchin, P. 1993. American slavery: 1619 - 1877. New York: Hill and Wang.

Kramer, M. 2004. WSU: Geard to the needs of a professional. Crains Detroit Business. November 8, 2004. 20 (45), Supplemental 39.

Landon, F. 1920. The Negro migration to Canada after the passing of the fugitive slave act. The Journal of Negro History, 5(1), 22-36.

Larry Nevers has died. 2013. Larry Nevers, Detroit cop who went to prison in Malice Green incident, has died. Deadline Detroit. February 4, 2013. Available at: https://www.deadlinedetroit.com/articles/3617/larry_nevers_detroit_cop_who_went_to_prison_in_malice_green_death_has_died (Accessed: November 13, 2020).

Lassiter, M. 2021. Detroit under fire: police violence, crime politics, and the struggle for racial justice in the civil rights era. Policing and Social Justice History Lab. Available at: https://policing.umhistorylabs.lsa.umich.edu/s/detroitunderfire/page/1958-63 (Accessed May 16, 2023).

Lartey, J. & Cooper, W. 2023. Tyre Nichols' death: how Black officers alone can't stop brutal policing. The Marshall Project. Available at: https://www.themarshallproject.org/2023/01/28/tyre-nichols-memphis-black-police-brutality (Accessed: March 28, 2023).

Lawrence, E. 2020. Michael Eric Dyson: Floyd killing 'moved white people,' showed them racism in action. Detroit Free Press. October 27, 2020. Available at: https://www.freep.com/story/money/cars/chrysler/2020/10/27/michael-eric-dyson-george-floyd-killing/6044818002/?fbclid=IwAR0w_YPEQExe0Mkw8J7KcAoSXJwRNs1ks2axvKFc-zV8LuF3A7Jud4P-F54 (Accessed: November 5, 2020).

Lawrence, R. 2017. Blacks that wore the blue. Detroit: Roosevelt Lawrence.

LeDuff, C. 2015. A Black teen, a White cop, and a photo that changed the Civil Rights movement. Vice News. March 2, 2015. Available at: https://www.vice.com/en/article/mbw843/a-black-teen-a-white-cop-and-a-photo-that-changed-the-civil-rights-movement (Accessed: June 26, 2023).

Lee, B. 2012. Parents seek justice for unarmed son's killing. CBS Miami. March 10, 2012. Available at: https://miami.cbslocal.com/2012/03/10/parents-seek-justice-for-unarmed-sons-killing/ (Accessed: November 22, 2020).

Leinen, S. 1984. Black police, White society. New York: New York University Press.

Levin, D. 1992. Detroit suspends policemen in fatal beating of motorist. New York Times. November 7, 1992.

Levin, S. 2020. What does 'defund the police' mean? The rallying cry sweeping the US – explained. The Guardian. June 6, 2020. Available at: https://www.theguardian.com/us-news/2020/jun/05/defunding-the-police-us-what-does-it-mean (Accessed: July 12, 2023).

Lewis, C. n.d. Top quotes by C. S. Lewis. Quote Master. Available at: https://www.quotemaster.org/author/C.+S.+Lewis (Accessed: December 14, 2020).

Liars squads list, n.d. The implications of Brady-Giglio for law enforcement. National Institute for Jail Operations. Available at: https://jailtraining.org/the-implications-of-brady-giglio-for-law-enforcement/ (Accessed: December 10, 2023).

Linder, D. 2001. The trials of Los Angeles police officers' in connection with the beating of Rodney King. Retrieved from: http://law2.umkc.edu/faculty/projects/ftrials/lapd/lapdaccount.html (Accessed: November 6, 2020).

Lininger, T. 2004. Sects, lies, and videotape: the surveillance and infiltration of religious groups. Iowa Law Review, 89 (4), 1201-1286.

Lockwood, D. 2020. The Kenosha shooting didn't happen in a vacuum. CNN. August 25, 2020. Available at: https://www.cnn.com/2020/08/25/opinions/kenosha-shooting-jacob-blake-prison-injustice-police-lockwood/index.html (Accessed: September 25, 2020).

Logan, M. H. (2018). Stockholm syndrome: Held hostage by the one you love. Violence and gender, 5(2), 67-69. Available at: https://www.liebertpub.com/doi/full/10.1089/vio.2017.0076(Accessed: January 25, 2024).

Lopez, G. 2017. Cleveland just fired the cop who shot and killed 12-year-old Tamir Rice more than 2 years ago. Vox Media. May 30, 2017. Available at: https://www.vox.com/identities/2017/5/30/15713254/cleveland-police-tamir-rice-timothy-loehmann (Accessed: November 18, 2020).

Louis X. 1964. Boston minister tells of Malcolm - Muhammad's biggest hypocrite. Muhammad Speaks. December 4, 1964.

Louis X. 2021. White man's heaven is a Black man's hell. YouTube, uploaded by Reelblack One, December 21, 2021.

Available at: https://youtu.be/K-vElPV6onw (Accessed: June 1, 2023).

Love, A. 2010. Nation of Islam pioneer turns 80. Final Call. October 12, 2010.

Love, D. 2015. What Walter Scott's death reminds us. CNN. May 5, 2015. Available at: https://www.cnn.com/2015/04/08/opinions/love-walter-scott/index.html (Accessed: November 19, 2020).

Luibrand, S. 2015. How a death in Ferguson sparked a movement in America. CBS News. August 7, 2015. Available at: https://www.cbsnews.com/news/how-the-black-lives-matter-movement-changed-america-one-year-later/ (Accessed: November 20, 2020).

Madani, D. 2020. Derek Chauvin, ex-officer charged with murder in George Floyd case, released on $1M bond. NBC News. October 7, 2020.

Malcolm X. (1962). Addressing police brutality [Video file]. Available at: https://youtu.be/kboP3AWCTkA (Accessed: November 16, 2020).

Malcolm X. 1963. Malcolm X speech. Available at: https://www.digitalhistory.uh.edu/disp_textbook_print.cfm?smtid=3&psid=3619 (Accessed: August 11, 2023).

Malcolm X quotes. n.d. Malcolm X quotes. Goodreads. Available at: https://www.goodreads.com/quotes/6583798-the-media-s-the-most-powerful-entity-on-earth-they-have (Accessed: February 18, 2024).

Mandel, D. R. 2002. Instigators of genocide: Examining Hitler from a social-psychological perspective. Understanding genocide: The social psychology of the Holocaust 259–284. Oxford University Press.

Mann, S. 2022. Ohio cops are accused of dressing patrol horses as KKK - but sheriff argues they were meant to be 'ghosts' covered in sheets with their holes cut out for their eyes. Dailey Mail. November 2, 2022. Available at: https://www.dailymail.co.uk/news/article-11382395/Ohio-cops-accused-dressing-patrol-horses-KKK-sheriff-says-ghosts.html (Accessed: July 3, 2023).

Marable, M. 2011. Malcolm X: A life of reinvention. New York: Viking Penguin.

March on Washington. 2020 March on Washington: Thousands gather at historic civil rights march. BBC News. August 28, 2020. Available at: https://www.bbc.com/news/world-us-canada-53949460 (Accessed: October 1, 2020).

Mass shootings. 2023. How many US mass shootings have there been in 2023? BBC. May 26, 2023. Available at: https://www.bbc.com/news/world-us-canada-41488081 (Accessed: July 13, 2023).

Matiash, C.& Rothman, L. 2016. The beating that changed America: what happened to Rodney King 25 years ago. Time. March 3, 2016. Available at: https://time.com/4245175/rodney-king-la-riots-anniversary/ (Accessed: November 6, 2020).

May, T. & Yancy, G. 2020. Policing is doing what it was meant to do. That's the problem. New York Times. June 21, 2020. Available at: https://www.nytimes.com/2020/06/21/opinion/police-violence-racism-reform.html(Accessed: December 9, 2020).

McCormack, S. (2107). Cops Bought Dylann Roof Burger King Hours After Charleston Shooting. The Huffington Post. December 6, 2017. Available at: https://www.huffpost.com/entry/dylann-roof-burger-king_n_7645216 Accessed: October 5, 2020.

Maffly-Kipp, L. 2005. On the secret religious meetings of enslaved persons. National Humanities Center. Available at: https://nationalhumanitiescenter.org/tserve/nineteen/nkeyinfo/aarsecretmeetings.htm (Accessed: June 16, 2023).

McGraw, B. 1999. Protesters march by mayor's mansion. Detroit Free Press. March 22, 1999.

McKinnon, I. 2020. I was a police chief stopped by my own officer. After Floyd, we need change at all levels. USA Today. June 11, 2020. Available at: https://www.usatoday.com/story/opinion/2020/06/11/floyd-killing-police-must-change-former-detroit-chief-column/5341884002/ (Accessed: July 6, 2020).

McLaughlin, E. 2006. The new policing. Thousand Oaks: Sage.

MCOLES. 2008. Subject Control Continuum. Michigan Commission on Law Enforcement Standards. Available at: https://www.michigan.gov/documents/msp/Use_of_Force_Continuum_699292_7.pdf

(Accessed: November 29, 2020).

Mediapro, J. Year. 2019. The life of prophet Musa (Moses). San Francisco: Blurb, Inc.

Meisner, J., Gorner, J. & Schmadeke, S. 2015. Chicago releases dash-cam video of fatal shooting after cop charged with murder. Chicago Tribune. November 24, 2015. Available at: https://www.chicagotribune.com/news/breaking/ct-chicago-cop-shooting-video-laquan-mcdonald-charges-20151124-story.html (Accessed: November 28, 2020).

Melanson, P. 1991. The Martin Luther King assassination: new revelations on the conspiracy and cover-up, 1968-1991. New York: Shapolsky Publishers.

Mendoza Lao, E. 2021. Cariol Horne biography: 13 things about ex-cop from Buffalo, New York. Conan Daily. April 13, 2021. Available at: https://conandaily.com/2021/04/13/cariol-horne-biography-13-things-about-ex-cop-from-buffalo-new-york/ (Accessed: April 19, 2021).

Mertz, N. 2020. Instead of more cop shows, what if networks greenlit shows tried to explore police abolition? Chicago Tribune. June 3, 2020. Available at: https://www.chicagotribune.com/entertainment/tv/ct-mov-police-abolition-dramas-instead-of-cop-shows-0605-20200603-bc3pewq7i5cqnjg7gghmf2kkze-story.html (Accessed: July 13, 2023).

Meyers, H. 2021. No, US policing doesn't trace its roots to heinous slave patrols. New York Post. May 17, 2021. Available at: https://nypost.com/2021/05/17/no-us-policing-doesnt-trace-its-roots-to-heinous-slave-patrols/ (Accessed: May 5, 2023).

Michael Brown is killed. 2020. Michael Brown is killed by a police officer in Ferguson, Missouri. History. August 6, 2020. Available at: https://www.history.com/this-day-in-history/michael-brown-killed-by-police-ferguson-mo (Accessed: November 16, 2020).

Michigan Penal Code Act 328. § 750.520d. 1931.

Minister Abdul Bey Muhammad. 2022. The best of minister's – Mosque no. 99 honors Nation of Islam pioneer, Minister Abdul Bey Muhammad. The Final Call. October 25, 2022. Available at: https://new.finalcall.com/2022/10/25/the-best-of-ministers-mosque-no-99-honors-nation-of-islam-pioneer-minister-abdul-bey-muhammad/ (Accessed: July 21, 2023).

Ministry of Rage. 1994. Cover image. Time. February 28, 1994. Available at: https://content.time.com/time/covers/0,16641,19940228,00.html (Accessed: June 1, 2023).

Miller, T. & Allen, D. 2008. The perplexing promotion problem at the Memphis police department. Southeast Case Research Journal, 5 (2), 1-11. Available at: https://secrj-ojsshsu.tdl.org/secrj/article/download/174/92 (Accessed: March 28, 2023).

Miranda v. Arizona, 384 U.S. 436 (1966).

Mitchell, J. 2024. On this day in 1962. Mississippi Today. April 9, 2024. Available at: https://mississippitoday.org/2024/04/09/on-this-day-in-1962-cpl-roman-ducksworth-fatally-shot-by-white-police-officer/ (Accessed: February 9, 2025).

Monacelli, N. 2021. Detroit's top cop has message on overcoming racism. Click on Detroit WDIV News. February 16, 2021. Available at: https://www.clickondetroit.com/features/2021/02/16/black-history-month-detroits-top-cop-has-message-on-overcoming-racism/?fbclid=IwAR0l4Wnz_1lOTZg-473ZlzIjlK6FTg-L0ISh_Gf_1wMiaAPODTzyUe5DME0 (Accessed: February 26, 2021).

Morey, T. n.d. 6.7 Police misconduct, accountability and corruption. Pressbooks. Available at: https://openoregon.pressbooks.pub/ccj230/chapter/5-7-police-misconduct-and-accountability/#:~:text=The%20Bureau%20of%20Justice%20confirmed,news%20is%20not%20always%20true. (Accessed: July 3, 2023).

Morrow, J. 2013. Why was Jesus silent on the issue of slavery? Helping a New Generation Build a Lasting Faith. [Blog]. Available at: https://www.jonathanmorrow.org/why-was-jesus-silent-on-the-issue-of-slavery/ (Accessed: August 10, 2023).

Morse, S. 1982. Dearborn lowers its flag for its 36-year ruler. Detroit Free Press. December 17, 1982.

Muhammad, A. 2016. State of emergency - Black skins, White minds and false promises. Final Call. September 20, 2016. Available at: https://www.finalcall.com/artman/publish/National_News_2/article_103305.shtml (Accessed: November 19, 2024).

Muhammad, D. 2002. Redefining the role of the American police: eliminating slave catching tactics. Unpublished manuscript. College of Liberal Arts & Sciences, Wayne State University.

Muhammad, D. 2004. Religious policing: suppression of innovative social and political change. Unpublished manuscript. College of Liberal Arts & Sciences, Wayne State University.

Muhammad. D. 2007. Islam expansion in Africa and Black America. [Unpublished manuscript]. Department of Religious Studies, University of Detroit - Mercy.

Muhammad, Demetri. (2017). How to police the black community. Chicago: Nation of Islam.

Muhammad, E. 1965. Blood bath teachings: the suicide of Malcolm X. Cleveland: Secretarius Publications.

Muhammad, E. 1965. Message to the Blackman in America. Chicago: Muhammad's Mosque of Islam No. 2.

Muhammad, E. 1968. The Black policeman and what he polices. Muhammad Speaks. December 13, 1968. Available at: https://www.elijahmuhammadspeaks.com/black-policeman (Accessed: March 30. 2023).

Muhammad, J. (1992). Police wilding. Final Call. April 8, 1992.

Muhammad, R. & Muhammad, A. 2010. Farrakhan: Blacks are true children of Israel. The Final Call. June 28, 2010. Available at: https://www.finalcall.com/artman/publish/National_News_2/article_7089.shtml (Accessed: August 4, 2023).

Muhammad v. Taub-Co Management, 1997.

Mukwara, P. & Mongosho, T. 2016. Django Unchained: rediscovering racial relations during the slave trade. International Journal of African Literacy and Comparative Studies, 7 (20, 36-43. Available at: https://unisapressjournals.co.za/index.php/Imbizo/article/download/1852/1385 (Accessed: December 27, 2023).

Mullenix v. Luna, 577 U.S. ___ (2015).

Myrdal, G. 1944. An American dilemma: the Negro problem and modern democracy. New York: Routledge.

@myskincolorisnotacrime. 2023, July 22. Happy Birthday to the Bay Area's own actor, producer and activist Mr. Danny Glover. [Instagram post]. Available at: https://instagram.com/myskincolorisnotacrime?igshid=MzRlODBiNWFlZA== (Accessed: July 23, 2023).

Nalla, M. & Hummer, D. 1999. Relations between Police Officers and Security Professionals: A Study of Perceptions. Security Journal. 31-40. Available at: https://www.researchgate.net/profile/Don_Hummer/publication/247477725_Relations_between_Police_Officers_and_Security_Professionals_A_Study_of_Perceptions/links/56de490608ae46f1e99f9c8f.pdf (Accessed: October 12, 2020).

Napoleon, H. 2022). A badge, a gun, but no God: the problems with policing in America. Bloomington: iUniverse.

Narcissism. 2021. Oxford Learner's Dictionary. United Kingdom: Oxford University Press. Available at: http://oxfordlearnersdictionaries.com (Accessed: February 1, 2024).

National Advisory Commission. 1968. Report of the National Advisory Commission on Civil Disorder. New York: Bantam Books. Available at: http (Accessed: November 6, 2020).

National Advisory Commission on Civil Disorders. 2016. The Kerner Report. Princeton University Press.

Neavling, S. 2022. These 74 cops in Wayne County have been deemed

untrustworthy to testify in court? Metro Times. December 2, 2022. Available at: https://www.metrotimes.com/news/these-74-cops-in-wayne-county-have-been-deemed-untrustworthy-to-testify-in-court-31751994 (Accessed: December 10, 2023).

Nelson, J. 2000. Police brutality: an anthology. New York: W. W. Norton.

New data show. n.d. New data show dramatic increase in arrest and prosecutions of Black people for carrying a concealed weapon. Neighborhood Defender Service. Available at: https://neighborhooddefender.org/blog/new-data-show-dramatic-increase-in-arrests-and-prosecutions-of-black-people-for-carrying-

a-concealed-
weapon/#:~:text=The%20number%20of%20arrests%20on,the%20crime%20charged%20are%20Black. (Accessed: May 25, 2023).

Nhan, J. 2014. Police culture. The Encyclopedia of Criminology and Criminal Justice. January 22, 2014.

Nicholson-Crotty, S., Nicholson-Crotty, J. & Hernandez, S. (2017). Will more Black cops matter? Officer race and police-involved homicide of Black citizens. Public Administration Review, 77 (2), 206-216. Available at: https://onlinelibrary.wiley.com/doi/epdf/10.1111/puar.12734 (Accessed: March 29, 2023).

NLEOMF, n.d. Our Purpose. The National Law Enforcement Officers Memorial Fund. Available at: https://nleomf.org (Accessed: July 14, 2023).

Noble, G. [foreal]. 2020, May 19. El Hajj Malik El Shabazz (Documentary) [Video]. YouTube. Available at: https://youtu.be/mRtYluUXZ8Q (Accessed: June 23, 2023).

Noel, M. 2023. Black female officer says she was fired after trying to de-escalate a police encounter in California. Now she's suing the police department for discrimination. Essence. December 7, 2023. Available at: https://www.essence.com/news/black-female-officer-sues-for-discrimination/ (Accessed: December 27, 2023).

Oath of office, n.d. Muskegon police department. Policy 102. Available at: https://public.powerdms.com/MuskegonPD/documents/1703346 (Accessed: May 26, 2023).

Office of Community Oriented Policing Services. 2015. The President's Task Force on 21st Century Policing Implementation Guide: Moving from Recommendations to Action. Washington, DC: Office of Community Oriented Policing Services.

Oliver, W. 2009. The structural cultural perspective: a theory of Black male violence. Cambridge University Press.

Olmstead, A.& Rhode, P. 2018. Cotton, slavery, and the new history of capitalism. Explorations of Economic History. January 2018. 67, 1-17.

Orsagos, P. 2023. A police dog attacked a Black trucker on his knees. An Ohio city is dealing with the aftermath. Associated Press. October 22, 2023. Available at: https://apnews.com/article/k9-dog-attack-circleville-black-trucker-4fd3d4806a71cca6f1667d8dbe58ded0 (Accessed: January 2, 2024).

Overview of Investigation. 2020. Overview of investigation of allegations regarding the assassination of Dr. Martin Luther King, Jr. U.S. Department of Justice. December 17, 2020. Available at: https://www.justice.gov/crt/overview-investigation-allegations-regarding-assassination-dr-martin-luther-king-jr (Accessed: June 16, 2023).

Oxford Learner's Dictionaries. n.d. Neutralize. In Oxford Learner's Dictionary on-line. Available at: https://www.oxfordlearnersdictionaries.com/us/definition/english/neutralize (Accessed: June 19, 2023).

Palmer, M. 2004. Brutal legacy: history of the Nation of Islam. Mission Islam. Available at:

http://www.missionislam.com/conissues/malcolmx.htm (Accessed: June 19, 2023).

Parker, W. 2012. Dealing with stress in law enforcement: alcoholism, divorce and suicide. Fort Smith Police Department. Available at: https://www.cji.edu/wp-content/uploads/2019/04/dealingwithstress.pdf (Accessed: July 5, 2023).

Patterson, D. 1988. Police in the P.R.C. Police, The Law Officers Magazine. October 1988.

Paybarah, A. 2020. He Videotaped the Rodney King Beating. Now, He Is Auctioning the Camera. New York Times. July 29, 2020. Available at: https://www.nytimes.com/2020/07/29/us/rodney-king-video-camera-auction.html (Accessed: November 6, 2020).

Payne, L. 2018. Civil Rights and Restorative Justice. Northwestern University School of Law. Available at: https://web.archive.org/web/20180227063518/http://nuweb9.neu.edu/civilrights/larry-payne/ (Accessed: March 28, 2023).

Pearson, C. 2016. Comment on: Fernandez, M., Perez-Peña, R. & Bromwich, J. Five Dallas officers were killed as payback, police chief says. New York Times. [Online]. Comment posted on July 11, 2016. (Accessed June 24, 2023).

Peeple, L. 2020. What the data say about police brutality and racial bias — and which reforms might work. Nature. 583 (2) 22-24. Available at: https://media.nature.com/original/magazine-assets/d41586-020-01846-z/d41586-020-01846-z.pdf (Accessed: December 1, 2020).

People v. Budzyn, 456 Mich. 77, (1997). Available at: https (Accessed: November 13, 2020).

People of the State of Michigan vs Derrick Bernard Bonner. 19-002363-01. 36th District Court for the city of Detroit. Preliminary Examination. April 1, 2019.

Perl, P. 1999. Race riots of 1919 gave glimpse of future struggles. The Washington Post.

Phillips, U. 1905. The economic cost of slaveholding in the cotton belt. Political Science Quarterly 20 (2) 257-275.

Philimon, W. 2020. Not just George Floyd: police departments have 400-year history of racism. USA Today. June 7, 2020. Available at: https://www.usatoday.com/story/news/nation/2020/06/07/black-lives-matters-police-departments-have-long-history-racism/3128167001/ (Accessed: December 27, 2023).

Picadio, A. 2019. The right to bear arms: a disfavored right. Pennsylvania Bar Association Quarterly. January 2019. Available at: https://transpartisanreview.org/bear-arms/ (Accessed: May 25, 2023.

Pierson v. Ray, 386 U.S. 547 (1967).

Police advisory committee, n.d. Wayne County Community College District. Available at: https://www.wcccd.edu/dept/cam_safety_services.htm (Accessed: May 31, 2023).

Polsky, R. n.d. Police K9 fatal dog attacks. Animal Behavior Counseling Services. Available at: https://www.dogexpert.com/police-k9-fatal-dog-attacks/ (Accessed: June 29, 2023).

Popli, N. 2023. Why Malcolm X's family is suing the FBI, NYPD, and CIA 58 years after his death. Time. February 22, 2023. Available at: https://time.com/6257699/malcolm-x-lawsuit-family-fbi-nypd-cia/# (Accessed: June 22, 2023).

Powers, J. 2000. Eroding the blue wall of silence: the need for an internal affairs privilege of confidentiality. Suffolk Journal of Trial and Appellate Advocacy, 5 (1), 19-35. Available at: https://dc.suffolk.edu/jtaa-suffolk (Accessed: July 24, 2023).

President Joe Biden. [@Joe Biden]. 2023, December 27. It was about slavery. [Tweet]. Available at: https://twitter.com/JoeBiden/status/1740221284284256645 (Accessed: December 28, 2023).

President's Task Force on 21st Century Policing. 2015. Final Report of the President's Task Force on 21st Century Policing. Washington, DC: Office of Community Oriented Policing

Services. Available at: https://cops.usdoj.gov/pdf/taskforce/taskforce_finalreport.pdf (Accessed: July 21, 2023).

Primary Documents in American History. 2020. Library of Congress. United States Government, February 18, 2020. Available at: https://www.loc.gov/rr/program//bib/ourdocs/northwest.html (Accessed: January 11, 2022.)

Prince, M. 2003. Recollections of Slavery by a Runaway Slave. The Emancipator. Available at: https://docsouth.unc.edu/neh/runaway/runaway.html (Accessed: January 30, 2022).

Pulley, B. 1998). Casinos bring Detroit hope and division. New York Times. April 11, 1998. Available at: https://www.nytimes.com/1998/04/11/us/casinos-bring-detroit-hope-and-division.html (Accessed: August 16, 1998).

Quinones, S. 1994. Police corruption. Police: The Law Enforcement Magazine. 18 (11), 59,62-63,74.

Raboteau, A. 1992. The secret religion of the slaves. Christian History Institute. Available at: https://christianhistoryinstitute.org/magazine/article/secret-religion-of-the-slaves (Accessed: June 10, 2023).

Radelet, L. 1986. The police and the community. New York: Macmillan.

Radke, B. 2020. American policing dates back to the formation of the slave patrols,' says Seattle police chief. KUOW NPR Network. June 19, 2020. Available at: https://www.kuow.org/stories/american-policing-dates-back-to-the-formation-of-the-slave-patrols-says-former-seattle-police-chief (Accessed: July 23, 2023).

Ramirez, C. 2024. Detroit schools cop guilty of making false 2021 carjacking report. The Detroit News. March 28, 2024. Available at: https://www.detroitnews.com/story/news/local/detroit-city/2024/03/28/detroit-schools-cop-guilty-false-carjacking-report/73129247007/ (Accessed: May 3, 2024).

Randall, K. 2000. The killing of Frederick Finley: sudden death in an American city. World Socialist Web Site. July 19, 2000. Available at: https://www.wsws.org/en/articles/2000/07/finl-j19.html (Accessed: August 17, 2023).

Read, B. 2020. Breonna Taylor Was Shot and Killed by Police in Her Own Home. The Cut. July 9, 2020. Available at: https://www.thecut.com/2020/07/breonna-taylor-louisville-shooting-police-what-we-know.html (Accessed: July 14, 2020).

Reed, R. 1966 Bloody Sunday was a year ago. The New York Times. March 6, 1966. P.76.

Reichley, J. 2000. The life of the parties: a history of American political parties. Lanham: Rowman & Littlefied Publishers.

Reimund, M. E. 2013. Are Brady lists (aka Liar's Lists) the Scarlet letter for law enforcement officers? A need for expansion and uniformity. International Journal of Humanities and Social Science, 3 (17), 1-6. Available at: https://citeseerx.ist.psu.edu/document?repid=rep1&type=pdf&doi=8e938f24fda1a014ca6d009392fcddf5d898cd7a (Accessed: December 10, 2023).

Rhodan, M. 2016. Why President Obama's police reform is a work in progress. Time. July 8, 2016. Available at: https://time.com/4398392/obama-police-reform-report-task-force-on-21st-century-policing/ (Accessed: August 3, 2023).

Rice, S. 2020. My 12-year-old son, Tamir Rice, was killed by police. I'm not allowed to be normal. ABC News. July 13, 2020. Available at: https://abcnews.go.com/GMA/News/12-year-son-tamir-rice-killed-police-im/story?id=71654873 (Accessed: November 18, 2020).

Richardson, L. 2017. An American crime fighter. United States: Mind-to-Manuscript Publishing.

Robinette v. Barnes, 854 F. 2d 909 (1988).

Robinson, C. & Scaglion, R. 1987. The origin and evolution of the police function in society: notes toward a theory. Law & Society Review, 21 (1), 109-154.

Robinson, D. 1990. The Missouri compromise revisited, Durham theses, Durham University. Available at: http://etheses.dur.ac.uk/6255/ (Accessed January 11, 2022).

Robinson, R. 2016. Zimmerman vs Martin: an analysis of sociological theory. Atlanta Dream Center. May 24, 2016. Available at: https://russiarobinson.wordpress.com/2016/05/24/zimmerman-vs-martin-an-analysis-of-sociological-theory/ (Accessed: November 23, 2020).

Rock, C. 2014. How to not get your ass kicked by the police. YouTube, uploaded by Indycrat, August 23, 2014, https://youtu.be/OEvMc-K8XHY.

Romanowski, M. 2012. Case Report. 120005635. Birmingham Police Department: patrol unit.

Ross, R. 2017, November 17. IACP 2017 opening ceremony [Video]. YouTube. Available at: https://youtu.be/5rRws7f_jXc (Accessed: July 7, 2023).

Rubin, J. & Blankstein, A. 2013. In wake of Dorner shootout, questions over use of the burner. Los Angeles Times. February 14, 2013.

Runaway Slaves. n.d. Women and the American Story. Available at: https://wams.nyhistory.org/settler-colonialism-and-revolution/settler-colonialism/runaway-slaves/#:~:text=One%20of%20the%20most%20powerful,prevent%20them%20from%20running%20again. (Accessed: May 5, 2023).

Runkle, A. (1994, January 27). Suit alleges police harassed men, used racial slurs. Dearborn Press and Guide, p. 1A.

Ryzik, M. 2020. Dave Chappelle's Netflix special: three key references to know. New York Times. June 12, 2020. Available at: https://www.nytimes.com/2020/06/12/arts/television/dave-chappelle-netflix-special.html (Accessed: January 2, 2021.

Sainz, A. 2023. Tyre Nichols' brutal beating by police shown on video. Associated Press. January 28, 2023. Available at: https://apnews.com/article/tyre-nichols-video-memphis-police-e3ee8e6698faae16df3f41d09234b09f (Accessed: March 24, 2023).

Schmidt, M. & Apuzzo, M. 2015. South Carolina officer Is charged with murder of Walter Scott. New York Times. April 7, 2015. Available at: https://www.nytimes.com/2015/04/08/us/south-carolina-officer-is-charged-with-murder-in-black-mans-death.html (Accessed: November 19, 2020).

Scheck, B., Neufeld, P., & Dwyer, J. 2000. Actual innocence: five days to execution, and other dispatches from the wrongly convicted. New York: Doubleday.

Scott, J. 2022. Black LAPD officers reported racism. Chief Michael Moore took 6 months to address it. KNOCKLA. September 17, 2022. Available at: https://knock-la.com/lapd-social-media-racism/ (Accessed: July 10, 2023).

Second police officer. 2023. Second police officer files claim against the city. Pasadena Now. December 13, 2023. Available at: https://www.pasadenanow.com/main/second-police-officer-files-claim-against-the-city-2 (Accessed: December 27, 2023).

Seigel, R. 2000. Activist split over Fairlane protest strategies. The Michigan Citizen. A5.

Sergent, J., Loehrke, J., Padilla, R., & Hertel, N. 2020. George Floyd protests: How did we get here? USA Today. June 1, 2020. Available at: https://www.usatoday.com/in-depth/news/2020/05/29/george-floyd-protests-how-did-we-get-here/5283225002/ (Accessed: June 19, 2020).

7 of the most corrupt police. n.d. 7 of the most corrupt police cities in history. BET. Available at: https://www.bet.com/photo-gallery/czj3ir/7-of-the-most-corrupt-police-cities-in-history/ts1t2j (Accessed: July 3, 2023).

Shapiro, A. 2020. What it is like to be a Black police officer. NPR. June 18, 2020. Available at: https://www.npr.org/2020/06/18/880513767/what-it-is-like-to-be-a-black-police-officer (Accessed: December 21, 2020).

Shapiro, N. 2004. North Alabama's response to the fear and facts of slave revolts. Huntsville Historical Review, 30 (1), 15-40. Available at: https://louis.uah.edu/cgi/viewcontent.cgi?article=1423&=&context

=huntsville-historical-review&=&sei-redir=1&referer=https%253A%252F%252Fscholar.google.com%252Fscholar%253Fhl%253Den%2526as_sdt%253D0%25252C23%2526q%253Dfear%252Bof%252Bfreedom%252Bslave%252Binsurrection%252Brebellion%2526oq%253Dfear%252Bof%252Bfreedom%252Bslave%252Binsurrection%252Brebe#search=%22fear%20freedom%20slave%20insurrection%20rebellion%22 (Accessed: June 2, 2023).

Shelton, J. 2020. How the U.S. police was founded as a slave hunting organization. History Dailey. June 7, 2020. Available at: https://historydaily.org/how-police-founded-as-slave-hunting-organization/5 (Accessed: May 29, 2023).

Siese, A. 2021. Former Buffalo officer who stopped fellow cop's chokehold on suspect will get pension after winning lawsuit. CBS News. April 15, 2021. Available at: https://www.cbsnews.com/news/cariole-horne-former-buffalo-police-officer-pension-lawsuit-win/ (Accessed: April 20, 2021.

Siegel, L. & Worrall, J. 2014. Introduction to criminal justice. Belmont: Wadsworth.

Sigurvinsdottir, R. & Ullman, S. 2015. Social reactions, self-blame and problem drinking in adult sexual assault survivors. Psycho Violence. 5 (2) 192–198. Available at: https://www.ncbi.nlm.nih.gov/pmc/articles/PMC4562326/ (Accessed: November 13, 2020).

Silverman, E. 1999. NYPD battles crime: Innovative strategies in policing. Boston: NW University Press.

Simmons, K., Bowers, T., & Ruiz, J. 2003. Pre-employment psychological testing of police officers: the MMPI and the IPI as predictors of performance. International Journal of Police Science & Management, 5 (4), 277-294. Available at: https://citeseerx.ist.psu.edu/document?repid=rep1&type=pdf&doi=95c11502e91c77fe2d03dcae6d7b2b4d0fd0a62f (Accessed: December 28, 2023).

Siwicki, D. 2024. Detroit Public Schools officer convicted of phony carjacking report. Patch. March 28, 2024. Available at: https://patch.com/michigan/detroit/detroit-public-schools-officer-convicted-phony-carjacking-report (Accessed: May 3, 2023).

Skaflestad, P. February 25, 2021. How slavery caused the American Civil war [Video]. https://youtu.be/vb9u4CKxOLE

Sklansky, D. 2006. Criminology - Not your father's police department: Making sense of the new demographics of law enforcement. Journal of Criminal Law and Criminology. 96 (3) 1209 – 1244.

Skolnick, J. 1975. Justice without trial: law enforcement in a democratic society. 2nd ed. New York: Wiley.

Skolnick, J. 2002. Corruption and the blue code of silence. Police Practice and Research, 3 (1), 7-19. Available at: https://lawcat.berkeley.edu/record/1186375?ln=en (Accessed: July 24, 2023).

Skolnick, J. & Fyfe, J. 1993. Above the law: police and the excessive use of force. New York: The Free Press.

Slave patrols NLEOMF, n.d. Slave patrols: an early form of American policing. The National Law Enforcement Officers

Memorial Fund. Available at: https://nleomf.org/slave-patrols-an-early-form-of-american-policing/ (Accessed: July 14, 2023).

Smith, M. 2013. Suspect's grudge dates back to 2007 complaint. CNN. February 10, 2012. Available at: https://www.cnn.com/2013/02/07/us/lapd-attacks-dorner/index.html (Accessed: January 1, 2021).

Smith, S., Wu, J., &Murphy, J. 2020. Map: George Floyd protests around the world. NBC News. June 9, 2020. Available at: https://www.nbcnews.com/news/world/map-george-floyd-protests-countries-worldwide-n1228391 (Accessed: June 19, 2020).

Smothers, R. 1992. 2 Nashville officers dismissed in beating. New York Times. December 19, 1992. Available at: https://www.nytimes.com/1992/12/19/us/2-nashville-officers-dismissed-in-beating.html (Accessed: December 26, 2020).

Sollenberger, R. 2020. Race baiting filth: Carlson criticized for claiming a Black Lives Matter mob will come for you. Salon. June 9, 2020. Available at: https://www.salon.com/2020/06/09/race-baiting-filth-carlson-criticized-for-claiming-a-black-lives-matter-mob-will-come-for-you/ (Accessed: September 28, 2024).

Spivey, W. 2022. The hanging, dissecting, and beheading of Nat Turner. Black History Month 365. September 11, 2022. Available at: https://medium.com/black-history-month-365/the-hanging-dissecting-and-beheading-of-nat-turner-bc3af88b817c (Accessed: June 12, 2023).

SPLC. n.d. Louis Farrakhan. Southern Poverty Law Center. Available at: https://www.splcenter.org/fighting-hate/extremist-files/individual/louis-farrakhan (Accessed: June 1, 2023).

Spruill, L. 2016. Slave patrols, pack of negro dogs and policing Black communities. Phylon. 25 (2), 400-435. Available at: https://is.cuni.cz/studium/predmety/index.php?do=download&did=139755&kod=JMB215 (Accessed: June 27, 2023).

Sprunt, B. 2020. The history behind when the looting starts, the shooting starts. NPR. May 29, 2020. Available at: https://www.npr.org/2020/05/29/864818368/the-history-behind-when-the-looting-starts-the-shooting-starts(Accessed: December 9, 2020).

Stamper, N. 2016. To protect and serve: how to fix America's police. New York: Nation Books.

Stern, M. 2020. The police lie. All the time. Can anything stop them? Slate. August 4, 2020. Available at: https://slate.com/news-and-politics/2020/08/police-testilying.html (Accessed: July 3, 2023).

Sternisha, E. (2010). Security Officer Training Manual: News Headlines & Review. Morrisville: Lulu. Available at: https://books.google.com/books?id=RV1XAgAAQBAJ&dq=fairlane+hired+black+security+dearborn+park+boycott&source=gbs_navlinks_s (Accessed: July 6, 2020).

Stewart, S. 2020. Man's best friend? How dogs have been used to oppress African Americans. Michigan Journal of Race and Law. 25, 183-207. Available at: https://repository.law.umich.edu/mjrl/vol25/iss2/4 (Accessed: June 27, 2023).

Stodghill, R. 1998. The Motown motormouth. CNN. August 17, 1998. Available at:

https://edition.cnn.com/ALLPOLITICS/1998/08/10/time/fieger.html (Accessed: August 29, 2023).

Stone, G. 1989. A private mod squad sets out to prove police harassment—and stirs a fight over Its tactics. People. December 11, 1989. Available at: https://people.com/archive/a-private-mod-squad-sets-out-to-prove-police-harassment-and-stirs-a-fight-over-its-tactics-vol-32-no-24/ (Accessed: December 27, 2020).

Stroshine, M. & Brandl, S. 2021. The impact of foot pursuits on police use of force. Policing: A Journal of Policy and Practice. 15 (4), 2355–2371. Available at: https://doi.org/10.1093/police/paab054 (Accessed: May 3, 2023).

Sutch, R. 2018. The economics of African American slavery: the cliometrics debate. National Bureau of Economic Research. Number 25197.

[TAQWA995]. 2020, October 9. Pharaoh's (Ramesses II) mummy: sea-salt traces prove the miracle of the Holy Quran [Video]. YouTube. Available at: https://youtu.be/ETe__zwPT_I (Accessed: August 5, 2023).

Taylor, U. 2003. Elijah Muhammad's Nation of Islam: Separatism, regendering, and a secular approach to Black power after Malcolm X (1965–1975). In: Theoharis, J., Woodard, K. (eds) Freedom North: Black Freedom Struggles Outside the South, 1940–1980. New York: Palgrave Macmillan.

Temin, P. 2020. From Eric Garner to George Floyd: how history repeats itself. Institute for New Economic Thinking. Available at: https://www.ineteconomics.org/perspectives/blog/george-floyd-and-eric-garner (Accessed: May 17, 2023).

Tennessee v. Garner, 471 U.S. 1 (1985).

Terry v. Ohio, 392 U.S. 1 (1968)

The Associated Press. 2009. Two killed in murder-suicide at Henry Ford Community College in Dearborn. MLive. April 10, 2009. Available at: https://www.mlive.com/news/2009/04/person_with_gun_reported_at_mi.html (Accessed: August 17, 2023).

The Holy Quran (Maulana Muhammad Ali, Trans.). 2011. Ahmadiyya Anjuman Isha'at Islam Lahore Inc.

The Jefferson Monticello. n. d. Quotations shown on the Jefferson Memorial. Available at: https://www.monticello.org/site/research-and-collections/quotations-jefferson-memorial (Accessed: December 15, 2020.

Thiessen, R. 2016, January 21. Did Jesus condone slavery? Allen Creek Community Church. [Blog]. Available at: https://ac3.org/2016/01/did-jesus-condone-slavery (Accessed: August 19, 2023).

Three years since George Floyd. 2023. Marking three years since George Floyd's murder, legacy civil rights leaders urge passage of his namesake Justice in Policing Act to bring accountability to law enforcements. National NCNW News. Available at: https://ncnw.org/marking-three-years-since-george-floyds-murder-legacy-civil-rights-leaders-urge-passage-of-his-namesake-justice-in-policing-act-to-bring-accountability-to-law-enforcement/ (Accessed: July 30, 2023).

Tolnay, S. 2003. The African American "great migration" and beyond. Annual Review of Sociology. 29, 209-232. Available at: https://www.jstor.org/stable/30036966?read-now=1&seq=1#page_scan_tab_contents (Accessed: May 17, 2023).

Tolnay, S., Beck, E. & Massey, J. 1989 Black lynchings: the power threat hypothesis revisited. Social Forces, 67 (3) 605-623.

Transcript Rodney King. 2005 Transcript of Rodney King's statement. Associated Press. October 11, 2005. Available at: https://www.tampabay.com/archive/1992/05/02/transcript-of-rodney-king-s-statement/ (Accessed: November 13, 2020).

Travis, J. 2015. The future of community policing. Testimony before the task force on 21st century policing created by President Barack H. Obama on February 24, 2015 in Washington, D.C. City University of New York John Jay College of Criminal Justice. Available at: https://academicworks.cuny.edu/jj_pubs/99 (Accessed: August 2, 2023).

Turk, A. 1982. Political criminality: the defiance and defense of authority. Beverly Hills: Sage.

Tyler, T. 2003. Procedural justice, legitimacy, and the effective rule of law. Crime and Justice. 30, 283-357. Available at: https://www.jstor.org/stable/1147701 (Accessed: July 21, 2023).

Umar, H. 2021. 50 best Imam Ali quotes sayings and wisdom. Names of Allah. June 27, 2021. Available at: https://namesofallah.co.uk/imam-ali-quotes/ (Accessed: July 11, 2023).

U.S. Const. amend. Amendment # II

U. S. Department of Justice. (1995). "Positional asphyxia – sudden death." National Law Enforcement Technology Center. June 1995. Available at: https://www.ncjrs.gov/pdffiles/posasph.pdf(Accessed: October 21, 2020).

Vielkind, J. 2014. Cuomo promises 'soup-to-nuts' review of justice system. Political. December 4, 2014. Available at: https://www.politico.com/states/new-york/albany/story/2014/12/cuomo-promises-soup-to-nuts-review-of-justice-system-000000 (Accessed: October 15, 2020).

Vitello, P. 2014. Joseph D. McNamara, father of community policing, dies at 79. New York Times. September 24, 2014. Available at: https://www.nytimes.com/2014/09/25/us/joseph-d-mcnamara-father-of-community-policing-dies-at-79.html (Accessed: July 21, 2023).

Wagner, R. 2020. Spare a thought for the good cops. Forbes. May 31, 2020. Available at: https://www.forbes.com/sites/roddwagner/2020/05/31/spare-a-thought-for-the-good-cops/?sh=4e276792f19c (Accessed: July 8, 2023).

Wahrhaftig, P. and Assefa, H. 1992. Move/Philadelphia bombing: a conflict resolution history. Sociological Practice, 10 (1). Available at: https://digitalcommons.wayne.edu/socprac/vol10/iss1/15 (Accessed: December 6, 2024).

Walker, S. 2001. Sense and nonsense about crime and drugs. Belmont: Wadsworth.

Walsh, C. 2021. Solving racial disparities in policing. The Harvard Gazette. February 23, 2021. Available at: https://news.harvard.edu/gazette/story/2021/02/solving-racial-disparities-in-policing/ (Accessed: July 8, 2023).

Warikoo, N. & Bailey, R. 2000. Thousands protest mall death as racial. Detroit Free Press. July 7, 2000. Available at: https://www.cnn.com/2000/LOCAL/eastcentral/07/07/det.mall.death/index.html (Accessed: October 8, 2020).

Watson, R. 2020. Local family pursues excessive force claim against Columbus police. WLTZ News. June 2, 2020. Available at: https://www.wltz.com/2020/06/02/local-family-pursues-excessive-force-claim-against-columbus-police/ (Accessed: October 23, 2020).

Watts, M. 2019. Leslie Dean Jones, Memphis police officer who killed Larry Payne in 1968 sanitation strike, has died. USA Today. April 4, 2019. Available at: https://www.commercialappeal.com/story/news/breaking/2019/04/04/leslie-dean-jones-officer-killed-larry-payne-memphis-sanitation-strike/3358151002/ (Accessed: March 28, 2023).

Waxman, O. 2017. How the U.S. got its police force. Time. May 18, 2017. Available at: https://uuhonolulu.org/wp-content/uploads/2021/04/The-History-of-Police-in-America-and-the-First-Force-_-Time.pdf (Accessed: May 29, 2023).

Waxman, O. 2020. What Martin Luther King Jr. said at the march on Washington about police brutality. Time. August 27, 2020. Available at: https://time.com/5882308/march-on-washington-police-brutality/ (Accessed: July 24, 2023).

WCCCD Increases Security. 2014. WCCCD increases security standards with MCOLES police certification. IACLEA Campus Law Enforcement Journal. May/June 2014, 44 (3), 16.

WCCCD oath, n.d. Law enforcement officer's oath. Unpublished document.

WCCCD Police Authority CCTV. 2019. DTC Main NW Entry Police Authority. March 11, 2019. [Video]. Report number 19-0123DT.

Wedell, K., Kelly, C., McManus, C. & Fernando, C. 2020 George Floyd is not alone. 'I can't breathe' uttered by dozens in fatal police holds across U.S. USA Today. June 25, 2020. Available at: https://www.usatoday.com/in-depth/news/investigations/2020/06/13/george-floyd-not-alone-dozens-said-cant-breathe-police-holds/3137373001/ (Accessed: October 22, 2020).

Weigel, D. 2020. The Trailer: Biden says most cops are good. Trump goes way further. The Washington Post. September 3, 2020. Available at: https://www.washingtonpost.com/politics/2020/09/03/trailer-biden-says-most-cops-are-good-trump-goes-way-further/ (Accessed: October 15, 2020).

Welding, L. 2023. Shootings at colleges: U.S. statistics. Best Colleges. May 11, 2023. Available at: https://www.bestcolleges.com/research/college-shootings-statistics/ (Accessed: August 17, 2023).

Wells, I. 1892. Southern horrors: lynch law in all phases. New York: New York Age Print.

White House. n.d. White House. United States. [Web Archive] Available at: https://obamawhitehouse.archives.gov/issues/civil-rights/selma (Accessed: December 27, 2023).

Wilkes, J. 2024. Why did John Wilkes Booth kill Abraham Lincoln? And how was he caught? History Extra - BBC History Magazine. March 15, 2024. Available at: https://www.historyextra.com/period/victorian/why-john-wilkes-booth-shot-killed-lincoln-how-caught/ (Accessed: October 23, 2024).

Williams, C. 1994. Trial date set in suit against Dearborn cops. The Detroit News. p. 1B. January 26, 1994.

Williams, E. 1944. Capitalism and Slavery. University of North Carolina Press.

Wills, M. 2023. The police dog as weapon of racial terror. JSTOR Daily. February 9, 2023. Available at: https://daily.jstor.org/the-police-dog-as-weapon-of-racial-terror/ (Accessed: August 11, 2023).

Wilson, A. 2018. 10 Dr. Amos Wilson Quotes. The Black Detour. July 24, 2018. Available at: https://theblackdetour.com/10-dr-amos-wilson-quotes/ (Accessed: August 10, 2020).

Winkler, A. 2022. Racist gun laws and the Second Amendment. Harvard Law Review, 135 (8). June 21, 2022. Available at: https://harvardlawreview.org/forum/vol-135/racist-gun-laws-and-the-second-amendment/ (Accessed: May 25, 2023).

Wirtschafter, V. 2021. How George Floyd changed the online conversation around BLM. Brookings. June 17, 2021. Available at: https://www.brookings.edu/articles/how-george-floyd-changed-the-online-conversation-around-black-lives-matter/ (Accessed: July 12, 2023).

Wood, R. 2021. The Ray Wood story: confessions of a Black NYPD cop in the assassination of Malcolm X. Madera Enterprises.

Wood, S. 2014. Ex-Philly police captain protests in a Ferguson, blast American policing. Philadelphia Inquirer. November 26, 2014.

Worthy, K. 2019. People of the State of Michigan vs Derrick Bernard Bonner. 19-002363-01. Wayne County Circuit Court for the County of Wayne. Notice of intent to introduce other acts of domestic violence pursuant to M.C.L. 768.27b. June 19, 2019.

Wren, A. 2024. Trump says 'violent day' of policing will end crime. Politico. September 29, 2024. Available at: https://www.politico.com/news/2024/09/29/trump-violent-day-policing-crime-00181619 (Accessed: November 19, 2024).

Wright, B. 2023. RIP Mark LeSure: ex-Memphis cop who criticized police after Tyre Nichols' killing is 'found shot and dead': report. NEWSONE. July 11, 2023. Available at: https://newsone.com/4638770/mark-lesure-found-dead/ (Accessed: July 12, 2023).

Wright, J. 2001. Reverend Wright transcript: the day of Jerusalem's fall. ABC News. September 16, 2001. Available at: https://abcnews.go.com/Blotter/story?id=4719157&page=1 (Accessed: August 9, 2023).

WWJ Newsradio. 2024. Detroit Public Schools police officer convicted of filing false carjacking report. Audacy. March 27,

2024. Available at: https://www.audacy.com/wwjnewsradio/news/local/school-police-officer-guilty-of-reporting-false-carjacking (Accessed: May 3, 2024).

Young, B. 2019. Initial Case Report. 19-0123DT. Wayne County Community College District Police Authority Department: Investigative Unit.

Young, M. (2024, May 1). When you destroy someone's life with lies, take it as a loan, it will come back to you with interest. [Image/post]. Facebook. Available at: https://www.facebook.com/1023445423/posts/pfbid0a4Rc6djPfBCTqjvK2eKuDiVvbAjTWzqZuBwBgxc8ZwhzVzn2FcdYHq1cJphWtH7nl/(Accessed: May 1, 2024).

Zadrozny, B. 2015. Here's what happens when a Black man open Carries gun. U S News. May 29, 2015. Available at: https://www.thedailybeast.com/heres-what-happens-when-a-black-man-open-carries-gun (Accessed: May 25, 2023).

Zagier, A. 2010. Mo. Corrects record on 1923 college-town lynching. Associated Press. November 8, 2010. Available at:

http://archive.boston.com/news/education/higher/articles/2010/11/08/mo_corrects_record_on_1923_college_town_lynching/
(Accessed: October 21, 2020).

Made in the USA
Monee, IL
08 November 2026

67968599R00280